NO BETTER
Land

Roberta L. Bagshaw
June 15, 1996

Engraving of the Right Reverend George Hills, *ca.* 1859,
Bishop of British Columbia 1859-1892

NO BETTER
Land

The *1860* Diaries of
the Anglican Colonial Bishop
GEORGE HILLS

EDITED BY

Roberta L. Bagshaw

VICTORIA, BRITISH COLUMBIA

Sono Nis Press

Canadian Cataloguing in Publication Data

Hills, George, 1816-1895
   No better land

   Includes bibliographical references and index.
   ISBN 1-55039-067-8

   1. Hills, George, 1816-1895—Diaries. 2. Church of England—
Bishops—Diaries. 3. Church of England—Missions—British
Columbia. 4. Indians of North America—British Columbia—
Missions. 5. British Columbia—Description and travel. I.
Bagshaw, Roberta L. (Roberta Lee) II. Title.
BV2813.H54A3 1996   266'.3711'092   C96-910068-X

Publication of this book has been financially
assisted by the Canada Council Block Grant Program.

COVER IMAGE: *Windy Point* by Pat Service
acrylic and oil on canvas, 1991.

Published by
SONO NIS PRESS
1725 Blanshard Street
Victoria, British Columbia v8w 2j8

Printed and bound in Canada by
MORRISS PRINTING COMPANY LTD.
Victoria, British Columbia

For Bob,
Drew, Glen and Jeffrey

Acknowledgements

Research for this book has been funded by the Anglican Foundation of Canada, the Anglican Diocese of British Columbia and the Archives Committee, the Diocese of New Westminster, the Diocese of Caledonia, the Diocese of Cariboo, the Diocese of Kootenay, and the H. R. Mac-Millan Trust Fund.

Contents

The soil is good generally, a light kind, some very good black loam, a great deal of this latter principally in the valleys . . . there is no better land in British Columbia that I have seen, nor in Vancouver Island. There is considerable wood to be cleared, but extensive open ground [is] covered with fern. The timber is not heavy or thick. There is good water from wells. Grouse are to be had. Deer in abundance & good. Fish plentiful.

6 September 1860
Salt Spring Island

Preface

GEORGE Hills, the first Church of England bishop in British Columbia until 1879, was installed in London in 1859, the same year that the Colony of British Columbia was founded. His diocese consisted of all the British territory between the Rocky Mountains and the Pacific Coast, north of the American border. Under the authority of the Letters Patent, jointly issued by the Church of England and the Crown, Hills was vested with the responsibility for all aspects of the Church of England in the colonies of Vancouver Island and British Columbia. This included the power to own and purchase lands, to determine the location of Church of England churches and schools, and to appoint the clergy and missionaries connected with the Church of England.

Although the residence of the colonial bishop was in Victoria, his administrative duties involved journeys to most of the settled areas in both colonies of British Columbia. During the thirty-three years Hills was Bishop of British Columbia (1859-1892) he kept a private record of his journeys, observations and experiences.

In the latter part of the nineteenth century Hills took the diaries to England along with other private possessions when he resigned as Bishop of British Columbia in 1892. After his death three years later, the diaries were left in the care of his nephew the Reverend William Henry Percival Arden, who had worked under Hills in Victoria.

In 1909 Rev. Arden loaned the diaries and other papers to a newly created society that was founded to support the Church of England; eventually it became the British Columbia and Yukon Church Aid Society. In 1959 it ceased operation and the diaries, along with other books, papers and copies of the Columbia Mission Reports, were given to the Archives of the Anglican Theological College, now the Archives of the Ecclesiastical Province of British Columbia and Yukon. Later, the National Museum of Canada made microform copies of the diaries and prepared typed transcripts for the years 1860 to 1892 and these were also given to the ecclesiastical archives.

The diaries provide a first-hand commentary on a great variety of subjects. They cover a period when major events occurred in British Columbia, from the time of the lower Fraser River gold rush, to the end of the colonial period, and into the last decade of the nineteenth century. They contain accounts of discussions Bishop Hills had with a great variety of people, including miners, farmers, women, natives, government officials and the inhabitants of remote places in the Colony of Vancouver Island and the Colony of British Columbia.

The diaries served Hills as notes on the day's activities. It appears they were written either at the end of each day or a few days later, but all the entries were recorded close to the time of the events they describe. The entries exhibit a distinct subjective view. The events, conversations and observations contained in the 400 handwritten pages of the 1860 diaries represent what Bishop Hills considered important.

As one historical geographer, H. Roy Merrens, explained, once the idea that there can be only one view of the past is dismissed "what remains from the past is a congeries [a disorderly mass] of views of the setting . . . each with its own distinctive bias reflecting the objectives, values and interests of the recorder." This approach, applied to the Hills diaries, acknowledges the limitations of Hills' subjective view of the past, and opens a way for readers to use the material comparatively, along with the various perspectives of Hills' contemporaries.

During the past ten years I have repeatedly read and analyzed the Hills diaries, both for their importance as documents of the colonial period, and because they are interesting to read. The full text of the 1860 diaries will bear close examination both for its value as a historical document and for repeated enjoyable reading. The diaries open a window from which to observe daily life during the first major wave of European settlement and the impact of this movement on all levels of society.

The preparation of the full text of the 1860 diaries for publication, and the focus of the commentary and postscript, has been influenced by a desire to find a place for Hills' voice in the discussion of the colonial period. Although he was well known among his contemporaries, little attention has been given to the role of the churches and very little exists to make Bishop Hills known to general readers. The complete text of the diaries portrays a more balanced view than one that could be created from excerpts of the diaries.

One of the first editorial problems that arose from the decision to prepare a full diary text was how to break the long manuscript into a series of comfortable portions for readers and yet be consistent with the way Bishop Hills viewed his work during the year. He made no breaks in the original manuscript, except for the dates that separate the entries and the change to a new volume when it was necessary. The diary material is a long stream of events without internal pauses, far too long to be read without the introduction of some breaks in the text.

When Hills' correspondence was examined, I found that he had written several lengthy letters to his family in England so they could share the news of his activities. Two of the letters that focus on his voyages, from England to Victoria (17 November 1859 to 6 January 1860) and to the gold mining region (19 May to 8 August 1860) in the Colony of British Columbia, were sent to his sister Caroline Arden.

The summer journey was the basis for one letter. Hills chose extracts from his diary, enlisted a woman in Victoria to copy these into a notebook, and then sent it as a Christmas gift for his sister and her family to read around the fireplace. He apparently intended to send Caroline another letter concerning his trip to Barkley Sound (19 to 29 October 1860). Whether this occurred is not clear because there is no record of its existence in the archival collections.

Hills sent a third letter to another member of his family, his brother-in-law, the Reverend Herbert McSwiney, who had been a curate under Hills at Great Yarmouth in England. This letter concerns the trip to Barkley Sound and contains a summary of his impressions for the year. Hills' use of long sections of the diaries in letters to his family is the basis for my decision to separate the material into chapter divisions that coincide with the dates of journeys he made during 1860.

Chapter one covers the first two months that Hills was in Victoria and includes his first visit to New Westminster; chapter two begins with his return to Victoria and ends with Hills' evaluation of the first four months of the work. Chapter three begins with Hills' arrival in New Westminster in May, at the beginning of his lengthy trip to the gold mining region in the Colony of British Columbia; chapters four, five, six, and seven are concerned with this three-month journey. Chapter eight begins in August on Hills' first day back in Victoria and it includes material about his short trip to Admiral Island (Salt Spring Island) and Nanaimo. Chapter nine commences with the consecration of Saint John's Church, Victoria and contains details of a brief trip to the disputed San Juan Island. Chapter ten describes the visit to Barkley Sound aboard the *Grappler*. The final chapter concerns the last two months of 1860, which Hills spent in Victoria, except for a brief trip to New Westminster to consecrate Holy Trinity Church.

One consequence of dividing the diary material into chapters was that I needed to find titles for each chapter. These have been supplied by using phrases from Bishop Hills' comments within each chapter division. They were chosen to identify what appears to be the main activity of each chapter.

The first chapter begins on 4 January because the first page of the original manuscript begins on that date; Hills was still aboard the *Pacific* on the Columbia River near Astoria (Oregon). Therefore, the text for 1860 begins with that date, rather than on the first day of the year, or on the day of his arrival in Esquimalt, January 6. The end of the second volume of the handwritten diaries for 1860 coincides with the end of the year.

The editorial work has been accomplished by two large steps. First, I consulted the handwritten diaries and unpublished manuscripts and then prepared a text based on my own reading of Hills' handwriting which is, in many instances, difficult to decipher. The second part of the work has involved changes to punctuation and spelling. I have added punctuation to clarify the meaning of some sentences. Also, I have cautiously replaced the dash that Hills frequently used to change the phrases into sentences. I have employed square brackets to indicate that a word has been introduced to clarify what appeared to be intended, or an undecipherable word has been omitted. In most cases the omitted words have little influence on the sense of what is written in the original manuscript. I have, for the most part, left Hills' frequent use of ampersands. This seems consistent with the informality of Hills' writing style and with his comment that the diaries contain "jottings made at the time." They were private notes not intended for publication in their original state.

With regard to the spelling of names of places and persons, whenever possible, the "correct" spelling has been added in square brackets immediately following Hills' first mention of the name; thereafter the corrected spelling is used in the text without notation. In some cases it has not been possible to establish a correct spelling. There are several reasons for this. At times, the handwriting is unclear and there is no known record against which to determine what is correct. Consequently some words could not be read. The names of people Hills mentioned have proved difficult to determine in some cases. Names of miners and settlers were not always clearly written and these are impossible to determine with certainty because there is now no way of tracing most of the early settlers and miners that Hills encountered.

The spelling of place names was also different when Hills wrote. For example, he mentioned W. E. Banfield, after whom Banfield was named. Hills' spelling conforms with that used in Walbran's *British Columbia Coast Names* and some local people still recall it by this name. However, in current popular use the name has been altered to Bamfield. Another instance of the difference in place names is that used for what was later known as Lillooet. There were at least three spellings used: Cayuse, Cayoosh and Kayoosch. Hills used Cayuse and Cayoosh.

The names of natives and native words have presented similar problems. Hills mentions the nephew of a Haida chief named "Edensor"; his spelling is close to "Edensah" used by the *Colonist* newspaper in 1861 that is quoted in Akrigg's *British Columbia Chronicle 1847-1871: Gold and Colonists.* He most likely referred to the well-known Chief Edensaw or Edenshaw.

14

Hills usually wrote native words in syllables, and included symbols for pronunciation of the words, based on the sounds he heard, and these are different from recent spellings. In order to establish a consistent spelling for the names of tribes and bands, I have used those that are listed in Wilson Duff's book *The Indian History of British Columbia: Vol. 1, The Impact of the White Man.* I have also consulted several published Chinook glossaries in order to make the spelling of the trade jargon consistent.

In places where Hills' handwriting is cramped, the words are unclear, or the writing is squeezed into the margins, I have found that, with patience, it is possible to decipher almost all that was written. When a sentence was convoluted, I found that adequate punctuation, or the addition of a few words, clarified the meaning. However, this did not always solve the problem and at times it was not possible to determine what was intended. Although I have endeavoured to reproduce exactly what he wrote, some errors are inevitable.

The titles that appear in each dated entry were written by Bishop Hills and these were left in their original state, except for ensuring a consistent placement of dates and days in each entry. The short titles reflect what he considered the central idea of each section.

The introduction that precedes the text is intended to convey only the broad outlines of numerous subjects in the 1860 diaries. It does not attempt to evaluate Hills' work. This decision was made because the period covered in the diaries is only one of the thirty-three years that he was Bishop of British Columbia. It therefore seemed inappropriate to make far-reaching conclusions. The postscript is a response to questions surrounding the pervasive negative image of Hills. It suggests that the dominant image of Hills as eccentric and aloof is the result of interpretations based on a few isolated events in Hills' life. When Bishop Hills' evaluations of his episcopacy and the comments of his contemporaries are taken into consideration, the focus widens and a more balanced view is possible.

The illustrations are intended to support the diary text. The works of artists have been used to enrich the verbal descriptions in the diaries. The cover illustration, loaned by Pat Service, is a modern interpretation of the British Columbia landscape. The maps are also used as illustrations of the diary text, to show the extent of the diocese and the places Hills visited during this time. They reflect Hills' perceptions of the places he visited.

A number of people have been very supportive of this project and my thanks go to them. My initial graduate research on the Bishop Hills diaries began in the Geography Department of Simon Fraser University under Paul M. Koroscil in 1984 and I appreciate his encouragement.

Garth Walker was the first person I encountered with the dream to publish some of the early Hills diaries; he has provided valuable advice during the time I have worked on the diaries. Chad Donald provided computer assistance. Nuria Marti-Barneda assisted with the later stages of the research. Many people at Vancouver School of Theology have been helpful. The staff, faculty and Principal, Bud Phillips, of Vancouver School of Theology have supported this project by providing office space and their good wishes; William R. Crockett is the liaison between the Hills Diaries Project and the school. His comments have also been helpful. I would particularly like to thank Doreen Stephens, archivist for the Ecclesiastical Province of British Columbia and Yukon, and Mary Barlow, archivist for the Diocese of British Columbia, for generous access to the material on Bishop Hills in their collections. Thanks are also due to Susan Harris who cheered me through the ups and downs of the work, to Jean Wilson for advice and to Charlotte Sutton, Patricia Knight, Maureen Selwood and Ann Watson for their interest in the work.

ROBERTA L. BAGSHAW

North Vancouver, 1996

Jottings Made at the Time

THE Colony of Vancouver Island was formed several years after the international boundary was determined by the Oregon Treaty in 1846. However, there were few settlers in the British territory until gold was discovered. Only a small number of people had settled in the Colony of Vancouver Island and the difficult terrain on the mainland made that area generally undesirable to the few who came to the west coast. When James Douglas (1803-1877), the second Governor of the Colony of Vancouver Island, conducted a census of the island's residents in 1855, there were 774 residents; most were between twenty and forty years of age.[1]

The discovery of gold on the mainland caused rapid changes in the Colony of Vancouver Island. Large numbers of men of various nationalities passed through Victoria on their way to the Fraser River. One estimate was that 25,000 miners came to British Columbia by the end of 1858.[2] Many of the miners were American. The population increased so rapidly that Governor Douglas informed the British government there was an urgent need to establish a British presence on the mainland or it would likely fall into American hands.[3]

The government responded to the crisis by creating a second colony named the Colony of British Columbia. Officials for the colony were appointed in 1859. The Governor of Vancouver Island, James Douglas, was named the Governor for the new colony. Colonel Richard Clement Moody (1813-1887), the Chief of the Royal Engineers, and a corps of 150 men were sent[4] to work as surveyors, architects and military troops. Matthew Baillie Begbie (1819-1894) was appointed Chief Justice for the colony. At the same time an Anglican bishop was appointed and given jurisdiction over both colonies. The first Church of England bishop, George Hills, left England in November. He arrived on January 6, 1860.

Background of Bishop George Hills

George Hills was born at Eythorn, Devon, England, on June 26, 1816. At the time of his birth, Hills' father was a captain in the Royal Navy.[5] In 1840 Hills was ordained Deacon and then Priest. He studied at Durham University and received his theological education and D.D. there. His first curacy was at Tynemouth in Northumberland.[6] He then went to

Leeds where his parish work was influenced by a well-known innovator of urban parish work.[7] Under Walter Farquhar Hook (1798-1875), Hills was exposed to modern methods of parish management, which included the appointment of lay men and women to serve in the ministry of the church.[8] Between 1849 and 1859 he was the incumbent at Great Yarmouth. It was during this time that Hills established his reputation as a leader among clergymen.

The Reverend George Hills was appointed Bishop of British Columbia by Royal Letters Patent, issued January 12, 1859. The diocese was named the Bishopric of British Columbia[9] and gave Hills ecclesiastical responsibility for the Anglican church in the colonies of Vancouver Island and British Columbia. Hills was consecrated on February 24, 1859 at Westminster Abbey, when he was forty-three years old.

In the ten months that followed his installation Hills toured England, Ireland and Scotland to raise funds for the missionary society he founded, the Columbia Mission. During this time he gave 114 sermons and attended 177 meetings.[10] In November, he left England. He arrived in Esquimalt on the *Pacific* on January 6, 1860.

Hills' first return voyage to England was in the spring of 1863. During this lengthy furlough he married Maria Philadelphia Louisa King (1823-1888), the daughter of Rear Admiral Sir Richard King. After the marriage in 1865, they returned to Victoria. They had no children and no relatives who permanently resided in British Columbia. However, two of his nephews were in the colonies during Hills' episcopate. Arthur Reid Lempriere, the Royal Engineer who designed Holy Trinity Church in New Westminster, was in British Columbia for several years.[11] William Henry Percival Arden, who was the son of Hills' sister Caroline[12] and who came to work under Bishop Hills in 1891, stayed after Hills resigned.

In 1888 Bishop Hills' wife died and was buried in Ross Bay Cemetery, Victoria. In 1892 he resigned as the Bishop of British Columbia and returned to England. He died in 1895 at the age of seventy-nine.[13]

Hills remained the only Anglican bishop in British Columbia from 1859 to 1879, until the diocese was divided into three. He was responsible for all the activities performed in the name of the Church of England, including missionaries funded by the three main Anglican societies, the Society for the Propagation of the Gospel (SPG), the Church Missionary Society (CMS) and the Continental & Colonial Church & School Society. In 1879 Hills divided the one diocese into three, the Diocese of New Westminster, the Diocese of Caledonia, and the Diocese of British Columbia. He retained his original title but with a vastly reduced area of responsibility, consisting of Vancouver Island and several small islands.

From the time of his arrival Hills planned to spend much of his time "in the neighbouring colony because the greater distances, larger population and more numerous clergy" required "more personal visitation."[14] Consequently, between 1860 and 1863 he attempted to visit as many places as possible. In the summer of 1860 three entire months were spent visiting in the Colony of British Columbia, in addition to shorter trips to both colonies during February, September, October and December.

The Hills Diaries

Although the first extant Hills diary was written in 1838, and there are some short diaries of his travels, more regular entries were made in the diaries after his appointment as Bishop. The diaries that pertain to British Columbia were written between his installation and the year Hills resigned as Bishop of British Columbia, that is between 1859 and 1892.[15] The lengthiest entries were made in 1860; consequently, they reflect his first impressions of a wide variety of events and experiences. The first five years of the diaries consist of nearly 1500 pages of handwritten material.[16] After that time many of the entries were shorter, but Hills continued the diary entries throughout the thirty-three years he was in British Columbia, and during the last three years of his life when he resided in England.[17]

In addition to the diaries, Bishop Hills also wrote numerous letters, and kept record books concerning his activities and decisions on matters affecting the administration of the diocese. He divided these into subjects such as "Private Memoranda on the Character & Work of the Clergy," "Notes & Heads & Thoughts" and "British Columbia Including Vancouver's Island: 1858-1860."[18] Parts of the diaries formed the basis of Bishop Hills' reports and requests for additional funding.[19] The Columbia Mission reports, published at least once a year, contained excerpts from Hills' diaries and the diaries kept by some of the local clergy. The individual reports were discussed at the meetings of the Columbia Mission Society in England and they were published to raise additional funds and to keep subscribers informed.[20] At times, these excerpts were also quoted by boosters of British Columbia.[21] Some of the material was published in the form of sermons, and some of his letters were published by newspapers in Victoria.

In 1860, the "Occasional Paper" described some of Hills' journeys and his observations about the accomplishments of the church in the two colonies. It was published in June along with the sermon Hills gave at the first annual meeting of the Columbia Mission in London before he left.[22] Copies of the 1860 paper were also available in Victoria.

Excerpts of the diaries appeared in books that were widely circulated in England and consulted by emigrants and travellers. Richard Mayne's

Four Years in British Columbia and Vancouver Island contains a chapter on the "Religious and Educational Condition of the Colonies." Mayne provided some background information on the development of these institutions from 1857, and gave most of his attention to the work done by the Church of England. Mayne's book also included extracts from the Hills diary regarding the 1860 trip to the gold-fields.[23] The extracts contain information intended to assist those considering the journey to British Columbia. He also recommended the Columbia Mission reports for further information.[24] Rev. Matthew Macfie's 1865 book *Vancouver Island and British Columbia: Their History, Resources and Prospects* included information about Hills and the Anglican churches and schools in Victoria in a discussion of public institutions.[25] Both Richard Mayne and Matthew Macfie knew Hills and their names are mentioned in the 1860 diaries.

The diary material that relates to natural history is not extensive; it reflects mainly what impressed or interested Hills. In addition to listing the names of plants and birds,[26] Hills wrote a detailed description of a beaver dam he saw while visiting the troops on San Juan Island.[27] Many Nineteenth Century people saw the natural world as "the handiwork of God"[28] and Bishop Hills also regarded nature as God's creation,[29] but this was not the central purpose of the diaries.

The large amount of written material that Hills produced was partly due to the requirements of his occupation and partly the result of his financial situation. He needed a record of his activities and anecdotes of everyday life for the reports he sent to England and the diaries served this purpose. Hills' economic position allowed him more time to write than most other settlers who had to struggle to maintain their daily existence.[30] For example, when Hills left England for the colonies he brought a married couple, Mr. and Mrs. Bridgman, to be his full-time housekeepers.[31] He also had an iron house and church shipped from England; in the spring of 1860 the prefabricated house and church arrived and Hills was able to hire workmen to construct these.[32] Some of the entries in the 1860 diaries indicate that Hills spent the greater part of his day writing.[33]

The diaries contain personal observations written close to the time the events occurred.[34] In their original state there is no indication that the entries were altered with an aim to improve or correct what was written, except for an occasional word which appears to have been changed as Hills wrote.

The Introduction of a Colonial Bishop

Prior to the appointment of a colonial bishop it was customary for the Hudson's Bay Company (HBC) to hire a chaplain to serve the needs of employees at the company forts. Under this arrangement the clergyman was relatively free to conduct his activities as he thought best, provided these did not conflict with the chief factor.

George Simpson (1786-1860), Governor of the Northern Department of the HBC who was "not enthusiastic about appointing a chaplain to serve in the country west of the Rocky Mountains," nevertheless agreed to their appointment with the stipulation that the clergymen should be "under the protection of the chief factor" and "look up to that gentleman for support and assistance in almost everything as a superior" in order to maintain good relations between the two.[35] This was the arrangement under which Rev. Herbert Beaver (1800-1858) was sent to Fort Vancouver in 1836 and later, in 1849, when Rev. Robert John Staines (1820-1858) was appointed chaplain for Fort Victoria.[36] Both clergymen had strong conflicts with the HBC chief factors and returned to England because of their disagreements. The Rev. Edward Cridge (1817-1913) arrived to replace Staines in 1855.[37] He was the last chaplain appointed for Fort Victoria and his relationship with the HBC was much more positive than that of his predecessors.

As the official chaplain, Cridge, and the previous clergymen, conducted services, taught school, performed marriage ceremonies, baptised infants and conducted burial services.[38] The regular activities of the clergy were defined by licences issued by the Church of England before coming to Victoria. There was, therefore, no local Anglican clergyman with the right to perform confirmations and ordinations because these were the prerogative of the bishop. Although a visiting bishop could perform these functions, such visits were rare and the growth of the Church of England was limited by the lack of a resident bishop.

When Hills was installed as Bishop of British Columbia the relationship between the HBC, the local chaplain and the men who represented Anglican missionary societies in the diocese immediately changed. In 1859, in advance of Bishop Hills' arrival, the authority of the colonial bishop was outlined in a directive sent to Governor Douglas.

Rev. William B. Crickmer (1830-1905) arrived late in the year in 1858 and was sent by Governor James Douglas to Fort Langley to start a new church; it was expected that the capital for the new colony would be located at Langley. Shortly after this, the Colonial Secretary, Sir Edward Bulwer Lytton, wrote to Governor Douglas explaining that the missionaries who were arriving in the colony had not received any funds or privileges from him and that "owing to the terms of the Bishop's licence,"[39] Douglas should wait for the arrival of the Bishop before any assignments were made.

> I must instruct you that no permanent ecclesiastical arrangements can be made till they shall have received the sanction of the bishop of B. Columbia who may be expected shortly to arrive in the colony.[40]

Crickmer remained at Langley until Hills moved him to Yale, shortly after his arrival in 1860.

The responsibilities and trust given to Bishop Hills were characteristic of those granted from the time the first colonial bishop was appointed, in 1778. After a round of negotiations between the Crown, the Church of England and the candidate an appointment was made. It was legally based on a Royal Letters Patent, which designated the rights and duties of the colonial bishop. Generally the entire territory of the colonial possession was treated as one diocese and all clergy connected with the Church of England were subject to the bishop.

Colonial bishops were responsible to the Archbishop of Canterbury and considered bishops of the Church of England in foreign parts. Their presence in the colonies was an integral part of British government policy; it was authorized by church and state, but funded through grants and private donations.

A colonial bishop was also expected to raise funds for the diocese.[41] Some colonial bishoprics had benefactors to assist with endowment. Angela Burdett-Coutts provided the initial funding for the colonial bishoprics of Cape Town, South Africa, Adelaide, South Australia and British Columbia.[42]

When a clergyman was considered suitable for an appointment, he was contacted by the Reverend Ernest Hawkins (1802-1868), who in 1858 was the Secretary of the Colonial Bishoprics Council and the Secretary of the SPG.[43] He contacted Hills sometime during 1858.[44]

The first stage of inquiry was conducted on behalf of the Archbishop of Canterbury who formally recommended candidates to the Crown. During this period of negotiations a commitment from the candidate was secured. The appointment was offered on the condition that, if the man was found to be suitable, the candidate would promise not to reject it.[45]

After 1868, when a resolution was passed by the Church of England, colonial bishops could not become a bishop in England after serving in the colonies. The resolution stated that "the use of ex-colonial Bishops was to be deplored, first because it postponed reform, secondly because it tended to encourage resignation of colonial sees, and thirdly that if a man resigned a colonial see it made a presumption that he ought not to be performing episcopal functions in England"![46]

A letter that Hills received after his appointment as Bishop-Elect of British Columbia indicates how his appointment was received by one of his associates.

I hear of a change in your prospects, your destination seems strange & awful. Such an uncivilized & distant region! What a loss you will be to Yarmouth and indeed so by a much wider circle who benefited by your labours. . . . I sincerely wish you every success, although I cannot in truth congratulate on what seems such a desperate undertaking & I must add such a waste of your usefulness—I shall be sorry not to see you again in this world.[47]

Although a successful appointment was accompanied with privileges, it also had considerable disadvantages for the individual selected. There were risks of ocean travel between England and the colonial diocese, the certainty of a rough life in undeveloped territories and often dangerous environments, and the responsibility of transplanting the Church of England in colonies where settlers were sometimes more hostile than supportive.

The Colonial Bishop and Missionary Societies in British Columbia

The regular appointment of colonial bishops was the result of the eighteenth century conflict between the American colonists and the British government. Many colonists rejected the Church of England at the time of the American Revolution because the church was perceived as more loyal to British than to American interests.[48] During the entire American Colonial period no resident Anglican bishops were appointed and the introduction of resident bishops in the British North American colonies was expected to prevent further losses to the British church and state.[49]

The colonial bishops scheme replaced the previous method of licensing chaplains and missionaries through the Bishop of London.[50] It initiated a new concept. Instead of waiting for settlers to become sufficiently prosperous to request a bishop be appointed, the colonial bishops were sent as part of "the actual pioneer force."[51]

By 1859, when Reverend George Hills was named Bishop-Designate of British Columbia, there were six colonial bishops in British North America, and one in Newfoundland.[52] The system had already been in use in colonial Canada and other British colonies for eighty-one years.

Most of the missionaries who were active in colonial British Columbia were sent by the two largest English societies founded to minister to settlers and natives in British colonies. The Church Missionary Society (CMS) and the Society for the Propagation of the Gospel in Foreign Parts (SPG) were the largest missionary societies in Britain as well as the two most active groups in colonial British Columbia.[53] These missionary societies supported single and married men with families, most of whom were ordained clergy.

The orientation of the CMS in the middle of the nineteenth century was the result of policies generated by the wave of pietism that had challenged the established Church of England in the previous century.[54] For the CMS the most important aspect of a missionary was personal piety and, consequently, the role of the bishops in the missionary endeavour was greatly diminished.[55] The CMS did not think that "every missionary undertaking needed to have a bishop at its head, or a bishop to decide which persons should be sent as missionaries."[56]

Two men were sent by the CMS to the Colony of Vancouver Island before 1859. Both left the Church of England in the 1870s because of conflicts with bishops. They were the Rev. Edward Cridge who went to Victoria in 1855 and William Duncan (1832-1918), a catechist, who arrived in 1858. They were well respected for their work and were influential representatives of the colonial Anglican church.[57]

William Duncan was widely known for his work with the Tsimshian Indians at Metlakatla. In 1860 he resided at Fort Simpson and visited Victoria several times.[58] By the 1870s he came into conflict with the Bishop of Caledonia (Ridley). As a result he left the Church of England and moved the natives of Metlakatla to a new site in Alaska.[59]

Reverend Cridge was licensed by Bishop Hills as Rector of Christ Church in 1860. Later, he became the Dean of Christ Church Cathedral, Victoria. During the first years that Hills was bishop relations between the two were cordial,[60] but by the 1870s their differences were beyond repair. In 1874 Cridge left the Church of England after a lengthy and well-publicized battle with Bishop Hills. His disagreements with Bishop Hills were focused on the role of the bishop.[61] Cridge became the Bishop of the Reformed Episcopal Church of America in Victoria.

Missionaries sent out by the Society for the Propagation of the Gospel in Foreign Parts (SPG) followed British colonial expansion.[62] They worked with settlers and natives, but their main focus was with settlers. All these missionaries were sent with the understanding they would be under the direction of the bishop.[63] After 1853, the funds for SPG missionaries were sent in block grants to the colonial bishops for distribution as they deemed appropriate.[64]

The first SPG missionary sent to colonial British Columbia arrived in Victoria in 1859; the Reverend Richard Dowson (1827-1876) worked mainly with natives in the rural area near Victoria.[65] In 1859, the Reverend James Gammage (1822-1893) went to the town of Douglas, the Reverend David Pringle (1828-1908) to Hope, the Reverend John Sheepshanks (1834-1912) to New Westminster and the Reverend Robert James Dundas (1832-1904) to Victoria. In 1860 the Reverend Alexander C. Garrett (1832-1924) came with his wife and two children; he was licensed as missionary clergy to work with natives in Victoria. The Reverend Richard L. Lowe (?-1905) and his wife were assigned to the

Female Collegiate School as well as the Reverend Charles T. Woods (1825-1895) and his wife. Mrs. Woods was the Principal of the Female Collegiate School. Catherine Penrice and her sister Ann came as "female missionaries under the special patronage of Miss Burdett-Coutts."[66] The Penrice sisters had worked under Bishop Hills when he was Curate of Great Yarmouth.[67]

In the same year, the Reverend Octavius Glover (1830-1905),[68] a Hebrew scholar, arrived and was assigned to teach at the Collegiate School for Boys which Bishop Hills founded. The Reverend Robert. C. Lundin Brown (1831-1876)[69] also arrived in 1860 and he was sent to Lillooet. The Reverend Christopher Knipe (1834-1896) was sent to the Colony of British Columbia and Hills assigned him to Yale to assist Reverend Crickmer and to work as an itinerant clergyman among the miners in the area.[70] The majority of missionaries who assisted Bishop Hills in 1860 were supported by the SPG.

Church and State in Colonial British Columbia

In 1859 Bishop Hills outlined a plan for transplanting the Church of England in British Columbia.

> The plan we propose [is] . . . first, to take the hand of the European population by occupying the towns as they rise up . . . and in the unsettled districts of [the Colony of British] Columbia [to supply] ministers constantly itinerating. . . . Thus, nobly supported from the Mother Church and the Mother Land, we may plant from the first in its full integrity the whole institutions of the Church.[71]

His approach was influenced by what had already occurred in the Church of England in other colonies of British North America and by Hills' experience in England.

In places such as Nova Scotia and Upper Canada, the Church of England was the official church by law, or established, at the time of its introduction.[72] However, events in Upper Canada influenced the manner in which the Church of England was introduced in other British North American colonies.

Through the first half of the nineteenth century, there was a long battle between the Church of England and other protestant denominations in Upper Canada concerning the land set aside as an endowment for the church, the Clergy Reserves.[73] When the controversy ended in 1854, "the whole concept of a church establishment in Upper Canada" came to an end.[74] This change had implications for the way the Church of England was introduced in colonial British Columbia. In a letter that Hills wrote to Governor Douglas, he explained that his duty was "to carry out the principles and reproduce the exact resemblance of the Mother Church modified only by necessary circumstances of our colonial position."[75]

Hills planned to build an urban centred-church, implanted at the same time the towns were constructed, without the aid of church establishment. The churches were to be strategically placed in important towns.[76]

In order to determine where permanent churches were to be built, Bishop Hills had to estimate the viability of towns, to decide where clergy should be sent and maintained and where there were sufficient numbers of lay people to support the churches. Thus, his visits to the towns, mining bars, agricultural areas and to rural communities were made because he required first-hand knowledge of the diocese to implement his plans.[77] This is the thread that connects the journeys made in 1860. The three-month journey to the gold mining region and the trips he made with the naval vessels to San Juan Island, Nanaimo, Admiral Island (Salt Spring Island) and Barkley Sound provided opportunities to gather information.

Three factors influenced the location of the Anglican churches in colonial British Columbia: (1) the funds available for development of churches, schools and mission stations, (2) information Hills gathered through discussions with those he encountered after he arrived, and (3) the plan that he had devised before he left England.

In 1859 the Columbia Mission Report published Hills' plan for the new diocese.

> The following is the organization I propose to carry out: First—The Living Agency:
>
> | 1. The Bishop | 5. Lay-Deacons, or Readers |
> |---|---|
> | 2. The Priests | 6. Teachers |
> | 3. The Deacons | 7. Visitors |
> | 4. Probationers | 8. Lenders [of religious books] |
>
> Secondly—The Material Agency:
>
> | 1. The Consecrated Church | 3. Schoolrooms |
> |---|---|
> | 2. Mission Chapels | 4. Mission Stations[78] |

The priests, deacons and probationers held the major responsibility for worship services and teaching. The work of visiting was delegated to ordained and lay people, including women: "Visitors-Females" were to "attend the sick, look up children, care for the Indian females, &c."[79]

The "material agency" indicated the physical structures the church used and how they were to be developed from temporary stations to chapels and finally to consecrated churches. The "consecrated churches" were to be "set apart for ever for public worship, and entirely the property of the church"; the mission chapels were "some stores or other buildings, lent for religious purposes"; the schoolrooms were to be "any place suited for education." The mission stations were "any isolated spots in which a few can be gathered where the Readers [qualified laymen] will go. *Each consecrated church will have its several mission chapels and mission stations. The stations will develop into chapels, and the chapels into churches*" (italics mine). In addition, Hills intended to visit every place in the diocese every year, and to work as a "parochial clergyman in some chief place."

In 1859 Bishop Hills had increased the number of clergymen for the work; the following year he increased the number of churches. When Hills arrived in Victoria in 1860 there was only one Anglican church, the Victoria District Church.[80] By the end of the year Saint John's Church, known locally as the "Iron Church," was consecrated in Victoria. In the mainland colony, the first Anglican church, Holy Trinity, was built and consecrated in the colonial capital, New Westminster. Between 1861 and 1862 three more churches were consecrated, Saint Mark's in Douglas, Christ Church in Hope, and Saint Mary's in Lillooet. Anglican church services were held in a store at Yale during this time.[81]

The number of schools in the Colony of Vancouver Island increased after Hills' arrival. Bishop Hills opened the Boys Collegiate after he purchased the former Congregational meeting house. He began a Female Collegiate School, which later became Angela College. Also he began a school for natives on the Songhee reservation; in 1861 an octagonal building was constructed and the school was operated by Rev. Garrett.[82]

In the mainland colony, all the consecrated churches built by 1863 were located in towns the Royal Engineers had laid out. In rural areas, like Salt Spring Island and Saanich, where local people had requested a clergyman and even offered land, Hills did not move quickly to build churches.[83] It appears he was more concerned to develop the churches in urban areas and new townsites first.

For example, Hills' general impression of Ganges Harbour on Admiral Island (Salt Spring Island) was positive. He praised it as the finest place he had seen for settlement, but the favourable impression did not seem to end in a promise to send a clergyman or build a church.[84]

When Bishop Hills visited Lytton during his spring trip to the gold mining region he found it very unattractive. When he left he remarked "We left Lytton without regret. It is a cold, windy, unsheltered flat & the people are more alien than any place I have been in."[85] His impressions were more negative than those of any other place. There was little local interest for a church in the town of Lytton in 1860 and in 1862 when Hills visited Lytton, he noted that "as before" he "found no encouragement to propose" building a church.[86] But Lytton had a church by 1867 while the church on Salt Spring Island was built in 1892.[87]

With regard to Lytton and Salt Spring Island, Hills' approach was similar. He talked to most of the people who lived there and evaluated the long-term prospects of the place for building a church, but his decisions regarding where to construct churches seemed to follow his plan, not his impressions of which place was the most attractive for settlement.[88]

The Diverse Population in the Colony of British Columbia

The sudden influx of population, the frequent migration to areas of new gold discoveries, the racial diversity of the population and the absence of British loyalty presented new opportunities and problems for the Church of England. Many of the miners who came had worked in the Californian and Australian gold rushes and had followed the rumours of gold to British Columbia.

The town of Hope was one that suddenly became important when gold was discovered and then declined after gold discoveries in the Cariboo drew the residents away. They boarded up their homes and left.

When Hills first visited the town of Hope he was impressed with the natural beauty of the place,[89] but it was the strategic location of the town that convinced him to build a church there. Hope was "near the head of navigation" and "where the river mining district began."[90] The town was expected to develop over time due to its proximity to the gold mining area. Consequently, Christ Church was built and consecrated the following year in Hope.[91]

In 1862, when Hope began its decline, Hills at first thought it might be a temporary change,[92] but by September he was more pessimistic.

> I do not see any immediate prospect of the recovery of this place. There are not above twenty persons left in it. . . . It is just possible there may be during the winter a return of some of the inhabitants who have houses and other property here, but after that should things continue as at present, the Society's [SPG] missionary should be employed elsewhere.[93]

The movement of the resident population from place to place was partly due to seasonal patterns; miners usually moved to the gold mining area in the Spring, but back to a town for the winter because of the lack of regular supplies. There was no means of predicting when, or if, the residents who owned buildings and had business investments would return. A resident clergyman and a consecrated church were signs of progress and stability, but the church had to follow the population movement in order to survive.

The town of Douglas had a population of about two hundred men but only thirty-five were British citizens; the remainder were "German, French, Italians, Africans, Chinese, Spanish, Mexican and American."[94] The largest number of inhabitants were American, second Chinese and then British.[95]

American miners were sometimes hostile because the presence of the Church of England indicated the development of British settlement. When a successful American miner was asked to contribute money toward the construction of St. Mark's church in Douglas, he refused. He told the local clergyman, Gammage, that he would not contribute because Gammage had assured him the construction of the church would "advance the interest of the country & be an improvement."[96]

The Chinese population that arrived at the time of the gold rush comprised another large group of immigrants. Chinese men had been employed as contract labourers in British Columbia as early as 1788, but immigration increased significantly in 1858.[97]

A merchant in Lytton told Hills that there were at least 3000 along the Fraser River "from Fort Hope & upwards" and another 2000 were expected to arrive during the summer of 1860.[98] Those who immigrated from California were fleeing heavy taxes and the prohibition of further Chinese immigration.[99]

Many of the Chinese miners Hills encountered were extracting gold from claims that had already been worked by Europeans: they were "content with a dollar or two dollars a day & frequently [made] much more. They have been buying up claims & paying as much as from 500 to 4000 dollars."[100] Others worked as labourers and gardeners and two men he met operated the toll bridges near Ensley's Flat.[101] At Yale, Hills spoke to a Chinese miner who said that he had a wife and children at Canton: "I asked why he did not bring [them] here. He said he had no means. Another Chinaman who stood by said this country was no place for China [Chinese] ladies, their feet were too small, they were too fine for this place."[102]

The racial diversity was a problem for the Church of England because it made it more difficult to unite the "hostile & discordant elements" in a population that had little or no knowledge of the "Christianity of England": it was "a remarkable feature & a difficulty in dealing with the population."[103]

> There is another reason . . . the National church should strike its roots deeply and firmly in Columbia. . . . I allude to the un-English character of the population. . . . In that respect this colony stands quite alone, there never having been a case, I believe, where so large and preponderating a portion of the population has not been drawn directly from the mother country, but has poured in from, or through neighbouring settlements, and has thus been Americanized in its passage and lost its British habits and feelings.[104]

Hills recognized the indifference of many in the Colony of British Columbia toward religion. He noted that the level of interest in religion among the miners was as low as it could "possibly be among civilized people" and that this condition was "not to be seen elsewhere in a British territory."[105]

There were also positive responses to the Church of England. These are indicated in Hills' accounts of his conversations with miners. He was relaxed and invigorated by his contact with them.

When Hills was at Lillooet, he was welcomed by many who did not usually attend church services. Sunday services, held in a saloon in Lillooet, were attended by miners and natives. The owner of the saloon was pleased to have the services held there.[106]

Several miners remarked that they were surprised to find the bishop in such a remote area, and that although they had not been in a church, or attended services in ten or fourteen years, they were happy to attend his Sunday services.[107] At Canada Flat, near Lillooet, the miners offered to support a minister if Bishop Hills would send one to them.[108]

Bishop Hills and Natives

Bishop Hills began collecting information about the natives in North America before he left England. In 1859, he consulted government reports, newspaper articles and individuals who had some experience with natives in North America.[109] By the time Hills arrived in colonial British Columbia, natives and Europeans had been in contact for at least two hundred years.[110] The negative effects of European contact were well known and obvious to those who lived near natives.[111]

Hills saw the Church of England as an institution of enlightenment for natives. From his perspective teaching English, providing the natives with instruction in civic values, training them for employment and economic sufficiency, and teaching the Gospel were the means to redress the problems caused by white civilization.[112] These ideas were not exclusively Anglican. The Colonial Office and Governor Douglas also endorsed a policy of "civilizing and Christianizing" the natives.[113] In general, western cultural ideals were assumed to be superior to native cultures.[114]

Hills soon had first-hand evidence of the plight of natives when he visited the Songhees in Victoria.

> This misery the poor Indian knew not till the white man came. And the white man, professedly Christian, taught the poor Indian, nay entered & forced the poor Indian to drink, degraded him & ruined him, still more hopelessly than in his native state.[115]

Bishop Hills went to the reserve with Edward Cridge and Joseph D. Pemberton (1821-1895),[116] a magistrate who spoke Chinook jargon and acted as interpreter. The men addressed the Songhees and the natives spoke to them about their concerns for education, better housing and their fears of the Haidas that were camped in Victoria.[117]

A number of people were concerned about the needs of the natives[118] and in April Bishop Hills, Joseph Pemberton and Revs. Dundas and Cridge met to discuss the problems of those in Victoria. They drew up a list of regulations to improve the situation.

all the families should be registered,
[they] should be taxed a small amount,
order should be maintained,
houses should be placed so that sanitary
measures could be observed,
a superintendent [should be appointed],
native police [appointed],
an Institution under a clergyman,
a school [under a] teacher,
an orphanage,[and]
a hospital [provided].[119]

This list is remarkably close to the one that Governor Douglas and William Duncan worked on in the summer of 1860. It has been suggested that Douglas' ideas were likely influential in shaping the list of regulations, and that they served as the "germ of many of the ideas and policies" that Duncan adopted at Metlakatla.[120]

In order to communicate with natives Hills learned to speak Chinook and some words in other native languages.[121] He kept lists of native words and their English translations. In addition to Chinook, he collected words from natives in Barkley Sound, Cowichan, Saanich,[122] Lillooet and Hope,[123] at Yale[124] and at Fountain.[125]

Chinook jargon was in greater use before British Columbia entered Confederation.[126] During the colonial period it provided a limited means of communication between natives and whites. It was initially a trading language that was later used by missionaries to express theological ideas. Hills often used Chinook when he spoke to large groups of natives. Sometimes he, or another clergyman, spoke only the jargon; in other situations the clergyman spoke in English and a native who knew both the Chinook jargon and the local language translated the speaker's remarks either into Chinook or into the local language.[127] By 1904 the Chinook jargon was no longer in use, except for a number of words that came into everyday speech.[128]

The natives used Chinook in addition to their tribal languages and some of the natives Hills knew were quite proficient in English. Michelle, the Chief of the Katzi Indians that Hills met near Langley, apparently understood "a good deal of English" and was "a well known friend to the white man" who wanted his children educated.[129] A Songhee man who went to see Hills several times in Victoria had instructed William Duncan in Tsimshian. Hills commented that the man "had learned English, or rather improved himself in English at the same time. He can speak & write English."[130] On one of the visits John Clark (Clah) impressed Hills with his knowledge of the Christian faith. On another occasion, when Hills delivered the Prayer Book Clah had requested, the young man showed him a box that contained his "writing books & account books." [131]

Two of Hills' entries concerning natives clearly indicate his feelings and his understanding of their responses to his message. One account concerns the Chief of the Fountain Indians. Hills' comments suggest he had a strong sympathy for him and some of the chiefs at Barkley Sound.

According to Hills, the Chief was impressed with what had been said to his people.

> I am sure our addresses made an impression upon these interesting people, especially upon the thoughtful Chilhovsels. I wish I had a missionary to leave amongst them. The example of the white men amongst them is sad & they need every help. They are a simple people as yet, but the youth alas are growing up, of both sexes, precocious in vice. [132]

Hills seemed drawn to them and they appeared to respond to his interest. In October Hills travelled aboard the *Grappler* visiting various places along the west coast of Vancouver Island. On this trip he spent nine of the eleven days with natives who lived near the settlement that was founded by two businessmen, Captain Edward Stamp (?-1872) [133] and Gilbert Malcolm Sproat, in Barkley Sound. On the Sunday before Hills left the settlement, several chiefs attended the services.

> The last named Chief [Wiccanamish] brought me presents and I gave both him & the others a blanket each.
>
> In the evening [Chief] Hy-you Panuel was at the service & I spoke to the people, the settlers present, about the Indians calling on them for sympathy & pointing out the Indians in the very midst of them, ready to be instructed.
>
> I feel greatly interested by these poor people & sometimes I am impelled with a desire to come & live amongst them & devote myself much to their evangelization. [134]

His feelings for the natives extended beyond concerns to civilize and Christianize the natives.

Natives in both colonies presented gifts to Bishop Hills. His descriptions of the gifts they gave him and their expressions of gratitude convinced Hills they had genuinely responded to his overtures. In many instances, when the tents were taken down and the supplies packed to move on, it took hours to say goodbye to the local natives, because every one came to shake hands. The chief of the Fountain people, Chilhovsels, said to Hills that "his heart went with us & hoped our heart would follow him." [135]

In 1863 when Hills was on furlough in England, he gave numerous speeches about the work in British Columbia, and explained the misery that white contact had brought to natives.

It was well worth the while of Christians to inquire what was the process of this fading away of the native races. . . . It was neither more nor less than this, that the civilized man brought to the native race an accumulation of misery, and added that to the already crushing burden of heathenism. . . . Heathenism was, indeed, a heavy burden . . . but after came the civilized man, and what did he do? He brought additional misery to all this. They [Indians] knew how strong the love of home was to us English; but the Indian loved his home ten times stronger than we did . . . but the white man came and took possession of the land; he built and cultivated and fenced these places all round. He warned the Indians to keep off, not to come near; and thus a barbed arrow was driven into their breast, and not removed while the white man was there.[136]

These remarks were based on the understanding he gained through his contact with the natives he encountered in the colonies. Their situation was not simply the plight of a group of people; he knew the faces and names of many natives.

"Vexations & Troubles" in Victoria

After four months in Victoria, Hills noted, "I have had more vexations & troubles than in all my ministerial life before."[137] These troubles continued throughout 1860. Difficulties arose concerning comments he had made in the *Occasional Paper* published in England, the Roman Catholic Bishop Demers protested the construction of Hills' residence on the Church Reserve, and the support Hills gave to the black community in Victoria was criticized. These "attacks"[138] originated in Victoria and were confined to Victoria.[139]

The *Occasional Paper* published by the Columbia Mission Society in England was attacked by the *Colonist*. Hills' perspective was that their remarks were intended "to stir up the Americans & the Roman Catholics against us."[140] Another attack, also published by the *Colonist*, was a pamphlet: *The Occasional Paper: One Letter from the Honorable Lady Lavinia Skewton, London, to the Lord Bishop of Columbia*.[141] It parodied Hills' comments about the sinking of the *Northerner*, the vessel on which Hills was originally booked from California, and Hills' comments about the house he had rented in Victoria. The pamphlet suggested the Anglican Church, was in the colony to "crush out . . . papists, infidels and dissenters."[142]

The Roman Catholic Bishop Modeste Demers had a writ served on Hills in October, ostensibly because a fence had been constructed around part of the Church Reserve on which Bishop Hills' residence was located.[143] Christ Church, the parsonage in which Rev. Cridge lived, Hills' iron house, and the cemetery were on the same property.[144]

The Church Reserve in Victoria was the only piece of public land that was reserved for the Church of England by the Hudson's Bay Company. The land was originally more than 2000 acres and was just over 23 acres in 1860.[145]

In November, Bishop Hills discussed the writ he had received from Demers with the Governor. Douglas told him that he "could see nothing to object to. He had read Bishop Demers letter in the *Colonist* & could not understand what he meant."[146] Hills' view of the legal action was that it was intended to "try the question of the Church Reserve."[147] During all these controversies, Governor Douglas befriended Hills.[148] The relationship between the men was one of mutual respect. They met frequently to exchange information about the development of the colonies and the church, and from time to time for dinner.[149]

Hills also discussed the status of the Church Reserve with Donald Fraser (1810?-1897),[150] a member of the Council of Vancouver Island and a journalist. Fraser said that the land was a gift from the HBC to the church and that the company had first bought the site for £1 an acre and then sold some of the land as town lots for £60.[151] In another note, Hills wrote that the Assembly of Vancouver Island had agreed, in a resolution of September 1858, that the land belonged to the Church of England.[152]

Earlier, in February and March 1860, Bishop Hills had discussed the matter with Alexander Grant Dallas (1816-1882), a director of the HBC, and also with Governor Douglas. Both men understood that the property was intended for the Church of England. Dallas told Bishop Hills that he had recommended the grant be confirmed to the Church of England.[153] Governor Douglas told Hills that he thought the Church Reserve was to be the property of the Church of England because Christ Church was built on the Church Reserve.

> The application had been approved by the Home authorities & nothing was needed but the formal signing of the deeds. The H.B.C. have the legal title. . . . [They] have held back from signing until their claims have been recognized. An understanding has been come to & he supposes there will be no more delay. But the question of the disposition of the land to Ch[rist] Ch[urch] will not be open again. That is settled.[154]

The deed for the property was granted in 1864[155] and Christ Church Cathedral was consecrated in 1865.

The uncertainty connected with the deed delayed the consecration of the cathedral. To consecrate Christ Church as a cathedral, Bishop Hills required possession of the deed. The lack of clear title to the Church Reserve also opened the door to unfounded accusations on the part of people who were convinced the Church of England wanted to be an established church.[156]

Another issue that created trouble for Bishop Hills and similarly was centred in Victoria concerned the black community. In 1860 this divided the congregations in some of the churches in Victoria.

In 1858, a group of American negroes, anxious to escape racial discrimination in California, sent a delegation to Victoria.[157] When the delegation arrived they were welcomed by Governor Douglas and Rev. Edward Cridge. They were assured that they could buy land and, after seven years of residence, become British subjects.[158] A group of 400 negroes arrived in 1859.[159] Many among this group attended the Congregational Meeting House until 1860 when the white members of the church requested the two ministers, Rev. Clarke and Rev. Matthew Macfie, to provide a separate seating area for the negroes. The heated feelings surrounding this issue were strong enough to cause a split among the members of the Congregational Meeting House.[160]

Two prominent businessmen, Mifflin Gibbs and A. F. Francis, went to discuss the situation with Bishop Hills.

> They told me the coloured people had been excluded from the Philharmonic and the Young Mens' Christian Association.
>
> I said, from whatever society they were excluded I was excluded also, for I should belong to nothing where such unrighteous prejudices existed.[161]

Hills argued that they were equal to whites and should not be barred from participating in local events.[162] His position, and the welcome he offered to the blacks, displeased some of the residents in Victoria.

One man was so incensed that he withheld money he had intended to give for the construction of St. John's Church. "Mr. Dundas informed me that some respectable trader named Fellowes had not subscribed to St. John's Church. . . . Mr. Fellowes said the cause of his [not] sending a subscription was that he heard that the Bishop had invited Mr. Lester (a coloured gentleman) to luncheon on the day of the consecration."[163] Another response to Hills' action was to attempt to convince Hills that he should conform to the attitudes of American Episcopalians. In discussions with Mr. and Mrs. Trutch, they told Bishop Hills that "even American Episcopalians who are residing here [in Victoria] refuse to attend church because we make no distinction."[164]

In 1860 change was characteristic of daily life in colonial British Columbia. In Victoria new buildings arose out of the mud that had made it almost impossible to walk in the main part of town during the previous year. Entire buildings were moved, with the furniture still in place! The prefabricated house and church that were shipped from England to Bishop Hills were examples of modern building technology—portable buildings designed for rapid construction. Many people who came through Victoria stayed just long enough to purchase provisions for the months in the gold fields and then left.

In the Colony of British Columbia most of the change centred on the areas of gold mining activity and the nearby towns that supplied the needs of miners. Land values increased rapidly, and the population migrated seasonally between the two colonies.[165] New Westminster prospered as the colonial capital. Government policies were aimed toward gaining civic control over the fluctuating population and effecting permanent settlement. Magistrates and gold commissioners were appointed,[166] civic buildings were constructed and roads were built to improve access to the gold mining area. These were evidence that more change was expected.

The movement of population between the two colonies continued for the next several years. According to the colonial government's records, it was impossible to estimate the number of immigrants and emigrants: "there is a constant tide of both immigration and emigration from and to the neighbouring Colony of British Columbia and San Francisco, so that if it were practicable to exhibit figures under these heads they would convey no information of any value."[167]

Miners, frequently on the move and searching for better prospects, were subject to wide variations in their standard of living. They sometimes stayed because they were too poor to return to the homes they left behind. Much social chaos resulted from the arrival of large numbers of men who had come only to gain a fortune and had no intention of remaining in British territory.

Often, miners knew very little about the backgrounds and families of the men they worked with every day. In one instance, when a man came in search of a relative, the miners he spoke to who actually knew the missing person, and had worked alongside him, said they had never met him because they did not recognize his name. They knew him only by a nickname.[168]

Rapid change also influenced the natives. Many aspects of European contact contributed to the decline of native people. The increase in liquor consumption, the spread of European diseases, and the introduction of western cultural ideas took a heavy toll. There is evidence, in Hills' conversations with native men and women, that they were aware of the negative impact of white civilization[169] but had few resources to adjust to the changes.

"Do Not Publish My Letter. I Write Freely in Private"

Hills was influenced by the changes that occurred in colonial British Columbia. He discovered new ways of conducting services. They were held in saloons, in courthouses and hotels and in private homes. These were departures from the customs he was familiar with in England. Hills recognized the need for new approaches and great tact. He acknowledged that the task ahead for the church was a difficult one.

By the end of 1860 Bishop Hills had experienced a number of triumphs and endured some losses. In Victoria opposition to the presence of a colonial bishop seemed to grow during the year. Attacks in the *Colonist* newspaper and the writ from Bishop Demers came shortly after he returned from his lengthy trip to the Colony of British Columbia. This, and the weight of problems he had with clergy, added to his concerns.

In March, Hills sent Reverend Dowson, who had worked with natives in the Colony of Vancouver Island, back to England, due to problems with alcohol. In April, Mr. Harvey, who had come with the missionaries on the *Heather Bell*, was dismissed a week after his arrival because of his excessive use of alcohol.

Hills' insistence that blacks would be treated the same as whites by the Church of England gave him "serious trouble"; the stand that Hills took in the name of the Church of England "on behalf of the negroes" was "not only against the consensus of lay opinion in Victoria, but also against the practice of almost all other religious denominations."[170] The anti-black feeling was mainly confined to Victoria.[171]

Hills was involved with the efforts made to improve the conditions of natives in Victoria. The provision of schools for children and the work done by the "Improvement Committee" were intended to help natives cope with the pressures of white society.[172] In later years Hills continued to speak to the government about the needs of natives and the direction of government policy.[173]

The first year in British Columbia also changed Bishop Hills. He had left England in 1859 on a wave of success and admiration and by the end of 1860 he was aware that the task ahead of him was tougher than anything he had known in England. In a brief letter to his brother-in-law Hills reviewed the course of his entire year.

> I have been moving much about since I have arrived, now above nine months. I was three months of the Summer travelling in different parts of [the Colony of] British Columbia. The distance was not much, not above 850 miles, but very varied and rough. I walked a good deal.
>
> My object was to visit the mines & see the people. The mountain country was most difficult of access while the scenery was sublime. I found people of all races gathered into this British land. I was generally well received. On one occasion I arrived late at a wayside log house. The owner, an American not only gave us (Rev. Mr. Crickmer, William & myself) beds — or rather blankets (on the floor), but excellent supper & breakfast & free passage over the ferry, taking not a farthing. . . .
>
> At one place, Cayoosh, 250 miles up the Fraser River I encamped on a flat which was being mined. The gold miners often came & sat & talked. I had services with them. . . .

In coming back I had four horses. All is as in England in the middle ages, by packhorses & mules. Two carried my tents, blankets & provisions & two with saddles and saddle bags, we rode. . . . It was a happy life to lead, a continual pic-nic & with many opportunities of doing good.

I am thankful to say I have been enabled to see several important works fairly set going. Victoria is the chief town. When I came there was but one clergyman & he, though a good man, [was] overburdened & the whole state of things was depressed. . . . There was much neglect of religion amongst many professing to be of us.

I am now on a cruise in the *Grappler*. We are anchored in a bay, or rather harbour, thirty miles inland from the Pacific. A settlement is in [. . .] of formation & people have commenced to build houses. . . . There are about 2000 Indians connected with this place. They are an interesting people & well disposed. I am happy to be able to open a mission amongst them, the Sheshaat [Seshart] Indians. . . . I have been learning to speak the language of the Seshart. I have had one meeting & am to have another one tomorrow. I have had several interesting services amongst the white settlers. There are as yet only two women. . . .

I have twelve clergy, two more are on their way. . . . I only wish they had a more worthy head. Often I sigh after the more peaceful & less anxious work of dear old Yarmouth. Here are fierce opponents. . . . Pray, do not publish my letter. I write freely in private.[174]

The experiences Hills had during his three months in the gold fields were among the happiest of the year. When Hills arrived in Hope at the end of the trip, his clothes were in tatters, his shoes worn out and he looked much like any other miner. Hills, remarked, "I certainly have had a rougher time than I ever experienced . . . yet I have enjoyed my journey much."[175]

In Victoria Hills faced "fierce opponents." In November, he wrote in his diary, "Chrysostom says, 'a bishop is more agitated by cares & storms than the sea is by the winds & tempests.' It is some consolation to know that one is not singular in the burdens that weigh heavily upon the mind."[176]

Bishop Hills' 1860 diaries provide a view of the events and people he encountered and places he visited during the second year of his episcopate, his first year in colonial British Columbia. The observations are limited, as all such documents are. They offer only one perspective of the past, limited by the writer's ideas of what he considered important.

The diaries cannot answer all the questions that might be posed.[177] They are fragments from life in 1860, but they are also more than the sum of the answers to questions about the past. The natural flow of the diarist, recording mundane details of daily life alongside events of greater significance, creates an image of the man behind the words and an echo of his voice.

[1] W. Kaye Lamb, "The Census of Vancouver Island," *British Columbia Historical Quarterly*, 4 (1939-40), 55.

[2] Margaret A. Ormsby, *British Columbia: A History* (Vancouver: The MacMillan Company of Canada, Ltd., 1958), 140-41.

[3] *British Columbia*, 146-47.

[4] Frances M. Woodward, "The Influence of the Royal Engineers on the Development of British Columbia," *BC Studies*, 24 (1974-74), 14-15.

[5] Letter from the Rectory, Eythorn, Devon to "Dear Sir," 6 November 1934. British Columbia Archives and Records Service.

[6] Diary of Bishop George Hills (hereafter Diary), 24 February 1859. The information is from a newspaper article, n.d., n.p. Archives of the Anglican Provincial Synod of British Columbia and Yukon.

[7] *Ibid.*

[8] Owen Chadwick, *The Victorian Church: Part II 1860-1901* (London: SCM Press Ltd., 1987), 243.

[9] "Royal Letters Patent Founding and Constituting the Bishopric of British Columbia and Naming and Appointing the Rev'd. George Hills, D.D. the First Bishop Thereof." Date, Jan'y 12th, 1859 (copy) 86-13. Archives of the Diocese of British Columbia.

[10] Diary, 23 March 1864.

[11] Letter to "My Dear Uncle" from A. R. Lempriere, 12 June 1859 Archives of the Diocese of British Columbia. See also *Diary*, 7 August 1860 and Frances M. Woodward, 18.

[12] "Notes on the Ministry and Ordination—6 March 1861–17 August 1892." Archives of the Ecclesiastical Province of British Columbia and Yukon.

[13] H. P. K. Skipton, "A Life of George Hills, First Bishop of British Columbia," unpublished manuscript, 1912. Archives of the Anglican Provincial Synod British Columbia & Yukon.

[14] *Columbia Mission: Occasional Paper* (London: Rivingtons, 1860), 43.

[15] It appears that George Hills began to keep diaries in 1838 at twenty-two years of age, and that this was intermittent until 1859 when he was installed as Bishop of British Columbia.

[16] Bishop Hills went to England to renew subscriptions to the Columbia Mission because the pledges made in 1859 were for a five-year period. During this period there are gaps in the diary entries. He left Victoria in the spring of 1863. He returned in the spring of 1865. During this time he married Maria Philadelphia Louisa King (1823-88); she was buried in Ross Bay Cemetery, Victoria. See John Adams, *Historic Guide to Ross Bay Cemetery* (Victoria: Heritage Architectural Guides, 1983), 11.

[17] The last entry in Bishop Hills' diary is November 17, 1895. He died on December 10, at Parham, Suffolk, England. See Owsley Robert Rowley, *The Anglican Episcopate of Canada and Newfoundland* (Milwaukee: Morehouse Publishing Co., 1928), 37.

[18] See "Inventory of the British Columbia and Yukon Church Aid Society" (Internal Finding Aid, 1987), 1-5. Archives of the Anglican Provincial Synod of British Columbia and Yukon.

[19] *Columbia Mission*, n.p. This short letter from Bishop Hills, 8 May 1860, was published separately from the *Occasional Paper*.

[20] *Occasional Paper*, frontispiece.

[21] See W. C. Hazlitt, *The Great Gold Fields of British Columbia*, 1862, rpt., ed. Barry Gough (Victoria: Klanak Press, 1974), 107-12; and Richard Charles Mayne, *Four Years in British Columbia and Vancouver Island*, 1862, rpt. (Toronto: S. R. Publishers, Ltd., 1969), 532. My thoughts about the contemporary uses of colonial diaries have been influ-

enced by two articles: H. Roy Merrens, "The Physical Environment of Early America: Images and Image Makers in Colonial South Carolina," *Geographical Review* 59 (1969), 529-54; Paul M. Koroscil, "Boosterism and the Settlement Process in the Okanagan Valley, British Columbia, 1890-1914," *Canadian Papers in Rural History*, 5 (1986), 73-74.

22 "Occasional Paper," 1860. This contains a list of publications sold in aid of the Columbia Mission. Archives of the Anglican Synod of the Ecclesiastical Province of British Columbia and Yukon.

23 *Four Years in British Columbia*, 107-10.

24 Mayne, 305-52.

25 Matthew Macfie, *Vancouver Island and British Columbia: Their History, Resources and Prospects* (1865; rpt. Toronto: Coles Publishing Co., 1972), 80-85.

26 Diary, 20, 21 July 1860.

27 Diary, 10 October 1860.

28 Carl Berger, *Science, God, and Nature in Victorian Canada* (Toronto: Univ. of Toronto Press, 1983), xii-xiii.

29 In the description of scenery at Hope, Hills' remarks end with the expression "O Lord how manifold are thy works." Diary, 5 June 1860.

30 "The Physical Environment of Early America," 529-30.

31 Hills consistently spelled Bridgman without an "e." For an alternate spelling see Jean Friesen, "George Hills," *Dictionary of Canadian Biography, XII, 1891 to 1900* (Toronto: Univ. of Toronto Press, 1990). Mr. and Mrs. Bridgman accompanied him on board ship. See also the letter to Caroline [Arden], 3 December 1859, Archives of the Ecclesiastical Province of British Columbia & Yukon. Also see Diary, 19 July 1860.

32 For a description of the interior of the iron house, Bishops Close, see Dorothy Blakey Smith, ed., *Lady Franklin Visits the Pacific Northwest: Being Extracts from the Letters of Miss Sophia Cracroft, Sir John Franklin's Niece, February to April 1861 and April to July 1870*, (Victoria: Provincial Archives of British Columbia, 1974), 16, 118. For an explanation of the process of purchasing, and shipping the iron buildings, see Stuart Underhill, *The Iron Church: 1860-1985* (Victoria: Braemar Books, 1984), 4-5. For additional information on the iron church and photographs of the exterior and interior, see Barry Downs, *Sacred Places: British Columbia's Early Churches* (Vancouver: Douglas & McIntyre, 1980), 52-55.

33 See Diary 6, 31 July 1860.

34 In several entries Hills wrote that he had spent the greater part of the day writing. It is probable that on some occasions he recorded his activities the day they occurred, and on days when he was too busy to write, he made the entries several days later.

35 G. Hollis Slater, "New Light on Herbert Beaver," *British Columbia Historical Quarterly*, 6, No. 1 (1942), 15-16.

36 The Reverend Herbert Beaver had conflicts with Chief Factor McLoughlin and Rev. John Staines strongly opposed HBC's policy at Fort Victoria. See "New Light of Herbert Beaver," 16-28.

37 Dorothy Blakey Smith, "The Journal of Arthur Thomas Bushby, 1858-1859," 21 Nos. 1-4 (1958), 171.

38 Slater, 27.

39 "Correspondence Relating to Bishop Hills: 1859." Two letters from Colonial Secretary E. B. Lytton to Governor Douglas, 31 January 1859 and 24 March 1859. This letter shows that Governor Douglas was previously informed of the government's intention to establish a Colonial Bishopric in British Columbia. Archives of the Anglican Provincial Synod of British Columbia & Yukon.

40 Letter of E. B. Lytton to Governor Douglas, 24 March 1859. Archives of the Anglican Provincial Synod of British Columbia and Yukon.

[41] In 1787 the See of the Bishop of Nova Scotia "extended over the whole of North America, but was practically limited to Nova Scotia and New Brunswick." See *The First Century of the Colonial Episcopate, 1787-1887* (Westminster: SPG, n.d), 5-7.

[42] Edna Healey, *Lady Unknown, The Life of Angela Burdett-Coutts* (London: Sidgwick & Jackson, 1984), 155. See also *Occasional Paper*, frontispiece, which illustrates a drawing of both buildings; however, the buildings were located on different lots. Angela Burdett-Coutts provided a church which became St. John's Church, Victoria, a cottage which Hills named Bishops Close and £25,000 for the endowment of the colonial bishopric of British Columbia. The buildings were shipped to Victoria in 1860, see Diary, 2, 4 March 1860.

[43] T. R. Millman and J. L. H. Henderson, "Ernest Hawkins," *Dictionary of Canadian Biography*, 1861-1870, v. IX, 378-79.

[44] The Rev. Ernest Hawkins served as General Secretary for the S.P.G. between 1843 and 1865. He was the negotiator for the Bishop of Capetown (Robert Gray), in 1847, and when George Hills was appointed. Hills and Bishop Gray were close friends and Hills consulted Robert Gray for advice about what he would need to meet the demands of office. See Diary, 29 January 1859. See also, Pascoe, 835.

[45] For an explanation of the kind of negotiations Rev. Ernest Hawkins conducted, see Rev. Charles Gray, *Life of Robert Gray: Bishop of Capetown and Metropolitan of Africa, Volume 1* (London: Rivingtons, 1876), 100. Bishop Robert Gray was a close friend of Bishop Hills. See Diary, 29 January 1859.

[46] *The Victorian Church*, 344.

[47] Letter of Maria T. King to Rev. George Hills, November 8, 1858. Archives of the Anglican Provincial Synod of British Columbia & Yukon.

[48] The first colonial bishop to be appointed was Charles Inglis, Bishop of Nova Scotia, in 1787. C. F. Pascoe, *Two Hundred Years of the S.P.G.: An Historical Account of the Society for the Propagation of the Gospel in Foreign Parts, 1701-1900, Volume 2* (London: S.P.G., 1901), 758.

[49] *Two Hundred Years of the SPG*, 751-52. See also Ernest Hawkins, *Historical Notices of the Missions of the Church of England in the North American Colonies, Previous to the Independence of the United States: Chiefly from the MS. [Manuscript] Documents of the Society for the Propagation of the Gospel in Foreign Parts* (London: B. Fellowes, 1845), vi, 402.

[50] *Ibid*. See also Hans Cnattingius, *Bishops and Societies, a Study of Anglican Colonial and Missionary Expansion, 1689-1850* (London: S.P.C.K., 1952), 57-63, 231-32.

[51] *Bishops and Societies*, 199-200.

[52] *Two Hundred Years of the SPG*, 758.

[53] *Bishops and Societies*, 109.

[54] *Bishops and Societies*, 57.

[55] *Bishops and Societies*, 61-63.

[56] *Bishops and Societies*, 59.

[57] For discussions of the work of William Duncan, see Jean Usher, *William Duncan of Metlakatla: A Victorian Missionary in British Columbia* (Ottawa: National Museums of Canada, 1974); Robin Fisher, *Contact and Conflict: Indian-European Relations in British Columbia, 1774-1890* (Vancouver: UBC Press, 1977), 125-45; John Webster Grant, *Moon of Wintertime: Missionaries and the Indians of Canada in Encounter Since 1534* (Toronto: University of Toronto, 1984), 129-32; F. W. Howay, *British Columbia from Earliest Times to the Present, Vol. 1* (Vancouver: S. J. Clarke Pub. Co., 1914), 617-27 and Peter Murray, *The Devil and Mr. Duncan: A History of the Two Metlakatlas* (Victoria: Sono Nis Press, 1985). For a view of the early work of the Rev. Edward Cridge, see F. W. Howay, "The Negro Immigration into Vancouver Island in 1858," *British Columbia Historical Quarterly*, 3 (1939): 101-13. For a discussion of early missionary work in British Columbia see Frank A. Peake, *The Anglican Church in British Columbia* (Vancouver: Mitchell Press, 1959), 10-24.

[58] Diary, 30 May, 10, 12, 13 August 1860. See also *William Duncan of Metlakatla*, 55.

[59] *William Duncan of Metlakatla*, 59.

[60] Diary, 6, 8 January 1860. Bishop Hills was the godfather for Mr. and Mrs. Cridge's daughter, Mary Hills Cridge. She was christened on September 13, 1860, the same day that St. John's Church, Victoria was consecrated. See Diary, 13 September 1860.

[61] *Trial of the Very Reverend Edward Cridge, Rector and Dean of Christ Church Cathedral, Victoria* (Victoria: The Victoria Standard Office, 1875), iv. Archives of the Anglican Provincial Synod of British Columbia and Yukon. See the final chapter for further details regarding this conflict.

[62] *Bishops and Societies*, 207.

[63] *Bishops and Societies*, 219.

[64] *Ibid.*

[65] Diary, 13, 20 February, 6 March 1860.

[66] *Occasional Paper*, 20.

[67] *Ibid.*

[68] Simon H. D. Carey, "The Church of England and the Colour Question in Victoria, 1860," *Journal of the Canadian Church Historical Society*, XXIV No. 2 (1982), 64.

[69] Rev. R. C. Lundin Brown, *British Columbia: An Essay* (New Westminster: Royal Engineers, 1863). British Columbia Archives and Records Services. See also Carey, 64.

[70] 'Synodal Notes and Memorandum Book,' 19 January 1860. Archives of the Anglican Ecclesiastical Province of British Columbia and Yukon.

[71] "Meeting at the Mansion House," 1859, 24-25.

[72] Judith Fingaard, *The Anglican Design in Loyalist Nova Scotia: 1783-1816* (London: S.P.C.K., 1972), 2-3, 62.

[73] Alan Wilson, *The Clergy Reserves of Upper Canada* (Ottawa: The Canadian Historical Association, 1969), 3-10.

[74] J. L. H. Henderson, "The Abominable Incubus," *Canadian Church Historical Society*, 11, No. 3 (1969), 5.

[75] Letter from the Bishop of British Columbia to his Excellency Governor Douglas, Victoria, 4 January 1862, Archives of the Diocese of British Columbia.

[76] The Church of England was located in the centre of the plan for the town. Roberta L. Bagshaw, "Settlement and the Church of England in the Bishopric of British Columbia: 1859-1863," (MA Thesis, Simon Fraser University, 1987), 47-49.

[77] Reverends Sheepshanks, Pringle, and Crickmer came to visit Bishop Hills within six weeks of his arrival in Victoria, and they would have provided him with information about the towns in the Colony of British Columbia.

[78] "Occasional Paper," 1860, 9.

[79] *Ibid.* The information in this paragraph and the next one is from the same source.

[80] The Victoria District Church built by the HBC was eventually consecrated Christ Church cathedral in 1865. By 1859 there were other churches, but there was no increase in the number belonging to the Church of England until after Hills arrived. See also Edward Mallandaine, *The First Victoria Directory* (Victoria: Edward Mallandaine & Co., 1860), 54, Vancouver Public Library microfiche reel.

[81] Diary, 10 June 1860.

[82] *Lady Franklin Visits the Northwest*, 19.

[83] Bishop Hills was offered land to build a church in Saanich. See Diary, November 6, 1860.

[84] Diary, 23 July 1891. A mission church, Saint Mark the Evangelist, Salt Spring Island, was erected in 1889. Bishop Hills' letter to the Society for the Promotion of Christian

Knowledge dated 23 July 1891 requested funds for books for the church. Archives of Anglican Synod of the Diocese of British Columbia.

85 Diary, 3 July 1860.

86 Diary, 29 June 1862. In this entry Hills wrote that he had a plan for a church. St. Paul's Church was not built until 1865.

87 *Columbia Mission Report*, 1868, 98 and *British Columbia Church Aid Society Yearbook*, 1912, 67.

88 Diary, 24 October 1860. His visit to the settlement in Barkley Sound was conducted in a similar manner.

89 Diary, 7 June 1860.

90 Letter of Bishop Hills to Rev. Ernest Hawkins, 1 June 1861. Archives of the Diocese of British Columbia.

91 This is the only church that remains of those built between 1860 and 1863. It was constructed by the Royal Engineers.

92 Diary, 19 June 1862.

93 Diary, 24 September 1862.

94 "Bishop of Columbia Correspondence" 1859-1876, 10. Archives of the Diocese of British Columbia.

95 "Occasional Paper," 1860, 15.

96 Diary, 23 March 1861.

97 David Chuen-yan Lai, "Chinese Communities" in *British Columbia: Its Resources and People*, ed. Charles N. Forward (Victoria: University of Victoria, 1987), 335-37.

98 Diary, 29 June 1860.

99 Diary, 13, June 1860.

100 Diary, 13 June 1995.

101 Diary, 29 June, 23 July, 1860.

102 Diary, 15 June 1860.

103 Diary, 8 August 1860.

104 "Speeches," 1860, 110.

105 Diary, 8 August 1860.

106 Diary, 8 July 1860.

107 Diary, 7 July 1860.

108 Diary, 17, 18 July 1860.

109 Before leaving England, Bishop Hills read material written by Paul Kane and the report written by Sir George Simpson, North American Director of the Hudson's Bay Company. See "British Columbia Including Vancouver's Island: 1858-1860." Archives of the Anglican Provincial Synod of British Columbia.

110 See *Moon of Wintertime*, 119.

111 Captain James Charles Prevost was an officer on *HMS Satellite*. He was on the West Coast between 1857 and 1860. He has been considered the one responsible for the CMS sending William Duncan, who established the Metlakatla Indian mission. Captain Prevost transported Duncan free of charge in 1857. John T. Walbran, *British Columbia Coast Names: 1592-1906*, 1909; rpt. (Vancouver: Douglas & McIntyre, Ltd., 1971), 192, 400.

112 "Extracts of Speeches Delivered in England by the Bishop of Columbia," 1863-64, 19-20.

113 *William Duncan of Metlakatla*, 56.

114 "Meeting at the Mansion House," 1859, 23-24.

[115] Diary, 23 March 1860.

[116] Dorothy Blakey Smith, "The Journal of Arthur Thomas Bushby, 1858-1859," *BCHQ* 21 (1958), 190. Joseph D. Pemberton was a Churchwarden at Christ Church, Victoria. See also Diary, 8 January 1860.

[117] Diary, 17 January 1860. See also *House of Assembly Correspondence Book: August 12, 1856–July 6, 1859* (Victoria: Archives of British Columbia, 1918), 45-49.

[118] Diary, 3, 6, February, 23 March, 6 April 1860.

[119] Diary, 6 April 1860. See a discussion of the plan of improvement in *William Duncan of Metlakatla*, 55-57. See also Diary, 10 August 1860.

[120] *William Duncan of Metlakatla*, 56.

[121] Diary, 16 February, 10 July, 3 August, 25 October 1860. Also see Letter of Bishop Hills to McSwiney, 27 October 1860. Archives of the Anglican Synod of British Columbia.

[122] Among his papers are lists of words that were collected. "Words Collected by the Rev. R. Dowson, February 1859–March 1860." This list contains 36 words from "Barclay [Barkley] Sound," 69 Cowichan words, 51 Saanich words and 269 Chinook words with phonetic symbols. Hills' remarks on "word taking" are in the entries for 17, 19 January, 16 February, 10 July, 3, 8, August, and 25 October 1860. Also see *A Manual of Ethnological Inquiry: Being a Series of Questions Concerning the Human Race, Prepared by a Sub-Committee of the British Association for the Advancement of Science, appointed in 1851*, and Adapted for the use of Travellers and Others, in Studying the Varieties of Man (London: Taylor and Frances, 1852). Archives of the Anglican Provincial Synod of British Columbia and Yukon.

[123] 10 July, 3 August 1860.

[124] Diary, 25 June 1860.

[125] Diary, 10 July 1860.

[126] Robie L. Reid, "The Chinook Jargon and British Columbia," *British Columbia Historical Quarterly*, 6 (1942), 5-11.

[127] *A Bishop in the Rough*, 43-45. These references explain the process of translating English into Chinook and how simultaneous translation occurred at large gatherings. Bishop Hills encountered an Oblate priest in Victoria who used similar methods with the Snokomish Indians of Puget Sound; see Diary, 20 March 1860.

[128] "The Chinook Jargon," 5-11. By 1904 the Chinook jargon was no longer in use, except for a few words that came into ordinary speech in British Columbia. See also Barbara P. Harris and Andrea R. Giles, "An Annotated List of the Acquisitions and Holdings of the Chinook Jargon Project at the University of Victoria" (Victoria: University of Victoria, 1990).

[129] Diary, 27 May 1860. His method of gathering information from natives was outlined in a letter he wrote to one of his clergy in 1868. See letter of Bishop Hills to Rev. J. Xavier Willemar, 14 May 1867. Archives of the Anglican Provincial Synod of British Columbia and Yukon. See also "Ninth Annual Report of the Columbia Mission for the Year 1867," 103.

[130] Diary, 18, 21 January 1860. Hills wrote the name as John Clark. Clah is mentioned in *William Duncan of Metlakatla*, 43, and by F. W. Howay, in British Columbia *from Earliest Times to the Present, Vol. 1*, 619.

[131] Diary, 18, 21 January 1860.

[132] Diary, 15 July 1860. See 8-18 July for Hills' comments on Chilhovsels.

[133] "The Journal of Arthur Thomas Bushby," 194.

[134] Diary, 28 October 1860.

[135] Diary, 17 July 1860.

[136] "Extracts of Speeches Delivered in England by the Bishop of Columbia," 1863-64, 8-10. See also Diary, 26 May 1860.

137 Diary, 18 May 1860.

138 Diary, 5 October 1860.

139 Diary, 6 September 1860.

140 *Ibid.*

141 *The Occasional Paper: One Letter from the Honorable Lady Lavinia Skewton, London, to the Lord Bishop of Columbia* (Victoria: British Colonist, 1860). British Columbia Archives and Records Service.

142 *Ibid.*

143 Diary, 13-16 October 1860. The writ was served on Bishop Hills, Rev. Cridge, and Churchwardens Joseph Pemberton and Fred Wood.

144 Diary, 12, 13, 15, 16, 18 October 1860.

145 See correspondence of Douglas to Barclay 28 January 1852 and 8 April 1853 in Leonard Wrinch, "Land Policy of the Colony of Vancouver Island, 1849-1866," MA Thesis, University of British Columbia 1932, 235. Also see Dorothy Blakey Smith, editor, *The Reminiscences of Doctor John Sebastian Helmcken* (Vancouver, University of British Columbia Press, 1975), 148, footnote 3, and Plate 12. For another view of the Church Reserve in Victoria see Roberta L. Bagshaw, "Church of England Land Policy in Colonial British Columbia," ed. Paul M. Koroscil, *British Columbia: Geographical Essays in Honour of A. Macpherson* (Burnaby: Simon Fraser University, 1991), 52-55.

146 Diary, 2 November 1860.

147 *Ibid.*

148 Diary, 6 January 1860.

149 Diary, 2 November 1860.

150 *British Columbia Coast Names*, 190.

151 "Notes & Heads & Thoughts on Matters Affecting Christ Church," 27 January 1860, 1. Archives of the Anglican Provincial Synod of British Columbia and Yukon. See also Diary, 8 March 1860.

152 *Ibid.*

153 "Notes & Heads & Thoughts," 14 February 1860, 2.

154 "Notes & Heads & Thoughts," 2 November 1860, 68.

155 "Grant for the Site & Endowment of Christ Church &c. Victoria, Vancouver Island," dated 6 May 1864. Archives of the Diocese of British Columbia.

156 For a discussion of the view held by the Colonial Office and by Bishop Hills, see excerpts of a speech given by Chichester Fortesque, Under-Secretary of State for the Colonies, Columbia Mission: "Speeches," 1860, 18-19. For another view see Howay, *British Columbia from Earliest Times to the Present, Vol. I*, 616-17.

157 F. W. Howay, "The Negro Immigration into Vancouver Island in 1858," *BCHQ*, 3 (1939), 111.

158 *Ibid.*

159 "The Negro Immigration," 113.

160 Diary, 18 March 1860.

161 Diary, 26 March 1860.

162 Diary, 15, 18 March 1860.

163 Diary, 3 March, 4 October 1860.

164 Diary, 15 March 1860.

165 *British Columbia Blue Book: 1860-1871*, 147. No census was taken in the Colony of British Columbia in 1860. In 1861 the entry states that the number of emigrants and immigrants was "not computed," 153. Provincial Archives of British Columbia, microfiche.

[166] *British Columbia Blue Book, 1860-1871*, 155.

[167] *British Columbia Blue Book: 1860-1871*, 227. This comment was made for 1863.

[168] Diary, 28 June 1860. See also S. D. Clark, "Mining Society in British Columbia and the Yukon," in *British Columbia: Historical Readings*, ed. W. Peter Ward and Robert A. J. McDonald (Vancouver: Douglas & McIntyre Ltd., 1981), 216-17.

[169] Diary, 6, 21 April 1860.

[170] "The Colour Question," 65. See also Crawford Kilian, *Go Do Some Great Thing: The Black Pioneers of British Columbia* (Vancouver: Douglas & McIntyre, 1978), 60, 79-82.

[171] *Go Do Some Great Thing*, 84.

[172] Diary, 23 November 1860.

[173] Fisher, 170.

[174] Letter of Bishop Hills to Mr. McSwiney, 27 October 1860. Archives of the Diocese of British Columbia.

[175] Diary, 30 July 1860.

[176] Diary, 21 November 1860.

[177] Barbara Belyea, *Columbia Journals: David Thompson* (Montreal: McGill-Queen's University Press, 1994), 27.

CHAPTER 1

1860
Victoria is situated upon a rising ground
4 January – 29 February

January 4, Wednesday

We moved in the night from St. Helens [Oregon], having taken on board thirty oxen, 150 sheep and many [fowl], besides passengers & freight, part of which [were ...] 1000 boxes of apples for San Frisco, all from Portland. A fog came on & checked our progress down the river. We reached Astoria about two [o'clock].

ASTORIA

Washington Irving has given this [place] to fame. It was the seat of a venturous enterprise set on foot by Mr. Jacob Astor of New York early in the century. Many deeds of daring & much hard endurance attended its first years. It was taken by the English in the war with America & restored at the peace.

It never made progress. Its hopes now are revived by the increased traffic with the north & up the river.

A worthy elderly gentleman named Powers, the Deputy collector & a resident here, was one of our passengers. He said there [are] about 400 people. They have a Recorder & Corporation. They have no resident minister of any denomination. There is only one man [who is] a 'member' of any 'church' & five women. The mass are infidels. They had a resident Methodist preacher for a time but he left. Bishop Scott of Oregon had been there once or twice.

Mr. Powers lives in a picturesque house on the slope which is fringed, above [his house], with the forest.

We passed some waterfalls on our way. At length, [we] came to anchor in Baker Bay inside the bar, the surf upon which was too rough to cross. Close to us is what, on the map, has the grandiloquent title of Pacific City. It never had above one house or so. It has but one now, and that is deserted. There are many such delusions.

CURIOUS INCIDENT

At dinner today I happened to look at the letters on the knife by my plate when on it were these words, 'T. Matsons—Columbia Place,

Sheffield'! Here on the Columbia River was my knife from England & the spot of its manufacture, Columbia Place, & I bound to [British] Columbia. I showed it to my next neighbour who happened to be a Quaker gentleman from near Leeds in Yorkshire!

Had a long talk this evening with Captain Pattison upon religious matters. He is an intelligent & devoted churchman.

January 5, Thursday.

About nine [o'clock] we weighed anchor and crossed the bar of the Columbia [River] which is distant about 190 miles from Victoria. The coast presents no remarkable features northwards, the country inland is not of much value. It was this portion we contended for previous to the settlement of the Oregon Boundary in 1846. So far as this district is concerned we have not lost anything. There was involved, however, the southern side of the Strait of [Juan de] Fuca & Pugets [Puget] Sound which are important.

AN ACTOR IN SICKNESS

I visited in his cabin today a young man of about thirty-two years of age who is on his way to [San] Francisco, there to die of consumption. For ten years he has been on the stage.

Hearing he was ill, I tapped at his cabin door. He was in his berth, his wife was ill from sea sickness and there were two children.

He was glad, he said, for someone to read with him. He knew he could only live a few months. 'Are you cheerful as to the prospect?' 'No indeed,' he said. 'I am greatly fearful, I have lived a sad life. Oh, that I had never gone upon the stage! It is horrible to think of these past ten years, yet I never was happy. I would any time have taken fifty lashes to avoid going on to the boards, it was so degrading. I felt it so. I believe God makes the occupation possible to deter men from it.' As he spoke he rolled his eyes about & seemed racked with remorse.

I learned from him that he had been brought up a Baptist, that he had been converted, or thought so at the time he was & took pleasure in Sunday schools, city missions & other worthy objects, but came to California & all this feeling went away.

I read & spoke to him of the only remedy, of Christ's love & perfect work. His blood could cleanse *all* sin away, the sin of the backslider as well as other sin. Christ sought him, be sure, let him deepen penitence & quicken faith in Jesus, let him seek the Holy Spirit to give him this true [. . .] faith & then his heavenly Father would receive him yet. He expressed his wish to know he was saved, that he could feel saved. I urged not to seek that feeling but to seek Christ in a penitent spirit, look to Jesus. Many, in seeking persuasion, looked off from Jesus.

48

I am thankful to believe I was a help to this poor penitent who expressed regret I was to leave the ship at Vancouver [Island]. I promised to see him again that evening, but on looking in about half past seven, I found himself, wife & children all asleep.

God grant him peace!

TERMINATION OF VOYAGE

We are within a few hours of Victoria. That spot once so distant is now close at hand. This is the 49th day since leaving England. The time has been passed in the following stages:

Left Southampton	Nov. 17		
Reached St. Thomas	Dec. 4,-days	17	-3622 [nautical] miles
Left [St. Thomas]	5,-	1	-
Arrived at Colon	10,-	5	-1080
Left Panama	13,-	3	- 48
Arrived Francisco	26,-	13	-3200
Left Francisco	29,-	3	-
Reached Victoria	Jan. 6,-	8	- 800

50 [days] -8750 [miles]

I thank a merciful God for safety, for health & for a favourable voyage in all respects. May the influence of his Spirit go with me in the new career before me—guiding me—strengthening me. May I be faithful, bearing a true witness for Christ my Lord & laying in all their just proportions the foundations of his Church. May I myself more & more build upon the one foundation rock, rooted & grounded in him. So that, the voyage of life over, I may 'finish my course with joy, and the ministry which I have received of the Lord Jesus, to testify the Gospel of the grace of God.'

January 6, Friday, Epiphany.

ARRIVAL—THE BRITISH SQUADRON

Entered the harbour of Esquimault [Esquimalt] about half past nine o'clock. A beautiful & safe retreat for a large force. There lay four noble men of war from which floated the dear old ensign of England. The *Ganges* Flag Ship, [under] Admiral Baynes; the *Satellite* Frigate, [under] Captain Prevost; the *Tribune* & the *Plumper*. Boats from the two former vessels immediately arrived alongside with officers from the Admiral & Captain Prevost to offer me hospitality & any attention. The *Satellite*'s boat arrived first & I agreed to go then. I had some breakfast & wrote a letter which went back by the *Pacific*. The Admiral then was announced. He was indignant at my being taken possession of by the *Satellite* & spoke strongly to Captain Prevost, not however in my presence. I afterwards returned the Admiral's visit on board the *Ganges*.

My good friend & former Curate Dundas having appeared, the Admiral sent us ashore in his barge with Flag Captain Fulford. They wished to convey me round to Victoria but I preferred the walk, and walk it was, such as I had never taken before by a road, such a road, deep in mud the like of which no one in England could imagine. I had my long boots on & so far was fortified, but it was hard work, & thus mudded & on foot did I make my entrance into Victoria.

ESQUIMALT ROAD AND SCENERY

The road from Esquimalt is about 3 miles into Victoria, through a wooded & partly cleared district. There is much undulation & here & there is a view on the left or south of the bay & the Straits of [Juan de] Fuca. Beyond the Straits, about twelve miles off, rise up in all shapes the lofty ranges of American mountains with snow clad tops & wooded sides. They are very beautiful. The sea was placid & the sun shone brightly.

Approaching Victoria we came to the harbour of that place, crossing it by a bridge. Close on the Esquimalt side were villages of Indians. Many of these poor creatures were met.

VICTORIA

Victoria is situated upon a rising ground. It is much more spread out than I expected & bears every mark of substantial progress. The houses & stores are almost all of wood. It was a day of excitement, nomination of candidates for a general election. The way up to the house provided for me by Mr. Dundas was deep in mud. Yet there was progress making in improvement & everybody said this is nothing to what things were a year ago. Fort Street however now, 1860, January 6, is up to the knees nearly in mud. There are no pavements even of wood. It is heavy labour to walk even upon the side paths but to venture upon the road is to descend into a gulf of difficulty indeed. This is pretty much the character of all the streets excepting perhaps Government Street which is a trifle better.

MY HOUSE

[It] is a wooden one of 4 rooms below & the same above, with a verandah in front & a wooden paling to the street. The rooms are about twelve feet by ten. There are no grates, only hearths where wood is burned. It belongs to a coloured man. I pay 30 dollars a month, i.e., 6£—or at the rate of 72£ a year. It is rather a chilly place but I thank God for being housed at last. Having seen & arranged for immediate occupation, I departed to pay my respects to the Governor.

VISIT TO GOVERNOR DOUGLAS

I found His Excellency at the government buildings in a spacious room. He is a man of about 60. He was stiff & somewhat reserved in manner. We spoke upon general subjects. On my speaking of the enterprise & usefulness of the Americans as pioneers he exhibited his sensitiveness of any slight upon the Hudson's Bay C[ompany] people who had opened roads everywhere. I might have said they had founded no cities. The roads were intended for the hunter but not for civilization. Mr. Douglas' wife is a half caste between Indian & Canadian. She seldom appears but is, I understand, an amiable person.

On returning to my domicile I found all my goods had arrived, at least nearly all. Captain Prevost had kindly sent them round.

During the afternoon the Rev. Mr. Cridge called upon me. He is the minister of the only church in Victoria. He seems an amiable & good man.

January 7, Saturday.

The day fine. Received visits from officers of the fleet & others. Returned Mr. Cridge's visit. Arranged about the service for tomorrow. Much pleased with his tone. He had been accustomed to give the Holy Communion to a rail full at a time. This will be discontinued. He is most anxious to have all things in order as well as to edification. I explained my desire to see the regulations of the church fully carried out. If any appeal were ever made to me by members of a congregation or by the clergy my decision would be, must be, in accordance with the Prayer Book. There were some things which usage had sanctioned, though irregular, with which I should not interfere if the clergyman & congregation desired their continuance. At the same time, whenever my authoritative opinion were asked I should have no alternative but to condemn.

January 8, Sunday.

FIRST SUNDAY

The service began at Christ Church at eleven o'clock. There was a good congregation. Among them some coloured people, and a few Indians stood near the door. The Governor & suite were present as also Captain Prevost of the *Satellite* & officers of the fleet.

I found no prayer was offered usually for the Governor. I settled with Mr. Cridge that we should adopt that used in Canada, so for the first time this was done today.

I was much moved by the service. The organ played some well known tunes which struck upon tender chords. I have heard people say the Yarmouth Parish Church service affected them. Some strangers at first were overcome. I now could understand this from my own feelings. The organ is a barrel, but answers well. Amongst the choir in the gallery was the Chief Justice of B[ritish] Columbia. He is musical. This is a good way of using talents, for God's glory, for edification of others.

I preached from Romans 10:13-15 & was enabled to set forth leading principles of the Gospel & alluded to my presence there for the first time as Bishop. The Holy Communion was celebrated, at my desire, & about forty-two communicants were present, amongst them several coloured people. I offered thanks to Almighty God for safe voyage.

I was glad to find the spirit excited which I desired. Mr. Cridge remarked, 'this day will indeed be the commencement of new life. Now things will prosper. We have never before had a head.' Mr. Pemberton, the churchwarden, with tears in his eyes said, 'this is what we want. We have been long too much afraid to stand up for our church' & he thanked me.

God grant a real revival of true religion may be set on foot. May the Gracious Spirit be with us, giving us wisdom, faithfulness, boldness.

In the afternoon, i.e., immediately after service, I set out to walk to Esquimalt to the service commenced by Mr. Dundas.

The walk was tremendous. We arrived, however, only about a quarter of an hour late. There was a large attendance of officers from the fleet, also residents. Captain Fulford of the *Ganges* had brought his church band. The service was hearty. I preached extempore from the 'Visit of the Wise Men,' an Epiphany subject. A collection was made. The sight of the sailors made me think of dear old Yarmouth & the Seamen's Church.

Several gentlemen, settlers, walked home with us. We went by another trail part of the way. It is necessary to go in parties for fear of the Indians. The moon lit us back. It was wild life. A Mr. Jackson, son of a Baptist minister in Edinburgh, carried Mr. Dundas' bag. Captain Gordon carried mine.

I remained quiet that evening. Mr. Dundas & Mr. Cridge came in to tea.

January 9, Monday.

A fine day. Slight frost last night, numerous callers. Heard of the party feeling that prevails, Vancouver [Island] versus [British] Columbia. Hudson's Bay Company clique versus newcomers. American versus British—American versus coloured, etc.

January 10, Tuesday.

Snow about half an inch, slight frost. A fine day. Received a call from Captain Prevost & Captain Hunt, the latter Commandant of the American force on San Juan.

Dined with the Governor. Met his two daughters, Mr. Young, Acting Colonial Secretary; Mr. Dallas, Hudson's Bay Company Representative; Captain & Mrs. Gossett; Rev. Mr. Dundas & two marine officers.

January 11, Wednesday.

At ten saw Mr. Cridge for an hour & half upon the subject of church attendance. He brought me a list, also [one] of communicants. We went through them. I told him I should wish to preach in the mornings at Christ Church. He a little hesitated, naturally. He came back a second time to express regret at ever hesitating a moment & how glad he was for the plan to be carried out. I trust we shall go on well together.

Chief Justice Begbie called. I spoke about church matters & mentioned my intention, as I expressed to Mr. Cridge, of stating my views on Sunday as to the formation of a new congregation. He smiled. I asked why. He confessed it was at the idea of proposing another church from Mr. Cridge's own pulpit! How little did he allow to Mr. Cridge the credit of desiring the general good of the church. How often have I proposed from my own pulpit of Yarmouth the opening of services in other places which to some people might appear likely to weaken the old congregation. It was the contrary. So here, God willing, the opening of new churches will revive the church spirit of the town, indeed create it, & benefit generally all church work.

I had a pleasant walk with the Chief Justice. The country round Victoria is lovely & we visited some beautiful spots.

The weather however was dull & slightly raining.

January 12, [Thursday].

A dull day. Took a walk with Captain Gossett & inspected a proposed site for church & collegiate institution. Admiral Baynes called.

January 13, Friday.

Rev. Mr. Sheepshanks arrived from [the Colony of] British Columbia.

I learned how anxious the people are in that colony that I should come & live there. There is much rivalry between the two colonies. I must endeavour to do what is right, both colonies are under my care.

ROMIST LIBERALITY

I was supplied with milk, the first day or two, by a milkman who drove his cart daily in the neighbourhood. One day no one came & no milk was there to be had. It was thought to be some mistake which would be rectified, again no milk. A fresh milkman was found. The cause of failure in the other, by his own account, was that as he was a Roman Catholic he could not think of supplying milk to a Bishop of the Church of England!

So that here matters are reversed. *Customers* in the old country are sometimes charged with exclusive dealing, but here the *dealer* discriminates & will only supply such customers as he chooses to favour!

The man is an Irishman. How many thousands of his countrymen in fever, famine & poverty have found friends in the Protestant clergy of England & Ireland.

January 14, Saturday. [No entry in manuscript]

January 15, Sunday.

Preached at Christ Church. Mr. Cridge read prayers. I read prayers in the afternoon [and] Mr. Cridge preached. Took a walk with the latter. In the evening, preached at the Court House. Mr. Dundas read prayers. It was an interesting service which does Mr. Dundas credit. My sermon was upon 'the grain of mustard seed.' I could not, somehow, work up to the mark of fervour & force. This is one of the difficulties of extempore preaching. You are not always in tune. Your animal spirits are down. God grant some good may yet have come from my feeble words. May some be drawn nearer in heart to Christ.

January 16, Monday.

Our first news this morning has cast a gloom over the town. The steamer *Northerner* from Francisco which has been expected [for] several days, proves to have been wrecked a short distance from Francisco with the loss of thirty-five passengers! Alas.

I feel more than usually interested. Had I booked through from England, as some advised, I must have come by this ill fated vessel. Or had I yielded to the kind solicitations of friends in Francisco I should have delayed my departure, with a like result. Some passengers who had come from England did so, as Mr. Bloomfield, & poor creatures met a watery grave. There was no strong reason why I should have declined these inducements. I was inclined to yield to them. Now, however, I see the mercy that was guiding my steps & saving me from that great peril. My God, numberless have been thy mercies to me from my childhood until now. Unworthy am I of the least of them. O may I have grace to live more & more unto thee, in my heart loving thy service, & fervently endeavouring to win many to their salvation in repentance towards thee & in faith towards our Lord Jesus Christ.

54

January 17, Tuesday.

Mr. [Augustus F.] Pemberton the Magistrate, & Mr. Cridge accompanied me to the Indian reserve on the Esquimalt side of the harbour. We happened on our road to meet the chief of one tribe, the Songish [Songhee], his name is 'Freesy.' At least he goes by that name. He pioneered us to his own hut. It was amongst a group of large wooden squarish erections, [built] of plank boarding & flat ill made tops, through which air & water could plentifully enter. They were, I should say, fifty feet square.

In one of them was Freesy's dwelling. It was parclosed off, the front was open and in the three sides were recesses under a sub roofing, or canopy. In these were layers of matting which formed beds. In the centre was a small wood fire at which were two women & a little boy. We took our seats on one [mat?]. I was placed in the middle as the Tyhee [Tyee] or chief. Presently more came in. There were three friends wrapped in their blankets, these were Freesy's counsellors & several other boys came. Mr. Pemberton was interpreter, the language was Chinook, or rather jargon, for it is no language, only a trading medium composed of words of different languages & cant terms.

Mr. Pemberton explained to them that I was a King George or English Tyee & that I was come to endeavour to do them good. He interpreted the expression of my good will towards them & my desire to educate their children. He also, as well as the Chinook could express, told them my desire for their spiritual welfare & to show them the way to heaven & to know the only true God & Jesus Christ.

They spoke several times in reply & said they were glad anyone would be their friend & do them good & they would like to be educated & have better houses. They had heard it said they were going to be removed. This grieved them much. What could they do if sent away? Now they could get work & dollars & food, but if sent away they must starve.

They also were constantly in fear on account of the Northern Indians, the Hydas [Haidas] who were allowed to be near them. They wished these to be removed away. We told them, as to such matters, Mr. Douglas the Governor was the person to go to. They said they did not like to go to Mr. Douglas too often.

The little boy Peter was examined. He & the others came on Sundays to the church [for] a class in which they were instructed. They all gave answers, their letters, numbers, [and] small words. I was struck with the facility of their pronunciation.

One little boy about eleven was like a little Englishman. He was a half breed but knew no other language than his mother's.

The parents & others present seemed delighted & proud at the way their children answered.

Freesy was dressed in coat & trousers & if seen in England would be taken for rather a shabby Irishman. The others had blankets wrapped round them. The women were making a rope.

I visited other compartments of their hut where two other families were located. In one, the woman was making a mat, weaving rushes & grass. Her wrists & hands were covered with rings. The husband was in bed. In another, the man was making a paddle. I was struck by the industrious character of these poor people.

From the Songhee Indians I went to the Northern Indian encampment. These have lately come. They are the Chymsyan [Tsimshian], from Fort Simpson & the Haida from Queen Charlotte's Island [Queen Charlotte Islands]. They are a fine & fairer race than the Songhee. Some of the faces were no darker than our own & had a healthy tint on the cheeks. We heard amongst the Tsimshian of the labour of Mr. Duncan. Many of them went to school with him at Fort Simpson. I had heard from Mr. Cridge of two [Tsimshians] who had attended church regularly, indeed I saw them at church. They had come from Fort Simpson where they had known & attended the school of Mr. Duncan. They now wished to return & the time seemed very long. They were getting sadder & sadder every day. Would it were a thirst for the Lord God!

One hut I entered was remarkably neat & clean. It had carpets, a nice stove, [and a] bed upon a frame. There was a desk. The wife [was] a nice clean young person.

January 18, [Wednesday].

Today an Indian came to see me. It was the young man of the clean tent I saw yesterday. He instructed Mr. Duncan in Tsimshian and had learned English, or rather improved himself in English at the same time. He can speak & write English. His name is John Clark [Clah] and his wife's Jarx[?]. He has come to trade. He complained much of the Haida Indians. 'Fight, Fight' is the word. 'Fight all day, all night. Drink bad, I get no sleep, my wife afraid my little boy cry.' He told me he prayed. He knew the leading points of the Christian faith & in all respects is a promising specimen of what may be done. He asked me for a Prayer Book, which I promised.

I, this day, dined with Admiral Baynes on the *Ganges* & met the captains of the vessel, Captains Fulford, Prevost, Hornby & Richards, Major De Courcy, etc.

Previously I visited the cemetery for sailors on a beautiful spot on an island, also the hospital. Slept on board in a cot.

56

January 19, [Thursday].

Through the kindness of Admiral Baynes, I went in his barge on shore at various points to make calls. Visited the farms of the Puget Sound [Agricultural] Company, held by Mr. Skinner, MacKenzie & Langford. Nothing could exceed the romantic beauty of the scenery, wild in the extreme. Huge pines frequently lying prostrate in the path.

At Craig Flower [Craigflower] I found Rev. Mr. Dowson, sent by [the] S.P.G. [Society for the Propagation of the Gospel in Foreign Parts] to the Indians. He has been here ever since his coming out, studying the language of the Saanich & Cowitchen [Cowichan] Indians whither he proposes to go shortly. A deputation of their chiefs came to him & invited him to come & live amongst them & they would give him land.

He had given medicine to one of the Indians, the wife of a chief. So grateful was this chief that he brought a sack of potatoes & other edibles to Mr. Dowson. This day, he [Dowson] was without meat. We found him cooking. He has hard rough work. His wife is ill, has had fever.

Mr. Dowson has service every Sunday. The Methodists used to come but have given up the post. The people are Scotch principally but some have become attached to our liturgy.

I visited the Boundary Party of Engineers in their winter barracks. The officer Captain Haig & Mr. Watson showed me some good photographs.

January 20, Friday.

Rain all day. Rev. Mr. Pringle arrived from Hope last evening. He has truly borne the burden & heat of the day in ministering to the gold diggers. He has lived in a cabin of wood, one room, has cooked & done everything for himself. The weather has been excessive cold, some days thermometer down to twenty [degrees Fahrenheit]. He has established a reading room & library. The miners looked upon him as their friend & invited him to hold services upon their bars of the river. All luxuries, such as butter & milk, he has not known.

January 21, Saturday.

Had a visit from a Quaker gentleman, Mr. Lindsay from Halifax Yorks[hire]. He is on a mission & attends meetings to preach & pray. There is silence for a time & then the Spirit, he thinks, always moves him directly to speak, the same thing everywhere. He is a worthy & well meaning person. I had met him on board the *Pacific*.

He had been up to New Westminster & Langley. He spoke about the Indians & wished to interest me in them. I told him a good deal which interested him, as to my own visit recently to Indians, of Clah and Mr. Dowson's work & the deputation to him & Mr. Duncan's good success at Fort Simpson. Mr. Lindsay also said, 'Friend, let me speak to thee freely. I was pleased with thee on board the steamer & liked thy liberality, now I have been up the river & they talk much about thee. Thee will excuse me speaking out.' 'Oh, by all means, let me hear everything you wish to say.'

'Well then, they say thee are a Puseyite, now I have done all I could to show them that thy mind does not seem to be in that direction, I hope not, I hope thee will not be a Puseyite.' 'My dear Mr. Lindsay, my principles are those of the Church of England which I sincerely believe are those of the pure Gospel & my desire is distinctly & honestly to preach Christ & lead ever to Christ according to his will. I cannot sink what I believe to be truth, or make an insincere compact for the sake of external appearance. Your desire that I should unite with the many sects around, my experience tells me, cannot be realized with edification, did not higher reasons intervene. You know yourself how difficult it is to unite with them. They will not unite with *you*, you know of the insinuations made & jealousies which prevail. At the same time I hope to join with all classes in every matter of benevolence, & this I will say, that my conviction is, & it is pleasing to have it, that whosoever is found at the last holding to Christ by a simple living faith, no matter what the difference be on earth, will surely be saved.'

Mr. Lindsay's idea of a Puseyite, hateful word, being a person who consigns all dissenters in bundles to the flames & proudly declines to know any of them socially even, in this world.

VISIT TO AN INDIAN

I went with Mr. Dundas to the Tsimshian ranch. We found the hut, or tent, of Clah to whom I had promised a Prayer Book.

He was in. There was also his wife Jarx & another, with his little boy. The tent had comforts not seen in others. There was a stove with cooking apparatus, a bedstead. He had also a desk. There were beautiful white loaves [of bread] which he had brought home, being Saturday & the whole *menage* was that of a respectable cotter in England on Saturday. He placed seats. We sat. I gave him the [Prayer] Book. He was pleased. He brought out a box with his writing books & account books. He writes a good hand & spells well, in English. He repeated the Lord's Prayer in a most reverent & touching way. He could tell of the dying of Christ for us & said he loved Christ. We had interesting conversation in which he evidently took pleasure. We all knelt down. He put his hands together & I prayed our Heavenly Father's blessing upon our plans, upon these poor Indians & that he would cause his blessed truth to be known by them that all might be partakers of the same hope & be meet for heaven through his dear Son.

January 22, Sunday.

NEW SERVICE

Weather fine. I preached twice at Christ Church & read prayers in the evening. In the morning my subject was death & I made allusion to the shipwreck of the *Northerner* & the loss of thirty five souls.

For the first time the church was lighted up for evening service. There was only short notice, yet the attendance was good. Four-fifths were men. Some evidently of the roughest sort, yet well behaved. I saw there men who knew not how to use the Prayer Book, but who made anxious efforts as though they had made up their minds after long neglect to serve God in his house. It was interesting to see their awkward yet earnest endeavours, being also shy. Mr. Cridge & the churchwarden said there were many faces they had never seen before at church, indeed the greater part were strangers. May God mercifully use this service for drawing many to himself & saving them in Christ.

January 23, Monday.

FIRST MEETING FOR ST. JOHN'S CHURCH

[There was] a meeting, the first, for the erection of the new church on the north side of the town. It was held at the wooden office of Mr. Alston, Barrister, in Yates Street at twelve o'clock. The Rev. E. Cridge in the chair. I made a statement of the cost & other particulars. Resolutions were passed to form a committee. The Rev. Mr. Dundas & Mr. Burnaby were appointed Honourable Secretaries.

January 24, Tuesday.

Day dull, but no rain. The *Pacific* steamer came in. Got my first letter from England, from my dear Aunt. Also there came others to poor Mr. Bloomfield, who, alas, lies on a strange shore. And there might I have been too, O gracious Father, but for thy mercy in ordering my course in another vessel & bringing me safely here.

January 25, Wednesday.

A lovely day. I visited the Dallas family in deep distress at the loss of their little one. I knelt with the father beside the beautiful corpse, as it lay like marble, cold & motionless upon its little bed. Mr. Dallas is the agent of the Hudson's Bay Company, a man who has lived in many parts of the world, passed through many dangers, but now softened with grief. We prayed together. He was submissive to the Father's will.

January 26, Thursday.

A lovely day. Had meeting of the St. John's Church Committee. Took walk with Mr. Cridge & Mr. Dundas. Saw for first time Mount Baker, far up a snowy height of 15,000 feet.

January 27, Friday.

Day dull, but no rain. Had conversation with Chief Justice Begbie about a Collegiate School. I wanted him to attend a preliminary meeting. He said schools were not in his way, but that he would aid me in any way in his line, such as advice about legal points, etc.

I saw also Mr. [Donald] Fraser (*Times* Correspondent) a very sensible man, had a long & interesting talk upon various matters.

January 28, Saturday.

Day dull in the morning. Fine afternoon. No rain. Received a visit from Major De Courcy who has charge of the British occupation of [San] Juan. He gets on, he says, very well with the American detachment who are under Captain Hunt, a man of superior mind, & also has a disgust for the proceedings of General Harney. He thinks the Americans will give up the Island.

January 29, Sunday.

Day dull, no rain. Good congregation at Christ Church. Collections for the hospital, total in the day $325.90, being above £60, which I consider good. The litany was used in the afternoon, omitted in the morning, the collection made in the morning with offertory sentences & Church Militant prayer, at the time of singing [the] hymn after [the] sermon, afternoon & evening. These alterations are practical & I think liked by the congregation. I preached morning & evening.

January 30, Monday.

At half past eleven received a deputation with an address from the inhabitants of Victoria & its vicinity, numbering above 800, congratulating me on my arrival. I read a written reply which Mr. D. Fraser, the *Times* Correspondent, immediately copied & sent off by the steamer just sailing.

Dr. Evans, the Wesleyan Minister, was one of the deputation, also Chief Justice Begbie.

There seems to have been an excellent spirit in this address, for which I am thankful. The mail [...] *Panama* took a copy to England this day.

The Rev. Mr. Clark [Clarke], Congregational Minister, called upon me today. I thanked him for the stand he had made in respect of the coloured people. His colleague Mr. McFie [Macfie] having split off from him with the American portion of the community. He told me he did not find but one English man in all Victoria a Congregationalist. Those of that religion were principally American. He said Mr. Macfie had ridden at first at the top of a buoyant wave but he was finding out now his weakness. His supporters were principally Americans whose only religion was to hate the negro & that he could not, when he began, number a single earnest man in his congregation. He said that the Christ Church congregation was four times greater than any other in the town.

January 31, [Tuesday].

[I had] a visit from the Quaker, Lindsay, accompanied by an American resident at Esquimalt named Gillingham, to ask for the use of the Esquimalt school room to hold a Quaker's meeting to which the public should be invited.

I declined on the ground:

1. It is usual in the Church of England to confine the use of places of religious instruction & worship to our own communion.
2. To grant the use to one body would open the door to any others, Mormons for instance, & the precedent would be inconvenient.
3. It is to be presumed that the peculiar principles, which are at variance, which are condemnatory of those of the Church of England would be taught. Honest men could not help stating their convictions. Hence we should be lending our own building to injure ourselves.
4. It is not wholesome to teach opposites in the same place, confusion of sentiment would necessarily follow. No one who had charge of religion & who conscientiously believed his own views were scriptural, could consistently sanction such a course.
5. It would be wrong for the church to sanction even in appearance what she has declared to be erroneous.

Such was the substance of my objections. I went into the peculiarities of Quakerism by way of showing the very different thing it is from the Church of England.

Mr. Lindsay at first was inclined to show off before his friend, kept his hat on till I told him to take it off. [He] talked of being sorry he should be obliged to report home the sad want of liberality, that the severe exclusiveness of England would not do in these Colonies where all religions are equal. [He] said he was not sectarian, etc.! He took at last a very different tone, principally, I think, because his friend rather went with me than with him.

As to 'reporting,' I told him I knew exactly the light in which he would put my refusal. I desired publicity for any truthful course, but he ought to consider what the rules & general principles were upon which my conscientious decision was based & give credit for them.

'All religions' were not equal anywhere in the eyes of religionists themselves. There were the same differences between them here as in England.

As to his not being sectarian, I elicited from him that he was accustomed to distribute tracts after the meeting explaining the peculiar tenets of Quakerism, which his friend thought certainly sectarian. He said he did not attack the principles of any other [religious] body. I said he had given me a tract which was an offensive attack upon the Church of England & of course I supposed he would distribute such again.

He spoke about a 'man made ministry.'

There was a great mixture of simple desire to do good which I heartily give him credit for & old inveterate & uncharitable prejudices. These our discussion afforded him opportunity to display. It was an interesting occasion, I trust a Christian spirit was maintained by myself throughout & am thankful I could be open & clear in the statement of my views though it would have been more 'popular' to have yielded. I do feel it of great importance that we should as a church here be well understood at this early stage. Latitudinarianism is the order of the day. Churchmen no doubt will be much affected by the contagion. It is the more necessary to be distinct & our principles being true, we need not fear the discussion of them, *magna est veritas & prevalebit* [great is truth and it will prevail].

I had a visit from the Governor of an hour & half. We spoke about Indians, Church Reserve, towns likely to increase, investments, etc.

Dined with the Governor. Met Mrs. Douglas for the first time.

February 1, Wednesday.

Had a meeting, two and a half hours, with Captain Prevost, Captain Fulford & Mr. D[onald] Fraser upon the subject of the Indians.

February 2, [Thursday].

Some rain most of the day. Walked with Dr. Tuzo to visit ground laid out for sale by the Hudson's Bay Company.

February 3, Friday.

Dull day. Had a meeting this evening at Mr. Fraser's for two objects: *Collegiate Institution, Indian Improvement.* Present, Captain Prevost, Dr. Tolmie, Mr. Finlayson, Captain Gossett, Mr. Wood, Mr. Fraser, Mr. MacKay, Revs. Mr. Dowson, Dundas & myself.

INDIANS

The tribes have much decreased since 1846, more than half of the Songhee are destroyed, principally from drink, also from dissolute habits. Those nearest to the whites are the worst. Women are purchased as slaves in order to [use them for] prostitution. A woman was killed in a brawl recently upon whose person was found 300 dollars, the wages of iniquity. Captain Prevost mentioned this & also that an Indian named Bear Skin made large profits from this traffic. The Tsimshian Indians had requested Mr. Duncan to take their children away, separate from the fort where they lived, in order to be free from the contamination of whites. Mr. Finlayson who speaks the language & whose wife was brought up among the Indians, spoke of the destructive habits of the chiefs in tearing up property. He had known a chief [to] buy a bale of blankets (fifty blankets) for 100 dollars, 20£, leave them in the store & at their feast come for them & distribute or tear them to pieces before their people.

Rev. Mr. Dowson had seen an Indian with a great stone destroy a beautiful canoe, his own.

I visited today Mr. & Mrs. Hall who take interest in the Indians. They have sometimes twenty children who come to be instructed. Ten go to Sunday School. They are all uncertain in attendance. [They] must have rice & molasses, [and] sometimes wish to go immediately after.

In a neighbouring house is an Indian woman, the wife of a white man named Cotsford. She is a nice clean & well ordered person [who] will not speak, but understands, English. I saw her little girl, a pretty child. You would not tell her from an English girl, speaking English well. The other day the mother of Mrs. Cotsford went out at eight o'clock, got drunk & died at ten. She was placed in a coffin with fifteen blankets. Her head did not lie easy & two new blankets were brought; they put inside a work bag, a looking glass, a box of matches & sundry other articles.

Mrs. Hall witnessed this. It looks like a belief in the resurrection, or instinct of a future.

The language uttered by the Indians is sometimes shocking, they will exclaim in violent oaths, but to our shame be it said the oaths are in the English language, which they have learned from the whites! They have no oaths in their own language. Two of the Indian children who come to the Sunday school were striving together & the older said to the younger, 'what the h— are you about.' Alas that their first English words are such as these! How different from what should be, as we read 'out of the mouth of babes & sucklings hast thou perfected praise.'

February 4, Saturday.

VICISSITUDES

Case 1

A young man called upon me this morning, Mr. G. Harding whose friends I know in England. He has suffered hardship & at length hired himself out for his board to clear land on Orcas Island. He has since been to another point on [Vancouver] Island where he has tended cattle & swine.

He now goes up to the diggings to Cameron's Bar in the employment of an American, under an engagement for nine months. There will be about sixteen [men] in all & he is the only Englishman. He will be pretty well paid, i.e., 2 dollars a day & his board, but this is less than an ordinary labourer demands here.

Case 2

I met today a fine young man who with his brother had built a hut in the wood on the north side of Victoria. He was from Cheshire. Mr. Pringle, the clergyman at Hope, was with me & was recognized by the gold digger with evident friendship. He had met him at the diggings. We went into the hut. There was no window & two berths in ship fashion were the beds, one over the other. He asked Mr. Pringle to take a drink from a bottle of whisky, which offered heartily, was declined kindly. He told me he had been ten years from England, had been in Australia & California & had suffered great hardships & the ten years seemed a lifetime. He was well spoken & intelligent.

Case 3

I visited today a lady & gentlemen named Wilby. They are respectably connected in England & Portugal. They are living in a small wooden house, in one room, with three children. This is their sleeping room, parlour & kitchen & all. There are rooms, or a room above, but the rain comes through as if there were no roof at all. The sides of the dwelling are propped up to keep it from being blown over. He drives a dray & a pair of horses. They have at last, after much suffering, taken to this. She & her children were in great disorder, certainly. Poor thing, she had not been well. They apologized for receiving me in that plight. Yet they bore their trial well & were determined to make the best of it. Yet the spectacle was a sad one. They had been in California but for their children's sake they dare not remain there & were thankful to be where at least a better example was set. The children were pretty & interesting.

Case 4

Just before dinner a young man came in named Moore. His family live near Bideford. His uncle is Colonel James of the surveying department in the [Royal] Engineers. Several of his family are in the ministry. He had given up a situation in England & had come out here with expectations of a government situation. From pillar to post had he been thrown. Nothing had prospered with him. He had been Special Constable up [the Fraser] River during the California rush & had to deal with terrible characters of whom he has many a story to relate. He was afterwards destitute & was glad to be a policeman in Victoria. He then became a labourer on a farm at 3£ a month & board, wages which no working man would take. The farm was at San Juan [Island]. From this he was discharged on reduction of their establishment. He had come back to Victoria not knowing which way to turn & had got a note at last from the Hudson's Bay Company agent to the farm agent to re-employ him but without a promise. He is about to cross & calls upon me as he knew his friends had communicated with me.

He was dressed in the roughest way, with red shirt, etc. There was something truly honest in his manner. I was going to dinner. He sat down & was a gentleman in all his deportment, though poor fellow it was strange. Amongst other troubles of poverty, he said, was the company a poor man was consigned to.

While going through all this hardship, his friends in England were writing to him as the rich man of the family, who being in the gold regions must be well off, they think. He sees a great deal of Americans. Their profanity is awful. He spoke of the loss of the means of grace. I found he observes Sunday carefully & reads portions of the service. I gave him a few hints & bid him take courage.

PETITION FROM YALE

I received this day a petition from the married people of Yale asking me to supply them with a school & churches. This town is the headquarters of the gold diggings & a few months ago notorious for its proceedings. I fear now the Sunday is much desecrated, but what can we expect when there is not a minister of religion amongst them. I take courage from

65

this address. May God cause the hearts of this people to love the truth & to follow gladly the service of their Saviour. Such, at least, will be an object of our teaching, our schools & churches, that many souls may be saved.

February 5, Sunday.

Preached at Christ Church morning & evening [&] Esquimalt [in the] afternoon. Holy Communion in [the] morning, assisted by Mr. Dundas [in the] morning & by Mr. Pringle afternoon & evening. Beautiful day, enjoyed walk to Esquimalt.

February 6, Monday.

Day dull. No rain. Had a walk with the Governor in the Park. He agreed to conveying the church sites, etc., to the See. He told me Bishop Demers was annoyed at the reception given to me when no notice of a like kind had been taken of himself these six years. Bishop Demers, to show his feeling, had voted for the anti-government & American Candidate, De Cosmos.

INDIANS

Captain Prevost & Lieutenant Roche called. They brought some statistics of Indians on the west coast. Last year the Nitinat Indians made a raid upon another tribe & took twenty heads which Lieutenant Gooch of the *Satellite* saw erected upon poles.

One tribe, the Loquat, were once the most powerful but now [are] the weakest & whenever there are young men, they are taken by hostile tribes for slaves. They are now reduced to a few old men & women.

The great trade now, since the whites have come, is in female slaves. These are bought for as high as 200 dollars, 40£ each. They are used for prostitution & fetch a much higher price than wives who are also purchased. There is a white man on the Fraser near Langley who owns such slaves & hangs out a sign over the house to signify the horrible iniquity therein pursued. Lieutenant Roche who had been there for some time on the business of the survey, stated this as a fact.

FISHING EXTRAORDINARY

Captain Prevost told me that in Semiahmoo Bay & on San Juan on two occasions, in three hauls, his men caught upwards of 600 salmon, averaging seven & eight pounds each. They might have gone on but had filled the tender, having enough. The fish, of all sorts, are inexhaustible.

The Indians have great provision on this island. In the Winter & Spring are innumerable wild fowl; in the Summer, five or six sorts of delicious wild berry fruit; and in the Autumn, the salmon. They have also abundant fish of other kinds, as herring & oysters always, also deer. In the salmon season they cure large quantities of dried fish for consumption the rest of the year.

February 7, Tuesday.

Had my first marriage in the diocese. The Admiral's barge was sent from Esquimalt to the Governor's Bridge, James Bay. We landed at ten at the shore about one and a half miles from Colwood. Mr. Langford, & Captain Richards of the *Plumper* walked with me. At half past eleven the marriage ceremony took place in the drawing room. Breakfast at half past one, over at three. Captain Fulford, of the *Ganges*, proposed the health of the bride & bridegroom, Mr. & Mrs. Bull, the latter an officer of the *Plumper*. I proposed Mr. & Mrs. Langford. Other toasts followed.

Colwood is romantically situated in the woods, seven miles from Victoria across the Esquimalt Harbour. I have seen scenery exactly similar in Scotland. I walked to the landing place, back with Captains Fulford & Prevost & returned in the Admiral's barge. The [marriage] licence was one issued by the Governor. The hearty English tones which prevailed, caused by the presence of many naval officers was exhilarating. There were seven bridesmaids.

February 8, Wednesday.

The *Pacific* steamer in today. Captain Nicol, Hudson's Bay Company agent at Nanaimo, called. That place is likely to become important. The coal is good & in Francisco, notwithstanding a duty of 30 percent, it is used in preference to other coal. Dr. Hector of the Exploring Expedition has been to see & test [it] & he pronounces it excellent, but not of primary formation.

There are about 100 people, the miners & families, [in Nanaimo].

ENGLISH LAW

Captain Nicol last year was Sheriff of British Columbia. He went the circuit with Judge Begbie. At one place there was a case in which a man had shot another. The deceased, intoxicated, had fired his revolver. It went far wide & it is doubtful if he meant to shoot the accused. His opponent, however, as he was running away out of the room, fired at him & hit him. The man went on. The accused fired at him again & again wounded him, pursued him as he was struggling & wounded him again bringing him to the ground & then again as he was dying snapping another barrel at him. The jury could not agree in their verdict, there being Americans who thought this justifiable. The question they had to decide was whether or [not] the accused was guilty of manslaughter. The jury were locked up all night for eight hours. It was a wooden house. Mr. Nicol nailed boards to the windows & put a sentry at the door. In the morning they were agreed. It was a special verdict which by American law would require a fresh trial. A 'judge' was on the jury & put up his partners to this expedient. They were foiled since in English law the special verdict was as good as another. They had virtually found the man guilty & he was sentenced to four years penal servitude. He now forms one of the convict gang employed in the streets of Victoria, an elderly man with a grey beard. They say he has shot many men. He is now very quiet.

This vigorous execution of justice has had a great effect. Men have been heard to say to [one] another, if this [place] were not under English law, I would shoot you.

February 9, Thursday.

Rain in the morning, fine afternoon. Walked to Mr. Cary's. Mr. Nicol from Nanaimo dined with me.

February 10, Friday.

Rain in the morning, fine afternoon. Dined at Mr. Woods'. Met Colonel Moody, Captain Palliser. The *Columbia* came in today from Francisco. No letters.

February 11, Saturday.

Had a walk with Captain Prevost.

February 12, Sunday.

Preached at Christ Church morning & evening. Esquimalt in the afternoon. Day fine.

February 13, Monday.

Day fine. Colonel Moody called.

Had this day a painful duty to perform, to announce to one of my clergy [the] rumours affecting his sobriety. He thanked me for the kind way in which I had dealt with him. How important is the utmost circumspection on our [part] as clergy. What would be but an indiscretion in others is a crime in us. It must needs be that offenses come but 'woe be to that man by whom the offence cometh. Ye are the light of the world, a city set on a hill cannot be hid. If the light that is in you be darkness, how great is that darkness.'

Alas in reproving a brother how condemned one feels oneself for many things. One would gladly be silent & look inwards & repent. 'First cast out the beam out of thine own eye,' but duty calls for such notice of the faults of others & speak we must. 'Oh my God cause me to be more & more watchful over my own evil heart & let thy Holy Spirit more & more fill me with love & faith & purity & truthfulness. Oh cleanse thou me from my secret faults.'

February 14, Tuesday.

Dined with the Governor. Met Colonel Moody. The *Athelstan* reported off the Sound.

Had conversation with Mr. Dallas, the agent of the Hudson's Bay Company here, about the Church Reserve. He said he had recommended the directors at home to confirm the grant to the Church of England. Day Fine.

February 15, Wednesday.

Day rainy throughout. The *Athelstan* not in. The *Princess Royal,* the Hudson's Bay [Company] annual ship, arrived. In former days this [was] a great event.

LETTERS OF INTRODUCTION

A letter of introduction was brought [to] me yesterday from a gentleman of high standing & reputation in England, introducing a friend, or rather the son of friends. The individual in whose favour the letter was written being of good family & of an honourable profession. He had arrived a few days [ago], had put up at the French Hotel. It is usual to present a letter of introduction in person. Not so in this instance. The letter was brought by a dirty German waiter of the hotel, together with a note of hand for some £20 or £30 signed by the gentleman with the cool request that I would either endorse or honour the note by paying part of the money. No letter or card or explanation. How little did the worthy writer of the introduction contemplate such a use of his kindness.

February 16, Thursday.

A lovely sunny day. The *Athelstan* not yet in.

At twelve I attended a gathering of children of the Songhee tribe. A treat of rice, molasses & cakes had been prepared. Mr. & Mrs. Hall had allowed them to assemble in a room attached to their dwelling. They were all come & looked like a number of little gypsies with their sparkling black eyes, long black hair & very dirty skins. There were twenty-nine, sixteen girls, thirteen boys, ages from about twelve down to six. Their dress was tattered & a piece of blanket was wrapped round. There were two men with them, related to some of the children.

The first thing I did was to take down all their names & hard work occasionally it was, for the pronunciation is difficult.

Some of the girls' names were peculiar. Katatch-tenah—How-was—Kah-kalah, Salak-tenah—Sese-Otza—Yia-Kotsa. The boys—Tchcloose—Tchall—Socteya—Nink-h—Itchayet—Sepoc—Tasseyo.

Some of the names were evidently derived from Europeans, as Susu—Cecil—Peter Freesy.

This operation was pleasing to them & gave me an opportunity of catching sounds. I was glad to find less difficulty than I expected. I believe the language can be acquired without much difficulty.

There were a few very bright & superior children. On the whole a good tempered set.

Their manners were quite as good as ordinary children & the older ones reproved the younger when making more noise than right.

We had only a dozen bowls. Those who were served last exhibited not the slightest impatience but meekly waited for their turn. They held their spoons beautifully, did not scramble & gave to others when they had more than they could eat.

The elder girls were modest & shy. All the little ones were very shy & occasionally could have run away to a hole had there been means of escape.

Before commencing to eat, I said grace. We had put on our hats that we might take them off as a sign of solemnity. They all stood up & I said in the Chinook language 'Sackally Tyee Papa Mercie Klosh Muck Muck.' The Chinook is a jargon understood by them & used throughout these regions as a trade language.

Sackally	Oh mighty
Tyee	Great Chief
Papa	Father
Mercie	Thanks
Klosh	for good
Muck muck	sweet things

We afterwards sang 'Praise God' to the Old Hundred tune. I first pronounced the words which they repeated. Rev. Mr. Cridge & Mr.

Dundas & Mr. Pemberton, the Police Magistrate, & myself then sang. We sang heart[ily] & the little voices were heard mingling with ours, & when we had finished we found a remarkable impression to have been produced. All were reverently hushed in a fixed & thoughtful manner. They were evidently touched in their little spirits & not one broke the silence till one of us did so.

At the close we sang the same again & the effect was just as before.

We thought how joyful will be the day when 'out of the mouths of these babes & sucklings' praise shall indeed be perfected. We had an omen of that happy day in the way these little ones were touched by the songs of Zion. After being with them about two hours we told them Klah-how-ya & went our way.

February 17, Friday,

Day fine. Evening wet.

INDIANS

I had this day a letter from Mr. Duncan in which he mentions having 200 in his school, but laments the sad effects of Victoria. Many were preparing to leave him on account of the better price they could get for their furs, for their labour & alas for iniquity. Some young girls of his first class had come sorrowfully to say they were going with their relations, too surely to infamy & to misery. Such is civilization.

February 18, Saturday.

Day fine.

February 19, Sunday.

Preached at Christ Church, [in the] morning. Ministered at the hospital [in the] afternoon. Read prayers [in the] evening at Christ Church. Day wet.

February 20, Monday.

Day fine, frost & clear. Marked out the exact position of the new church [St. John's, Victoria]. Saw Rev. Mr. Dowson & agreed to pay 100£ for his passage home.

February 21, Tuesday.

FIRST VISIT TO BRITISH COLUMBIA

Left Victoria at eight o'clock by the *Otter* for New Westminster. Colonel Moody with whom I was to stay, [was] a passenger likewise. The day was beautifully clear & fresh with a frosty touch.

71

We steamed out of the harbour with the range of Olympian Mountains standing out in bold & snowy outline on the opposite side of the strait. As we rounded the island we passed various farms. San Juan came in view & between it & the island we passed up in Haro Strait.

The width of this does not appear above four or five miles. It is wooded in most parts up to the summit. For it is an eminence in chief part. From this the course lay through a series of islands, of all sizes & shapes, mostly wooded with here & there park like openings. Sometimes the channel being very narrow & tortuous as at Plumper's Pass, by which the entrance is into the main Gulf of Georgia, nearly opposite the mouth of the Fraser.

We had a constant view of the icy peaks of Mount Baker on the mainland. It looked nobly exalted up in the heavens, on American ground. The 'Brothers,' a remarkable mountain near Hope, was very prominent, shining in snowy whiteness.

The river Fraser is entered without difficulty. The channel is wide between two sounds, without a bar & the gulf is generally smooth, Vancouver [Island] acting as a vast breakwater.

The banks are low & I think more interesting than the Columbia [River]. The river is about a mile & [a] half wide. We reached New Westminster about six o'clock. It was dusk. Lights amongst the trees marked where the new city stood.

A crowd was upon the wharf. There were three other steamboats. This was certainly great progress for one year. About the same time twelve months ago a dense &, to many, a hopeless forest covered the site.

A boat conveyed us about a mile up the river to the upper town where is situated the [Royal Engineers] Camp & Colonel Moody's residence.

A hospitable reception awaited me.

In landing upon this part of my diocese I am filled with a deep interest in its future. A vast city may one day pursue a world wide commerce here. What shall it be? A spot devoted to restless competition & thirst for gain, or shall it exhibit to the world a people not slothful in business, fervent in spirit, serving the Lord? How much may depend upon its early training! Upon the institutions founded in its infancy & nurturing it in holy & wise principles. God grant I may be a humble instrument for its good.

A SETTLER'S INTEREST IN EDUCATION

On board the steamer were many miners & others going up to Columbia. Among them was one man who was deeply interested in education. He said he hoped I would give myself much to that object. He had children & desired them to be educated. I might make myself a name by establishing a good system of education. 'Look at Wilberforce &

Nelson,' what names they had made. 'The man who distinguished himself in this new colony by establishing education would achieve more victories than Nelson. [A] minister in his life could save about ten souls. But an educator of children might save hundreds.' He was brought up in the Church of England. He was a native of Rugby. 'See what a noble school was there and all from land having been set apart at a distant period & become valuable in lapse of time. So you might get land set aside which in time would be sufficient for all the schools in the state.' I said, 'how will you get funds at present until the lands are valuable.' 'Oh Sir, [ask] the people, bachelors & all. I would even advocate the Prussian system & make all the children go to school. I value education, Sir, because I feel the want of it. I was neglected myself but I wish my children to be instructed & you are the person to take it up & do it for us.'

February 22, Ash Wednesday.

Beautiful day, frosty & clear. The view up the Fraser from Colonel Moody's house is really beautiful, an extensive reach of water with mountains beyond & fine forests on either side.

A SETTLER'S GREETING

A man named Murphy came in, a fine grey haired man who has squatted upon an island & has been fighting his way through difficulties. The flood one year carried away his produce, next year the frost destroyed his potatoes & vegetables. Yet he battles on. He shook hands & was delighted to see the bishop. 'I hope Sir you are going to stop amongst us & build your palace.' 'Palace,' said I, 'I have no thoughts of a palace.' 'Oh your Lordship you are next to an Archbishop & you must have a palace, it's quite proper.' 'A log hut,' said I, 'will do for me.' 'Ah yes? A bishop is a bishop whether in a palace or in a log hut, but Sir, I only hope you are coming to live with us.'

FIRST SERVICE IN BRITISH COLUMBIA

We had service at seven o'clock at the Camp, in the old survey office, now the school. There was a thin attendance. Mrs. Grant, wife of Captain Grant, was churched. Mr. Sheepshanks read the litany, I the communion service for Ash Wednesday. I preached & the Prayer for the Church Militant was read afterwards. Somehow, I was sadly cold & unimpressive. My first text was 'there is joy in heaven over one sinner that repenteth'! This is indeed a chief part of the message I have to deliver. May I have grace to love souls & seek to bring them home to Christ!

INDIAN CORRUPTION

In walking up from New Westminster to the [Royal Engineers] Camp I met Indians intoxicated. One poor fellow was made frantic & was whirling himself round & in a circle uttering oaths in English. His words were 'G-d d-m son of a b-tch.' Alas, alas how true of those who have taught these poor creatures. Thus is the reproach of the apostle to the Jews: 'the name of God is blasphemed among the Gentiles through you.'

February 23, Thursday.

NEW WESTMINSTER

Another lovely day, clear & frosty. Saw several of the officials of New Westminster. Captain Spalding, the Magistrate; Mr. Begbie, the Chief Justice; Mr. Hamly [Hamley], Customs; Mr. Brew, Small Debts Court Judge, etc.

Visited New Westminster proper. The site is certainly a remarkable one. The fine river flows before it, to the right is a second arm of the river. In the rear is [Burrard] Inlet, a magnificent harbour running up inland from the sea many miles. Here will be the naval station & here only can vessels of the largest size be sheltered. It will be a sort of Geelong [Australia] to New Westminster.

The site is on the slope of a hill in part, upon the top is a plateau. The thick & mighty forest covers the summit. I never in my life saw such enormous trees. Considering only one year has elapsed since this site was chosen, it is wonderful what has been done. Yet, no doubt, every discouragement has been given. Much ground has been cleared. Buildings have been erected. There are about 400 people. This in addition to the 300 at the [Royal Engineers] Camp.

Inspected the site of the church in Victoria Gardens! This spot now covered with fallen timber between two ravines. Fancy & faith & the map picture an attractive spot & surroundings. It is high & dry. May the church to be erected be the scene of many a thoughtful multitude lifting up an holy sacrifice of prayer & praise to the triune Jehovah.

February 24, St. Matthias' Day, Friday.

ANNIVERSARY

My thoughts recur to the most momentous occasion of my life, this day last year. I have before me that vast multitude in Westminster Abbey which gathered for prayer & praise & sympathy. I see the venerable, the Archbishop & Bishops of the Anglican church, solemnly entrusting to one most unworthy the sacred office of a Bishop & laying it on him with their hands and all its weighty responsibilities & cares. I call to mind my own heartfelt vows, yea my fears, my tremblings. Gracious God thou knowest I did not thrust myself into this high & solemn sphere. Thou knowest how, conscious of infirmity, I sought to be released & how only because thy will seemed clear I assented. A year has gone by. I have entered upon my work in this distant land. I am in the midst of anxious questions, requiring more learning than I possess, more ability, more courage, more faith, more fervency. Grant me pardon for my many shortcomings ahead, & help for the future. Without thy grace, the aid of the blessed Spirit, I can do nothing, be nothing that is good. Oh for Jesus' sake, pardon me, help me, guide me, strengthen me, Oh Heavenly Father.

A NEW ROAD

I walked with Mr. Sheepshanks along the new track towards Burrard Inlet. It was in a direct north line for about 5 miles from river Fraser to the inlet. This is to be the naval harbour of New Westminster. It is a deep water arm of the sea. At present, not a house is thereon. The land, however, in all directions is preempted. The road is just cut out of the mighty forest. It lay through the most profuse vegetation, on either side of lofty pines of 150 to 250 feet high with impenetrable undergrowth. Continually there lays a mighty giant which has come crashing down, there to decay & rot & mingle with the dust. You will see lofty trees like masts bare of leaf & destitute of life, erect in the midst [of the forest] & perhaps ready to fall when shaken by some tempest of wind. The fall of trees is frequently heard. It is like the repeat of a cannon. We heard one go & its fall was great. At the distance of about a mile is the Brunette, a rapid stream rushing from an inland lake. Over it a bridge had just been erected. A farmer from Canada was clearing his lot & I doubt not another year will show a plentiful harvest from the rich soil now opened to the light of day & to the sun.

INDIANS

On the opposite side of the river is an Indian village. I crossed over in a canoe with Dr. Setta [Seddall] & Captain Parsons. I made my first essay with a paddle. We had a check on a sand bank but [reached] the other side in safety & went to the village. We entered the Chief's house. He has built one with a gable roof in imitation of the house of Colonel Moody. Tschymnana was not at home. We found his three wives. They were all at work, as the women invariably are, sitting by a log fire. One was at needle work, another making a various figured cloth, a sort of thick woolen cloth wove[n] of dog hair for the warp, and torn up blanket yarn for the woof, & another was making a grass mat.

The price for the cloth was 10 dollars.

There was a baby of about six months old, a fine boy bound to a board hand and foot, like a mummy & upon his head the heavy bandage for the flattening process. All seen of the child was its mouth & nose. It was suspended in a horizontal position to the end of a bent stick placed in the ground & was rocked with a string [...]. The babe began to cry. The mother took it, board & all in her lap, & gave it milk. Afterwards she set the board up on its end against the side of the hut & the poor infant, with a very animated countenance kept looking round, turning its head first on one side, then on the other. The flattening bandage she took off.

We had not much to say. They did not understand Chinook much. They were good natured & more intelligent I think than the Indians near Victoria. They belong to the Musqueam tribe.

We found an old man near[by] making a canoe. He had a curious chisel & a granite mallet. He was hollowing it out of a single tree. He would take 'totelum dollar' (10) for it, when done.

We could not make much of him though he was good tempered.

We paddled again across the stream.

February 25, Saturday.

Returned some calls in New Westminster. Walked up the Douglas Street Trail, an opening in the forest just completed & looked at a ground to be selected as the cemetery. Magnificent trees rose majestically on either side.

In the town I was witness to the fall of a tree some 200 feet high. It was a pine. Two men had been cutting for some time. A crack was heard. The tree quivered, crash, crash & down it came, down to the ground which it struck with a sound of booming cannon & lay shaking in all its branches, a mighty giant prostrate & helpless. One had a feeling of almost pity, certainly of regret at the destruction of so sublime a growth of the ancient forest, after a life of at least 200 years.

I dined at the barracks. Showery.

February 26, Sunday.

Service [in the] morning [at the Royal Engineers] Camp. Preached, baptized two infants, children of Colonel Moody & Captain Grant, names Susan & Emily respectively. Subject [of] sermon, Colossians 3:1-4. Afternoon service at New Westminster, at the Treasury; about forty [people]. Mr. White, Methodist Minister, Chief Justice Begbie & others present, text—Joshua 24:15. 'As for me & my house,' etc. Evening [at the] Camp chapel, text—Romans 10:13-15. Morning & evening, extempore. Rainy day.

February 27, Monday.

Rain in the afternoon. I received an address from the people of New Westminster. The deputation consisted of Mr. Holbrook, spokesman, Messrs. Armstrong, [. . .], Captain Spalding,

Rev. Mr. Sheepshanks & Mr. White, Wesleyan Minister. The address was good & reverent in its tone. It was signed by above 200. I replied in writing.

February 28, Tuesday.

Visited the school at the [Royal Engineers] Camp, present eighteen children. Mr. Sheepshanks was instructing them in the catechism.

Called upon Mr. Holbrook. He was in the commissioned services in the Crimea & remained afterwards at Odessa, he is now a merchant here. Called upon Mr. White, Wesleyan Minister, a worthy man from Canada. His wife is a nice person.

INCIDENTS
Limbs of the Law

I saw two men chopping wood. They were in their shirt sleeves. On approaching I found they were Chief Justice Begbie & Captain Brew, Judge of Small Debts Court. They were procuring firewood for themselves. They live in one room & have no servant.

I took the axe from the Chief Justice & cut a log in two. It was harder work than I thought.

The Miner's Zeal

I passed on to a spot where several men were felling huge trees. They were miners, about [to be] going up to the mines. There were five of them. They lived in a log hut hard by. Three were Canadians and two Norwegians. They were making their contribution towards the new church. They were giving their labour to the service of God. The trees were enormous in size, such as English eyes never rest upon in the old countries, nor yet in Canada. They were standing upon the church site & these hearty men with real good will were clearing that ground by several valuable days labour, & labour here is gold & sometimes cannot even be had for that.

What is more, these five men have been regular attendants upon Mr. Sheepshanks' service. They have never missed. I was pleased to see the respect & even affection with which they regarded their zealous & worthy pastor. This was one way of showing their appreciation of his ministry.

They had all obtained Prayer Books. The Norwegians expressed themselves delighted with our liturgy as resembling their own. They had all asked for testaments & told us they hoped to winter thus again.

Mr. Pringle came in this evening from Hope.

February 29, Wednesday.

I was to have gone to Victoria. Three [o'clock] was the time named. I was there. Just at the last moment after all my things were on board the Captain said the *Otter* would not go tonight. They say, this is not infrequently the case.

A BACK WOODSMAN

I visited the clearing of a man named Holmes on the Burrard Inlet trail. I saw one of his companions. I met him today, I asked about his family. He said he had sent for them. His friends in Canada had written to say they thought him foolish for going where there were no people & into a wild & untrodden land. He said 'I shall tell them the bishop has been to see me & that I am sure will satisfy them.' He told me he was confirmed by the Bishop of Quebec when there was but one bishop. 'Now Sir they have bishops all over.' This man is a well conducted churchman. Honesty beams in his face. He comes in to New Westminster to the service in the Treasury.

CHAPTER 2

The Governor also called when I was out
1 March – 18 May

March 1, Thursday.

The *Otter* sailed, or rather steamed away at eight. The Chief Justice & the Collector Hamley, were on board. The former part of the voyage was in fine sunny weather. It rained towards the end.

THE MINERS

I conversed with a miner who with four other 'boys' have Mormons' Bar above Lytton. He is a New Brunswicker. He wintered at the bar last year. The difficulty was provisions, their 'grub' as they call it. Bacon was a dollar a pound. Then from want of vegetables, & with salt food, scurvy broke out. This winter the miners have come away. He had not done well himself. He thought this year all would do well, though not many would come, owing to the difficulty of getting to the mines. Those who had been there before knew the way. They were going up in canoes & taking about 600 pounds worth of provisions per man. This would save much expense. There are now more stores up the country.

The miners were mostly American & were full of complaints against England, but on the whole were quiet & well disposed men. They helped one another, assisting a miner who 'was strapped.'

The Hill's Bar boys had done the best of all from the first.

The miners had not much piety among them but did not work on Sunday. They did their shopping, however, on that day, going into the nearest town for goods. If I went [there], some, he thought, would come & hear.

We reached Victoria at half past four, eight and a half hours passage. Found two steamers had come in: *Panama*, Tuesday night February 28 and the *Pacific*, February 29.

Had letters from Mr. [John] Garrett, my Aunt & Bishop Kip & Mr. Garry. From the latter I hear alas the news of the death of my dear former curate, that noble creature, Rev. F. Johnson. How inscrutable the ways of providence. Strong apparently, in the high career of usefulness, beloved & on the eve of marriage, cut down in the midst of health & youth. If such are removed, who indeed may expect a day forward? Yet, without doubt, all is well, is for the best. Best for him, best for the bereaved. God give us all grace to submit to such decrees with resignation, with thankfulness.

My heavenly Father make me ready in Christ my Saviour that any moment I may be prepared to go, not fit except through thy mercy & Jesus' work, yet accepted [by] Him. Lord Jesus come quickly.

March 2, Friday.

Day fine. Of the two men sent out in the *Athelstan*, one, Hemming, has turned out a drunkard & a scapegrace. The father, to his shame, has played this trick, having engaged to send two skilled artisans whose passage money I have had to pay. He knew his son's failings, desired to get him out of the country & this was his method. How little one can trust anybody.

March 3, Saturday.

THE COLOUR QUESTION

The canvassers for subscriptions for St. John's church have met with several refusals because no distinction is to be made in the seating of white & coloured people. Mr. Dundas having had cause to expect, from the man himself, that a Mr. Waldron would give a subscription, on calling today, met with a distinct refusal.

March 4, Second Sunday in Lent.

Day fine. Preached morning & evening at Christ Church. Visited & ministered in the hospital, [in the] afternoon. The crew of the *Athelstan* came up in a body to Church, headed by my man Bridgman who went down to the ship to show the way. It was the proudest day, he says, of his life, that after so much talk & so much anxiety about coming here, that he should see all things safe & show the crew of the Yarmouth [ship] the way to the house of God where they would find their old pastor, in Vancouver [Island]!

March 5, Monday.

Day showery & cold. Captain Bracey of the *Athelstan* dined with me. It was pleasant to talk over old Yarmouth.

THE COLOUR QUESTION

When Captain Bracey mentioned to some Americans yesterday he was going to church, they said, 'oh do you wish to go to a place where they will put a nigger alongside of you?' Expressing their abhorrence of sitting next to a 'nigger' anywhere!

80

March 6, Tuesday.

Showery & cold. The Rev. Mr. Dowson called. I gave him his passage money. I called on Mr. Dallas, the Hudson's Bay Company director, to ask him to allow the Dowsons a first class passage at second class fare.

March 7, Wednesday.

I preached at Christ Church: subject, Pilate. There was an encouraging gathering & I enjoyed the service.

March 8, Thursday.

Rain all day. Went out to Mr. Cary's, the Attorney General, to look at some land. We walked about & visited spots of splendid views. Mr. Pearse, the land office official, was with us. He mentioned that the Hudson's Bay Company had appropriated to themselves the site of Victoria without payment to the government & had then sold it [at] the lot prices from 60 to 100£ an acre.

March 9, Friday.

[I had] a visit from Bishop Demers & one of his priests. He is a coarse looking, but good natured man. He apologized for not having called before. We talked about the Indians. He has been here since 1852, and for eighteen years amongst Indians. He came from Canada & is French & speaks broken or rather accented English.

He has no schools for Indian children. His missionaries have learned the language. He used, when in Oregon, to get on somehow with six languages or dialects. I asked about the French & Italian & other classes here who are Roman Catholic. He said they troubled him very little & were more intent upon making money than upon religion.

I told him I trusted socially we should meet as friends, but that our differences were fundamental & there could be no approach, as far as I was concerned, towards him in principles. This need not prevent a mutual respect as members of the same community. He assented & said this was all he desired.

This day has been fine and sunshine throughout.

I saw a butterfly for the first time.

AN IRREGULAR MARRIAGE

Mr. Cridge asked me if he might marry, out of the canonical hours, a couple who were obliged to go away to Port Townsend this afternoon. They had a Governor's [marriage] licence. I said I had no power to grant any indulgence from the rule of the canon, but as the case was one

81

of emergency & as we allow in some other cases [such] as sponsors exceptions, I should take no notice in this case, if on his own responsibility he chose to perform the ceremony.

March 10, Saturday.

Day fine. I walked with Captain Gossett.

March 11, Sunday.

Preached morning & evening at Christ Church. Took the full service at Esquimalt, [in the] afternoon. On my way, as I passed the village of Northern Indians there was a frightful scene of drunken confusion. The poor creatures were running about like crazy people in a lunatic yard. They were vociferating at each other & rolling & tumbling one against the other. Some of them had on the most fantastic dresses, bright scarlet jackets, feathers & ribbons in their hair, all costumed to increase the bedlam look of the scene.

A lovely day, the walk to Esquimalt [was] very warm.

March 12, Monday.

A Summer's day. Flowers have begun to appear. I saw several.

INDIAN DRUNKENNESS

Mr. Hall who goes a good deal among the Indians, told me [he] had often seen the way in which the natives deal with each other when intoxicated. They tie together the feet & the hands, behind the back, & tether the poor creature to a stump or tree. This is the common practice. The poor Indian when under the influence of drink is a menace.

March 13, Tuesday.

Walked with Dundas on the Saanich road & struck into a beautiful trail on the Victoria North Arm.

March 14, Wednesday.

Cold, rainy. The *Panama* & the *Pacific* came in, mail by the former. Heard from Miss [Burdett-]Coutts. Preached at Christ Church.

March 15, Thursday.

Received a call from two American officers, Captains Hunt & Woodruffe, commanding at San Juan [Island] & Semiahmoo. They are intelligent & pleasing men.

THE COLOUR QUESTION

I called on Mr. & Mrs. Trutch. She is an American though I should not have known it. They spoke of the colour question & the feeling about it in this place. He told me that even American Episcopalians who are residing here refuse to attend Church because we make no distinction. In America, in all denominations, excepting Romanists I believe, a distinction is made. Mr. Trutch himself, though an Englishman, confessed he had objection to sit near some black people, not that he felt any unkind sentiment, but because of the peculiar odour. She is against distinction & said how delightful it was to go into a Cathedral (meaning a Roman Catholic C[athedral]) & to see no distinction. Yet, she evidently believes the race is a different species of man & spoke of them rather patronizingly, with pity, [rather] than honour & respect as of fellow immortals & equal in the sight of God.

She spoke of the miseries of slavery & of the sad separation of families, children from parents, etc., when sold. Mr. Trutch had visited the slave market of New Orleans where the slaves are ranged in rows for inspection & where people come & feel them, tell them to open their mouths & let [them] see their teeth & then bid so many hundred of dollars for this boy, or this young woman! Just the thought sickens one.

Mrs. Trutch told me that Bishop Scott of Oregon does not deem slavery unlawful. His wife is an owner of slaves whom she will probably free at her death!

A MERCY

Just as we had finished prayers this evening, Bridgman came running into the room saying there was a great fire in the town. We opened the door & the whole street & neighbourhood was illuminated. We went out to see where it was & to our horror found we were on fire ourselves & the raging [element] was in our own frail & combustible dwelling. My first impression was there could be no possible chance but that the house in a few minutes must be laid in ashes. It was, however, confined as yet to the chimney, but pouring forth a column of fire like a volcanic eruption upon the wooden roof. Bridgman remembered in a little upper room was a hole in the chimney. He rushed upstairs & found a column of fire coming forth into the room. Immediately close to this was the ceiling which is dry canvas, & would burn like torch wood from a spark. He called for water. I had a pail full ready. He luckily poured it in with happy exactness. Wet blankets were then resorted to & stuffed in. This was a check. Our worthy black landlord, who had come to help, mounted the roof & with pails of water & wet clothes checked [the] progress there. Happily it rained in torrents & by twelve o'clock we had mastered the enemy. Our escape, however, was marvellous & deeply thankful we all felt to our Heavenly Father for his goodness to us.

March 16, Friday.

At eleven o'clock today [we had] a fall of snow. The first really I have seen, not enough however to lie upon the ground many minutes. The day continued cold & stormy. I visited a wreck on Rocky Point, that of the *Glimpse*, a bark from Francisco. She got on the rocks about twelve last night. Passengers & crew, all [are] safe. [It is] doubtful if she can get off. The tide & weather [. . .] will show before morning.

March 17, Saturday.

A cold, stormy, snowy, sleety, windy day from morning till night.

I went down to the wreck. The poor bark lay still upon the rocks.

March 18, Sunday.

Snow on the ground. Cold in the morning. Sunshine [in the] afternoon.

THE COLOUR QUESTION

This afternoon Mr. [. . .] came to tell me the troubles of the coloured people. Many had come up here expecting to find peace from the bitter prejudice & injustice which exists against them in America. They are fearful they shall not be free even on British soil. They are all very sad at things which have recently happened. A Mr. Clarke & a Mr. Macfie were sent out by the Congregational British Colonial Society. A chapel was erected. Mr. Clarke, in Canada, had been a marked friend of the coloured people. The chief adherents of the Congregational denomination here are Americans. They declared there must be a separate place in the chapel for the coloured people or they should leave. Mr. Clarke was firm. Mr. Macfie left him, took the whites & got money from Americans & in California, to build his chapel on the exclusive principle. Mr. Clarke appealed to the Society at home. The [Congregational] British [Colonial] Society upheld Mr. Macfie & dismissed Mr. Clarke.

Last Sunday the latter made the announcement to his congregation that he must leave Victoria. At this the coloured people are troubled as it seems a sign that exclusive principles are to prevail.

ROME AND THE COLOUR QUESTION

Another circumstance has happened in the past week. A merchant, Mr. Little, sent his daughter to the female school of the Roman Catholic

Sisters. There were at [the school] also some seven or eight coloured children, among which the niece of Mr. [. . .], a girl of fourteen. Mr. Little informed the Sisters that all the white children would be taken away unless a separation was made. The Sisters had then [made] a separate room for the coloured children. Upon this, the coloured children have been withdrawn & the parents are in perplexity [regarding] where to send them. The great want of a school for girls is seen by the fact that these very two children, the daughter of the merchant & the niece of my landlord, Mr. [. . .], would both come to us, both being in attendance otherwise at our church.

I told Mr. [. . .] he might rely upon it. The Anglican Church would never make any distinction. He said when Mr. Clarke left, the coloured people would come to us.

He thanked me with tears for the consolation he said I had given him, for all these things had made him nervous & very sad. For if on British soil rest & peace & justice to the coloured people were not to be had, where else in the world could they look?

I preached at Christ Church morning & evening. Mr. Crickmer preached in the afternoon.

March 19, Monday.

Cold. The Rev. Messrs. Cridge, Dundas, Crickmer dined with me. We had a pleasant evening & discussed many matters of the deepest interest. I felt revived & encouraged by the earnest spirit evinced by all in the great work before us, & by the sympathy with which they supported my plans. By God's blessing I trust we may make known with power the saving truths of the gospel to our fellow men & plant distinctively & solidly the foundations of the church.

March 20, Tuesday.

Took a class for Mr. Cridge, on confirmation.

Heard to my joy & thankfulness that the *Heather Bell* & its missionary freight had arrived well at Honolulu. The *Topaze* had left her there. The missionary party were met by the officers at an entertainment & were to follow in a few days. The Honourable Mr. Spencer & Captain Prevost I met on their way to call on me.

The Governor also called when I was out.

ROMIST PRIEST AND INDIANS

I walked out by the Bella Bella Indians & round the point of Victoria harbour towards Beacon Hill. Not far from the entrance is a bay. In it were two canoes & a party of Indians upon the sand. Upon the high bank behind some trees, sheltered from the wind, was a small group. As I approached, I saw a European with [the] Indians. They were sitting round a fire. He was talking & gesticulating. As I drew near, he rose & stood. He was a priest. I approached & he came & we conversed. He was instructing the Indians in religion. He told me he belonged to an order of Regulars called 'Oblaty' [Oblate] whose principal seat is [in] Marseilles. They are independent of other denominations, as for instance of Bishop Demers who is a Secular. Some devote themselves to missions amongst the Indians. He is one & has been six years in Oregon, principally near Fort Colville. He is supported by the Society for the Propagation of the Faith. He gets nothing from any other source. The headquarters of the mission are at Esquimalt.

He was instructing the Indians in Chinook, supplementing the deficiencies of that jargon by words of their own language. The Indians were from Puget Sound, amongst [whom] he was known, the Snokomish. Some of them however, paddled his canoe & he paid them. He had not in the six years acquired the native language, only the Chinook. His own language is French. English he speaks imperfectly. He had not made much [head] way with the tribes so far as changing faith goes. He had produced a good feeling towards himself & had got them to know this & that was right, the contrary wrong. He said it was utterly impossible to get them to send their children away to a place of instruction. He had tried with one boy, but in three months he was sick for home & ran away.

I asked if he thought they would send their children to [a] place near their village. He said he thought they would do that.

His way [is] to go round to certain Indian villages & spend a day at one & a day at another. He was generally four days from the mission & slept out on the ground. There was something simple & engaging about this young priest. I could not but admire the zeal. Yet alas, probably his zeal was expended in teaching these poor savages to look to the Virgin & other departed creatures instead of to the only true God & Jesus whom he has sent. Before I left & after finishing by many questions, he said, 'will you now tell me who you are?' I said, 'the Anglican Bishop.' 'Ah, I thought so,' he replied. 'So you know,' I said, 'how much we differ.' 'Yes but you sincerely believe your view to be right & I believe mine, God will accept us both.' 'I hope so,' I said. 'At least this is not the time to contend, in the presence of these unconverted heathen who are without a glimmer of truth & we ought to teach them some chief points of Christianity upon which we do agree.' I could not at such a moment, [when] his self denial & earnestness was in such contrast to our own cold neglect of these poor creatures, I could not say a word to pain him. Though I felt for his own sake & for the truth's sake it would have been right to have suggested some thoughts which would have set him thinking upon the errors of his church.

We parted. I to my idle walk & comfortable dinner & kind servants watching & anticipating every want. He back to his Indians, sitting in the cold, & not knowing where to lay his head that night.

I remarked the Indians to be boyish & good natured, there were two or three old ones who went away, but the rest played antes round the log, pulled each other's hair & repeated the very exact tricks which school boys do if the attention of the master is called away for a while.

I asked how he managed when some did not understand Chinook. He said the others explained to them.

He mentioned the Cowichans had their priest. I asked how long? He said a year. He himself has only come recently. The Romanists therefore, evidently are making an effort.

March 21, Wednesday.

GOVERNOR DOUGLAS

Had interview with the Governor. He read me a dispatch upon land grants to religious bodies recently sent to government, in which was made a strange jumble of terms. The Methodists being called Episcopal, & 'the four grand divisions of Christians': 'Church of England, Episcopal Methodists, Presbyterians, & R[oman] Catholics' being proposed for subsidies, 100 acres of land each in every place!

The Governor is a self made man. He has not been in England for many [years] & is unacquainted with the feeling there upon many points, hence mistakes in dealing with those who repeat here English society. Yet he is most anxious to do the right thing. He has been accustomed to be absolute in the Hudson's Bay Company & secret in his plans & to deal with inferiors. His position is difficult when in contact with accomplished men of the world, as our naval & military people, & where a legislature & council are concerned. He is resolute in his own view. In the case of New Westminster & Langley, he chose the latter as the Capital of British Columbia. It was an error in a strategical sense, being on the wrong side [of] the frontier. He was obliged to give way. But he clings to it & my belief is he will take every opportunity to forward it. It is pretty evident he has done all he could to check New Westminster. This feeling on his part & the uncertainty of his course acts against its progress.

March 22, Thursday.

Called upon the Admiral on board the *Ganges*, also upon Captain Spencer of the *Topaze*. Captain Bracey of the *Athelstan* dined with me & we had pleasant talk of old Yarmouth.

March 23, Friday.

THE COLOUR QUESTION

A respectable coloured person, Mrs. Washington, called on me. She is a communicant, but had felt an intruder, not having been called upon or recognized by the clergyman. She had been brought up a Methodist in Virginia. I was pleased with her simple piety, & also her intelligence.

I asked her if she could tell me what the ground of the American prejudice was against the coloured race. She said it had always puzzled her to tell.

She had heard that some consider the African race an inferior one & not ever intended to be equal to the white, that it was not possible it should be. It could not be the colour she thought, for some of her race were quite white & yet the same prejudice existed against them.

She believed they were afraid the race would become more powerful & therefore had to keep them down.

She spoke very sensibly, had a clear view of some great religious principles, [and was] of most pleasing countenance & altogether impressed me as one superior to the generality of white people. Occasionally, in speaking of the tribulations her people had to endure, she was affected to tears. She said they truly realized suffering for they are a sensitive race, & if any were permitted to enter heaven, it would [be] they had come there as the Scriptures had said, 'we must through much tribulation enter the Kingdom of God.'

I bid her cheer up. She might rely at least upon the clergy of the Church of England, but above all she would remember the words of Jesus. 'In the world ye shall have tribulation, but be of good cheer I have overcome the world.'

INDIAN TROUBLE

In passing the village of Northern Indians yesterday I heard lofty & pathetic speech. I saw an Indian woman gesticulating & loudly talking, sometimes as in anger, other times in affliction. She was wrapped in a blanket, one arm out & uplifted, hair wildly dishevelled. A man before her was on the ground. It was her husband. He was intoxicated, not sufficiently so but what he knew what he was about. He seemed rather to be in a state of inebriety which the poor creature might deem enjoyable. She was reproaching him. She was ashamed of him. She pitied him. She hated him. She feared him. She loved him. What she actually uttered I could not understand but the purport was plain & all these states of feeling were evident. There was something dramatic in the whole scene. She stood at a distance & scolded from afar. She relented & would come back as though to assist him home [but] on approach his folly created her disgust & she could not bring herself to aid him. At length, he was on his feet & made [a] rush after her. She fled afrighted, as though she feared something more than himself. A mystery was in that *pire chuck* [fire-water]. She looked back & he had fallen. Her pity was moved. Then her cries rent the air. She seemed to be appealing to heaven. There was a pathos & a nobility in her affective strain that moved one's heart. Here was misery. This misery the poor Indian knew not till the white man came. And the white man, professedly Christian, taught the poor Indian, nay enticed & forced the poor Indian to drink, degraded him & ruined him, still more hopelessly than in his native state.

THE INDIAN SCOURGE

In the same village & within the same hour I saw another similar instance of intoxication. A man dressed in European costume, he looked an athletic sailor, walked frantically past. He hastened to an Indian hut. He paced round. He sought entrance but was denied. He became furious, & then had all the actions of a wild beast. The hut was strongly made of pieces of timber. He crashed at the house. He tore down a timber. Another followed his arms which showed extraordinary muscle. Foaming & screaming he tore at the next obstruction & wedged himself in to get the greater purchase & presently would have found entrance. One [Indian] rushed up to him, [comforted], spoke to him, & stopped him. He eagerly ran to another part, where he was confronted by the Indian who seemed to have influence with him & who was himself distressed at the frenzy of the drunkard.

Such is the daily & hourly misery of these poor Indians.

Dined with Mr. Trutch. Met the Creases.

March 24, Saturday.

Beautiful weather. Packages landed from the *Topaze.*

March 25, Sunday.

Lovely spring day. Preached & read prayers three times at Christ Church. Mr. Cridge [is] away in [the Colony of] British Columbia.

March 26, Monday.

THE COLOURED QUESTION

Visited by Mr. Gibbs & Mr. Francis, two coloured gentlemen. In conversation they spoke of the unpleasant position they are in from the prejudice against their race.

As soon as this colony was formed & before any idea of the gold existed, they had come here to be in quiet & to find rest.

The feeling [against them] is even more bitter than in some of the states of America.

They were Presbyterians in [San] Francisco, now (Mr. Francis & Mr. G[ibbs]) attend [the] Church of England. They had asked Mr. Macfie and he had said it was true he was obliged to make distinction, for 'each church' (i.e. congregation) made its own regulations, was 'independent' & he only 'preached' to them.

They told me the coloured people had been excluded from the Philharmonic and the Young Men's Christian Association.

I said from whatever society they were excluded, I was excluded also, for I should belong to nothing where such unrighteous prejudices existed.

Mr. Gibbs said, 'people say of us we wish to intrude into social circles & force a position which may not be desired by others on social & private grounds. Nothing is further from the truth. We understand the rules of society quite well enough to know that social position must be made, each for himself & that character & influence & worth must make that position.'

I asked him what he thought was the real ground of the prejudice. He smiled & said, 'there is deeply seated in human nature [a . . .] to hate those you injure.' I could not but be struck with the superiority of these two men.

THE COLOUR QUESTION AND CONGREGATIONALISM

Mr. Clarke, the Congregational minister, called upon me to show [me] the correspondence between himself & the Colonial Society for the British Colonies [Congregational British Colonial Society]. A letter from the Secretary Mr. James, (brother of Angel James), enclosed resolutions of the committee approving of Mr. Macfie [and] disapproving of Mr. Clarke. They say they do not interfere or express an opinion if the congregations choose even to exclude altogether the coloured people & [they] censure Mr. Clarke for publishing his statement & [are] requesting him to suppress it.

A CONGREGATIONAL MINISTER UNSETTLED

I expressed to Mr. Clarke my sympathy with him. He had said he could no longer hold to the [Congregational British Colonial] Society & should resign his connection with it.

I found he was shaken as to the principles even of the body. He had previously asked if he could be of use in carrying out educational work with me. I asked how far he was wedded to the principles of Congregationalism. These circumstances were sent by God frequently, we might believe, to induce reflection & reconsideration of our position. I had a respect for his Christian character & the stand on principle he had made & would welcome him as a fellow labourer if under God's blessing a way was made for such a result.

He said he must confess he had, as he grew older, come to detest the unfairness of controversialists. He was dissatisfied with the grounds on which conclusions were based. He was no bigot. He found a want of central authority in his own body. People had said to him, 'does not this trouble between you & Mr. Macfie show something wrong in your system?' He felt it. I said that is exactly one difference between Congregationalism & the Church of England. He said he saw it.

I asked what points there were upon which he had scruples. He mentioned principally,

1. ch[urch] & state connection
2. want of free prayer
3. expressions in burial service
4. baptismal regeneration
5. episcopal absolutism
6. laxity of doctrine, such men as Jowett & Manning being allowed to remain
7. not freedom for conscience.

As to the first, he said it did not here exist & therefore need not trouble him.

As to the second, he did not object to a liturgy, but thought there should be scope for free prayer & he had heard the present Bishop of Huron use it before & after sermons. I told him I had no objection to it, if with it, on such occasions & in the way the Bishop of Huron used it, the liturgy was honestly & fairly dealt with.

As to the third, I explained that the expression was in 'sure & certain hope of *the*, not *his* or *her*, resurrection to eternal life,' but allowed from want of discipline many of us felt a difficulty.

Upon the fourth I showed the word 'regeneration' to be used in a different sense from his own. He allowed the explanation to be satisfactory.

[Upon the] fifth he said he really did not know the exact relations of Bishop & Clergy. I explained that the mode of government was, in many matters, [decided] by a church assembly which would be organized in due time & which regulated the affairs of the church in many important particulars, subject to the Bishop's veto.

[Upon the] sixth he could not see how the [Thirty-Nine] Articles could be subscribed [to] by so many various minds, & thought there must be laxity, but confessed such a matter ought not to be a difficulty as he could accept himself the Thirty-Nine Articles & each one must answer for himself as to the honesty of his subscription. I said no doubt there was want of thought upon some subjects. But this was rather an advantage in the Church of England that she allowed a breadth of thought & in a free country this was a wise adaptation to the wants of mankind which, limited as it was within certain clear lines, enabled her to win the more souls to Christ. Some extremes there would always be, treading upon the very edge of these lines & appearing to some to be outside.

[Upon the] seventh, conscience, I said latitude was allowed on points indifferent & the authority of the church was only exercised when manifest violation of the rules or doctrine took place, or the life was inconsistent.

I told him I thought one difficulty with him would be re-ordination. He said, 'no, most bodies followed that course.' We discussed the subject of the *due* call to the ministry. He was very weak upon the subject & I think he felt so, as he did not reply to my answers. He smiled at the 'apostolical succession' however & asked 'what good, even if a minister had it?' & whether ordination would be refused to any one who did not take the highest view.

I read the Article & the Preface to the Ordinal & said a Bishop should not require more to be believed than the Church did & though the highest view was not inconsistent, a lower view would not debar admission into the ministry.

In course of conversation he said he was much impressed with the stability of the Church of England. Notwithstanding the acknowledged abuses which had prevailed & the repeated attacks upon it, it was now stronger than ever.

He thought the Church of England had a fine career in this colony & that no body of Christians was likely to make the progress & do the good which was plainly within the reach of the Church of England.

As to Congregationalists, there was a very poor field & it was a fact there was but one English man disposed that way in all the place. The Americans were the chief adherents. As to his own people, they were principally coloured with a few whites who adhered not because of Congregationalism, but because of the principle he advocated.

I said these things, the fact of this rejection of a right cause by the Society he belonged to, his want of confidence in their principles, the breaking up of his charge, the trouble he was caused, were so many reasons for seeing the providence of God at work & justifying, indeed demanding, a reconsideration of his position.

He said whatever came of this he should ever feel grateful for the sympathy I had shown towards him. He was with me a couple of hours. May God direct him & make 'all things work together for good,' for his own glory & the saving of souls in Christ!

March 27, Tuesday.

A lovely day. I took Mr. Cridge's class of female candidates for confirmation. There was a much greater reserve & serious deportment than on the previous occasion. I thank God for this. Unless our confirmations are approached in a fervent spirit & with a real desire of self dedication to God & with a full appreciation of spiritual religion, they will be to us weakness instead of strength. I endeavoured to impress these young persons with seriousness & I trust I have so far succeeded. Of the baptisms which I enquired into, two had been baptized by Romanists, one by Presbyterians & one not at all.

I walked out today with Mr. Dundas to Mount Tolmie, from which the view is delightful, indeed sublime.

The foundations of St. John's [have] begun today.

March 28, Wednesday.

Mail steamer *Brother Jonathan* in. Colonel Hawkins & Captain Haig of the Boundary Commission called. Read prayers at Christ Church. Mr. Dundas preached an excellent sermon. Lovely day.

March 29, Thursday.

Mr. Cridge called, having returned from British Columbia. Arranged a confirmation paper. Engaged writing for the mail. Day fine, though windy.

March 30, Friday.

Fine day, a shower in the night.

DISSENT AND THE CHURCH

This day, I agreed to purchase the Congregational Meeting House. Some few months ago this was opened & its minister published attacks upon the Church of England. The building was erected upon the edge of the Church Reserve, lot 100 on Church Street. A space in front was marked out for a handsome & prominent 'Congregational Church,' facing the park. A few short weeks have been enough to create a split between the two ministers & the breaking up of this congregation is the result, together with the sale of the meeting house.

These things, though they exhibit the Church of England in favourable contrast as comparatively at peace & advancing, as compared with the sects around, yet are no matter of boasting. We have our own sad deficiencies & any day may see some division or sorrow sent to judge us. Besides the infidel rejoices & sees further ground which satisfies him in refusing to acknowledge what is so inconsistent to itself.

I feel much for Mr. Clarke, the much injured teacher of the Congregational body, who made the noble stand in behalf of the coloured, but who has suffered temporal loss in consequence.

March 31, Saturday.

THE COLOUR QUESTION

Mr. Clarke called & we completed the purchase of the Congregational Meeting [House]. He said he did not think Mr. Macfie could hold his ground. His congregation consisted partly of Americans, irreligious people, & partly of Scotchmen who adhere to him from clannish motives. These latter will be separated from him when a Presbyterian minister arrives & one is expected by every steamer. Mr. Macfie did not realize so much in California as he expected. Having gone for the purpose, [he] obtained only 400£. The Congregationalists in [San] Francisco gave him the cold shoulder & at a meeting in their vestry, [. . .] on his statement, they responded to the amount only of 13£!

As an instance of the effect of the decision of the Society upon individuals, one person had said to Mr. Clarke 'I adhere to you, not that I altogether agree with your principles on this question, but because I think you hardly & meanly used. If you are not supported by the Society I shall not go to the other party but shall go to hear the Lord Bishop.' On the news arriving of the Society's rejection of him, he said to his friend 'I suppose now you will go to the Bishop.' He found the effect produced was to confirm this person in his prejudice. He had not expected such an answer from England & would have been ashamed to ally himself to the Macfie party, but now finds confidence in yielding to his prejudice.

Another person who had supported him he heard was to be an usher to show persons seats in Mr. [Macfie's] chapel. He went to him & after conversation his friend with emotion jumped up & said 'what a fool am I. I profess to be a Christian & yet I have promised to aid in that which is utterly opposed to Christianity.' He wrote a letter to Macfie telling him he could not hold to his engagement & said his own sins & past life were far blacker than the complexion of his brethren he was called on to reject.

April 1, Sunday.

Preached morning & evening at Christ Church. Visited the hospital in the afternoon & ministered. Lovely day.

April 2, Monday.

A tempest of wind all day. Our first passion week service, this evening. About thirty in attendance notwithstanding the weather. The usual

Sunday music was played on [the] organ which is not strictly correct. Mr. Cridge preached. Mr. Clarke, the Congregational minister, [was] at church.

April 3, Tuesday.

Snow & wind. I preached at Christ Church in the evening on the 'Agony of our Blessed Lord.' There was an improved attendance, above forty.

THE CLERGY

I bid good bye to Mr. & Mrs. Crickmer who go to British Columbia tomorrow morning at five [o'clock]. Their nice house at Langley being broken up, I have been pleased at the readiness with which they have responded to my wish in going to Yale. They go with three children [in] this cold weather in the river steamers & part of the way in open boat to their new home. On arrival, they will find but poor shelter & a strange people. Yet they go cheerfully & mention not their hardship. They went on board the steamer tonight & it blows cold & stormy.

At Hope, Mr. Pringle is not better off. He has been living in a mere shanty & without a servant, doing everything, cooking & all for himself. At Douglas, Mr. & Mrs. Gammage have had to endure hardship & at New Westminster, Mr. Sheepshanks lives in a log hut.

Nothing, I feel sure, actuates these clergy but a sense of duty & God's blessing must be with them & with their work.

April 4, Wednesday.

Last night [we had] a terrific wind. At noon today it abated & the rest of the day [it was] fine.

PROGRESS — HOUSE WALKING

In walking down Fort Street today I met a house, positively & bodily on its way steadily down the street, a house of six rooms at least. It was about to take up its position in a different spot.

Bridgman was looking out for lodgings for my missionary band & called at a house he thought likely. The owner informed him that she had intended moving to another situation but as it was rather windy she put it off, but she was about to take her house to a lot in a different street. It would be removed on rollers & she should probably go inside with it & carry on her usual work!

The carpenter I am employing about the erection of my iron house proposes to place large boards under the chimney stacks in order that they may go safely when the house is rolled away to make room for a stone or brick building!

April 5, Thursday.

PASSION WEEK SERVICE

A fine but cold day. Preached this evening at Christ Church. There has been a gradual improvement in the attendance. On Monday thirty, Tuesday forty, Wednesday fifty, Thursday sixty. The weather has been cold & passion never observed before. Tonight the service was devout & the people really seemed to value the opportunity. One man has been present each evening who is, I know, hardly worked during the day & who drives an express wagon & two horses to Esquimalt daily.

A SWEDE

I had a conversation with a Swede. He lives alone in a small shanty of his own erection. He has been nine years from his country. He was a Presbyterian Lutheran, went to church sometimes. I gave him advice on neglect. I mentioned that one of his country women was well known in England, Jenny Lind. 'Oh sir my name is Lind, but no relation.'

SUCCESS

I was calling today upon a Mr. Russell who has cleared land & brought it into good order & erected a nice house. This man came out in the employ of the Hudson's Bay Company five years ago as a blacksmith, a mere workingman with the promise of fifty acres at the end of his engagement. He had acquired some land in Victoria when the rush came two years ago & now is worth at least 1000£ a year. He is a well conducted & good man.

CONFIDENCE IN BRITISH HONESTY

Mr. Russell told me [about] several instances showing how much more faith Americans place on the word of English traders than upon their own. They will actually bring their produce at an expense of transit from Oregon & sell cheaper to English merchants than they sell in Oregon to their own people, & why, because they are sure of their money with Englishmen.

April 6, Good Friday.

Excellent congregations morning & evening at Christ Church. I preached in the morning. The day cool but fine.

The mail came in & brought me letters, two from my Aunt. After evening service, Mr. Pemberton, Mr. Dundas & Mr. Cridge discussed with me the Indian subject. We agreed something should be done at once.

During the past few weeks so many disturbances have occurred that some police regulations are requisite:

all the families should be registered
should be taxed a small annual amount
order should be maintained
houses should be placed so that sanitary measures could be observed,
a superintendent [should be appointed],
native police [appointed],
an Institution under a clergyman
a school under a teacher
an orphanage [and]
a hospital [provided].

ARRIVAL OF THE "HEATHER BELL"

As we were discussing Indian affairs, Mr. Harvey one of the missionary party in the *Heather Bell* arrived amongst us. He had left the ship a few miles out & came with his wife to my residence. After seven months voyage, the land is grateful to them.

I thank God our prayers for the safety of the missionary band have been answered.

April 7, Saturday.

Easter evening. A goodly band again assembled in the house of God. I preached. I think God has caused his grace to attend these services. I can see a more devout spirit & real pleasure in some from joining with us. I trust those who may have thought Lent to be but a dead letter have felt the reverse. My earnest desire is to give reality to the system of our Church. Let people say 'we know by happy experience these arrangements are of God & that they are in truth the glorious ministration of the Spirit.'

THE COLOUR QUESTION — CASTE PREJUDICE

Mr. S. M. Catlin of New York, a worthy fellow passenger in the *S. L. Stephen*, arrived here yesterday for a couple of days. He dined with me today. Amongst other subjects, we talked of the colour difficulty. He had been to church & said it was the first time he had been in an English congregation & was much interested in the service. He was much surprised to see the coloured people sitting in all parts of the church & spoke of it as if something quite wrong. I asked his objection. He said, 'their colour showed it was not right & they had not been made equal to the white nor had they advanced even to equality & therefore it was not intended they should be equal'!

I gave the obvious answers to which he had no answer except to suggest how easy it was to have a place on purpose, a corner set apart.

He remarked, 'if you allow them this equality, how can you prevent amalgamation? There would be intermarriages.' I replied, 'that is a social question. You do not object to sit near a white poor person & yet you would not say there was danger of intermarriages in consequence.'

I could see in this worthy man the objection was grounded not upon reason but upon a prejudice of caste, similar to that in India, or amongst the Jews in Saint Paul's time. This caste prejudice the Gospel entirely opposes & a pure Christianity must have more effect upon the Americans than at present, if this unhappy prejudice is to be rooted out. Its existence in America proves how ready human nature is to fall.

April 8, Easter Day, [Sunday].

Weather fine. Congregation at Christ Church full. Sixty communicants, the largest number known, some usual communicants remained last Sunday & did not come [...]. We were five clergymen in Ch[urch], four officiated. I preached morning & evening. Mr. [A. C.] Garrett preached in the afternoon & evinced considerable power. I trust he may be a most useful, as well as energetic, fellow labourer.

One thing alone marred the pleasure of this great day. One of the party from England by the *Heather Bell*, the unordained member, appeared to have misconducted himself so much as to have brought great discredit upon himself, & I fear, the Church. His quarrels also had been many & there existed an unhappy feeling towards the two clergy. Already this was a subject of conversation in the town. I, therefore, sent him a note requesting him not to present himself at the Holy Communion.

I did this with much sorrow. I felt, however, that it was of great importance we should avoid scandal & not allow any one to enter our mission circle whose character was sullied. I know well how many faults I have myself & the precept is before me to exercise discipline with the spirit of modesty, considering myself. I hope I do so. God give me grace to be wise & gentle & humble.

April 9, Easter Monday.

At half past nine [I] saw Mr. Harvey who admitted he had erred in the voyage. The several points were such as to preclude his admission into Holy Orders. This announcement excited naturally his strong emotion, even to tears. Yet I felt I had no alternative. I must keep the sacred ministry free from blemish, alas how unworthy myself, as far as I possibly can.

I had today a call from His Excellency the Governor. He sat an hour.

Captain Prevost came in the evening.

Rain most of the day.

The iron house taken this day out of the warehouse & deposited on the five lots on Vancouver Street ready for erection. A white man and four labourers [are] clearing the ground.

April 10, Tuesday.

Weather showery. Marked out [the] ground for Bishop's residence on Church Reserve.

April 11, Wednesday.

Fine weather. Arranged with Mrs. Lowe to take charge of the Female Collegiate School. The disputes in the *Heather Bell* are much talked of & very humbling, a missionary ship unhappily the reverse of peaceful. May the scandal be [. . .] that our work be not hindered!

This evening the Rev. Mr. Garrett preached an excellent sermon on confirmation.

April 12, Thursday.

I was astounded this morning by a paragraph in a local paper ascribing intoxication, yesterday, to Mr. Harvey the unordained member of the party in the *Heather Bell*. On investigation, alas it was too true. I desired he would consider himself severed from the mission.

April 13, Friday.

Presented the Revs. Mr. Garrett & Lowe to the Governor. At three o'clock took place the laying of the corner stone of the new church of St. John. This was done by the Governor in the presence of a large concourse of people. I addressed them & felt painfully deficient in subject & language & manner. Many Indians were present.

AURORA

This evening at half past eight there was a beautiful exhibition of the northern lights. There was the warm red [. . .] in the north, but on the eastward of north was a remarkable pillar of fire in the midst of the heavens, perpendicular to the horizon. It remained a long time without much variation & created great attention the moment the eye caught it.

April 14, Saturday.

Day fine. Steamer in. No mail.

April 15, Sunday.

Preached on scandal at Christ Church. In the evening, on confirmation. Took service at the hospital in the afternoon. There [I] saw the workman [Mr.] Sharp with a dislocated thigh.

April 16, Monday.

Asked to print my sermon on scandal.

Met Committee of Collegiate Schools in the lecture room which was the Congregational chapel.

Dined at Mr. Cridge's. Met Captain Prevost.

April 17, Tuesday.

Day fine. House progressing.

April 18, Wednesday.

Day fine. Left home this morning at a little after eight with Mr. Cridge for a ride to Saanich. We got to Lee's [Leigh's] farm at nine. Had talk with him about some spot for Sunday service. We then rode through Cedar Plains & visited the settlers on the way. One woman expressed great desire, offered their house, & suggested an open air meeting such as she had seen in Scotland.

Tod's farm under Mount Douglas five miles [further], we then visited. Mrs. Tod [is] a communicant. Mr. John Tod had been brought up at the Red River settlement & knew well Archdeacon Cochrane [Cochran]. His mother who is a half breed is a communicant also.

We then retraced our steps & turned across to the North Dairy Farm. Here was a respectable elderly farmer's wife. She said she had not been in a church but once in seven years.

After several calls on the way we reached one of the Saanich settlers at half past three. The Deeks are from Essen, near Rockford. They seem hard working & industrious. We had a glass each of refreshing milk.

We pushed on a couple of miles further & came to other settlers. One Mr. Thompson, a most worthy young man who offered his house & every accommodation for a Sunday service.

FRENCH PRIESTS AND INDIANS

The Saanich settlers told us that several French priests have been instructing the Indians. There was an improvement amongst them in cessation from drink, but they had fallen away from work & a bad feeling had been given them towards the whites. A person was present at their instruction in an Indian Village. The priest took three pieces of stick, [these] representing English, American, French. He gave the merits of each in turn. The Americans were 'very bad,' the English 'better but bad.' These two he dashed to the ground & trampled them. French of course [were] 'very good' & taken care of as precious. He also showed English & American as doomed heretics for the fire of hell, the French as the true church destined to heaven.

We rode home by half past seven having had a ride of about thirty-five miles.

April 19, Thursday.

INDIAN PROGRESS

Visited the Songhee & Tsimshian Indians with Mr. Cridge. The latter told us many young men would come to school if one were opened.

A young man named Wahsh read a hymn in English. He has lately come from Fort Simpson where Mr. Duncan has been labouring so faithfully.

April 20, Friday.

Laid up with slight cold.

April 21, Saturday.

Walked with Mr. Cridge to inspect a spot he had selected for investment & to consider whether the college site should not be near, on the Park Line East of Beacon Hill.

YOUNG INDIAN

On Thursday, I met an intelligent young Indian & [he was] dressed well. On accosting him in Chinook, he answered in good English. He had been on board an American ship. I asked him how he liked going to sea. He replied with a knowing look, 'first rate.'

I asked if he ever prayed. He replied he knew not what it meant. Did he know who made him? He had never been taught. Intelligent & ready, this poor lad had learned much from the white man, to swear horrible oaths no doubt, but was left literally blank, worse than blank, as [to] the most momentous subject which can engross the thoughts of man.

AMBITION OF INDIANS

The Indians imitate the whites. You will see the young men dressed out in expensive cloth. One man is working for me; he has on a new pair of black superfine cloth trousers & to take care of them has a substantial pair of overalls outside.

You will see Indians with excellent shirts & even studs. The young women begin to deck themselves in fashionable attire. I saw a young woman at the Tsimshian camp with a gold ring on the wedding finger. She was washing her face & really looked pleasing with black sparkling eyes & rosy cheeks. Close to her was a female who had blackened her face to a demonical extent. Whether the other [was] washing her face preparatory to blackening it or not, I cannot say.

SORROW AND SICKNESS

In one lodge I entered was a young man in bed in a wasted condition. He had been a long while ill. He had had no doctor. We offered to send one. He assented. He looked very miserable.

Near this we heard howling. We entered & found an old woman making the most piteous moans with continual revivals to the extent of her lungs. It was real grief. Her big tears gushed forth & she seemed inconsolable. She was grieving for the loss of a son who had been killed by another tribe.

Poor creatures, how dark their prospects, how truly inconsolable, when they know not where to look for the only true succour, peace & hope!

UNEXPECTED

I approached a group of Indians. One of them said, 'if you will build a church for us we will all come to it.'

April 22, Sunday.

Day fine. Preached twice at Christ Church. The mail steamer in, *Panama*.

CONVERTED PRIEST

The mail steamer today brought the Rev. Louis Rivieccio, the same I had met on board the *Pacific* on my way here. He has thrown off the Romist yoke and joined the Church of England. He received the Holy Communion last Sunday at the hands of Bishop Kip in Francisco. He was Professor of Moral Philosophy in the Theological Seminary at the Mission Dolores in Francisco. He is twenty seven years of age. I believe him to be quite in earnest & clear from Romist error. He told me he left off praying to the Virgin eight months ago. He can preach in Italian (his native language) & French & Spanish. It seems something quite providential, his coming here & being ready to aid me amongst the many nations who are here represented.

April 23, Monday.

Day fine. Went to call upon Bishop Demers, met him & had [a] talk with him, he accepted that as a call.

April 24, Tuesday.

Had [an] interview with poor Mr. Harvey. He now complains of the conduct of his wife. Later in the day Mr. Alston told me he believed he had delirium tremens.

The churchwardens of Christ Church & Mr. Cridge called about the site for my residence on Church Reserve. Mr. Wood being a banker takes a commercial view & wished me to pay a larger sum, at least to pay interest at ten percent until the principal was paid, which could not be till the conveyance was made & this might be delayed.

CHAPTER

Had my first chapter meeting at the vestry at Christ Church, arranged work of different sorts. Four Clergy were present, Cridge, Garrett, Dundas, & Lowe. We commenced with prayer.

THE CONVERTED PRIEST

Mr. Rivieccio told me [that] years ago he was anxious for more reasonable satisfaction as to the doctrines of Rome. His teachers either would not or could not comply with his wish for information. He gave up these longings & took to philosophy. In 1858 he went to France. He resided in Paris for six months at a house which was a school. There was in this a fine boy of English parents who became attached to him & on parting said, 'I am a poor boy but I wish to give you a present. Here is the best thing I have.' It was a Church of England Prayer Book. This boy had been [. . .] by a student for conversion to Rome, but had manfully resisted.

Rivieccio came away to California. Here he studied the Scriptures, the Latin & the Douay, with the English prayer book. He became more & more dissatisfied. He left off all prayer to the Virgin & in confessions recommended no 'aves.' He became convinced the spirit of Christianity was quite different from the Church of Rome & that the fundamental principles of reason were contradicted. He sought interviews with Bishop Kip who loaned him Burnett on the [Thirty-Nine] Articles & Hopkins. He also got hold of [. . .], Pope & Maguire for instance.

Four months ago I met him on the steamer. I sympathized with him. I found him sound upon most points. I expressed the view he could not remain in Rome. We parted. He said he should write.

God has brought him step by step & he is now happy in the pure & apostolic Church of England, the church of his deliberate choice. He examined the principles of all. He found clearly this was the way of truth & peace.

May God lead him still further, to be useful in saving souls from error & sin, & to set forth & magnify the Lord Jesus.

April 25, Wednesday.

Walked to Esquimalt with Mr. Rivieccio. Called at the Engineers' barracks, saw Colonel Hawkins & the Boundary Commission officers. Visited the *Satellite* [and saw], Captain Prevost, who was laid up with indisposition.

April 26, Thursday.

A RIDING PARTY

Last evening, I received a note from the Governor asking me to join himself & the Admiral in a ride. We left at eleven o'clock, the party consisting of the three named together with two Misses Douglas, Mr. Fraser, Mr. [...], Mr. Hector (Sheriff) & a youth, the governor's son. We went to Tod's farm looking upon San Juan & then to Leigh's Farm. [Then to] Cedar Plains, Mount Douglas & home by the Dairy Farm (...), Mr. Work's & home at half past five. The day was delightful, the country exquisite.

April 27, Friday.

Stormy, windy, cold. Attended Indian Committee, resolved to begin work of education. Mr. Pringle came from Hope.

April 28, Saturday.

Visited the Indian reserve with the Indian Committee to consider a fitting spot for an Indian institution.

MARCH OF PROGRESS

We found in one round today, in the Tsimshian village, a group of Indians building a house. Standing amongst them were two Indian women dressed, I may almost say, in the latest fashion! Round straw hats with flowing ribbons & hooped dresses! Moreover an adornment of their peculiar kind in the shape of red paint profusely daubed upon their faces.

This day I had two interviews with poor Mr. Harvey, who unhappily pursues his drinking habits but who is much troubled as to his prospects. I have agreed to pay home to England the passage of his wife. This matter is to me a great affliction, yet I am every day more & more convinced of the propriety of my course & how fortunate was the discovery of intemperance before I admitted him to holy orders.

April 29, Sunday.

CONFIRMATION 1860—CHRIST CHURCH, VICTORIA

This afternoon was my first confirmation in my diocese. It was an anxious occasion. My wish is to have all the ordinances of the church so conducted as to edify & to be subject to no reproach. I made it therefore a rule that none be admitted except as intending to draw near the holy table, to become communicants at once.

There were thirty three candidates. Several of these were sailors from the fleet.

All behaved with great decorum & some were much impressed. The congregation was large. Indeed the church was completely full & there was great attention. The service consisted of the Litany, the Confirmation Office, two addresses from myself & four hymns, & lasted an hour & [a] half.

Mr. Cridge read prayers (Litany), Mr. Dundas, as Chaplain, read [the] preface. Mr. Lowe assisted in bringing up candidates.

I feel confident. I thank God for having grounds for such confidence, that His blessing did rest upon us today. Prayers went up from many hearts & the answer was sure. May the great & ever blessed head of his church keep all these now dedicated afresh to him from all evil & lead them on in greater measures of his Spirit until they come in his everlasting kingdom to the full measure of the stature of his fullness!

April 30, Monday.

Steamer in. No [mail]. Mrs. Harvey went off for England. Her husband saw her off.

ROME AND PAGANISM

Mr. Rivieccio told me he entered a Chinese temple at Francisco accompanied by two priests, one of these Roman Catholic priests exclaimed to the other 'upon my word, Simpson. Here is the Catholic Church.' The similarity was great between the dress & material of a pagan temple & a Romist church.

A JUST REMARK

Speaking of the ritual of the Anglican Church & with reference to the confirmation, Mr. Rivieccio remarked, 'The Church of England combines simplicity with decorum.'

We had this morning an interesting meeting of the clergy & arranged, after discussion, many things.

May 1, Tuesday.

A lovely day. Dined with Admiral Baynes on board the *Ganges.* Met the Governor, Chief Justice Cameron, the Attorney General & others. Stayed the night.

May 2, Wednesday.

Visited the Esquimalt Indians. The men had papers on which a temperance pledge was written, these [were] given by the mission priests. The children & women had crosses & crucifixes suspended round their necks.

May 3, Thursday.

Day fine, as yesterday. Wrote letters.

May 4, Friday.

Rain heavy most of the day.

INDIANS

We made a beginning & pitched tents on the Indian reserve in the hopes of gathering Indians from time to time for instruction.

May 5, Saturday.

Day fine. Took a walk to the neighbourhood of Ross & McNeil farms. The country was lovely & the flowers in wondrous profusion.

May 6, Sunday.

Fine day. Preached morning & evening at Christ Church, Holy Communion in the morning at which were many of the newly confirmed. I was glad to see several sailors of the *Satellite.*

This day we commenced open air preaching. Mr. Garrett spoke to a considerable crowd & the greatest order prevailed. One man, strangely dressed, who had probably not entered a place of worship for years was overcome to tears & afterwards came forward & desired to shake hands with the preacher.

By this means of open air addresses, I feel sure we shall reach many not to be got at in any [other] way. May God be with us & by his Spirit win many to their salvation in Christ. We had collection at Christ Church for the Sunday school, amounting to 128£ [or] 140 dollars.

May 7, Monday.

Part rain.

May 8, Tuesday.

Day fine. The tent for Indian school boarded by carpenters from the *Satellite.*

May 9, Wednesday.

Wet. Mail steamer *Panama* arrived.

May 10, Thursday.

Dined at Mr. Woods'.

May 11, Friday.

Mr. Sheepshanks & Dundas dined with me.

INDIAN EXECUTION

A week or two since an Indian was executed at New Westminster for murder. He said he supposed he had committed the crime, for the Indians said he did, but he was drunk at the time & knew not what he did. He was visited by Mr. Sheepshanks & paid most respectful attention to all he said & seemed to like much the visits. He evinced no fear. He was lame & walked on crutches but with the utmost cheerfulness & hopped up the steps & sat in the drop. He nodded to his mother as though he was going away for a few hours. The emotion of his wife was great. After looking round, he took the rope & put [it] round his neck & was launched into eternity.

He told Mr. Sheepshanks that he prayed to the Great Spirit. He asked Mr. Sheepshanks if he could give him a new heart. He said [at] times he had fled out of company to avoid his own anger & to try to master himself. He asked prayer to be made for him & had one request to make, that his body might be buried in a particular spot & might not be opened. His reason for wishing his body not to be opened was lest his heart should be seen. For he knew it was very bad.

May 12, Saturday.

Fine sunshine, but chilly in wind. Had a lovely walk amidst the beautiful solitudes of this neighbourhood. I found much comfort in communion with God. My depression is from the sense of my inefficiency. Sometimes I feel as if my mind has become impaired. I find myself unable to get through the mental work I once could, unable to converse with usefulness. I look back each day & see precious time thrown away & yet subjects upon which I ought to write are not treated. At least I take up first one & then another & nothing is got through.

I committed this deficiency to my God this day in prayer & earnestly sought to be sustained. He has graciously blest my ministry in former times. Souls have been won to Christ by the leading of the Spirit through my unworthy ministry. Thus he has been with me. I pleaded thus & sought that he would still bless my work & thought I need have no depression, no anxieties, all is light, if only I might be the means of saving souls, & being saved myself.

I was refreshed & much more happy after this conversing with my gracious & merciful Father. All around was beautiful. There were mountains & valleys & the sea & islands & quiet [meadows] & flowers in lavish profusion. But what are all these if the heart be sad.

I gathered today Larkspur, Lupine, Chambine, Calceolaria & a rose, all wild, I thought of old England & her happy homes & gardens.

May 13, Sunday.

Beautiful day, air chilly. Preached on board the *Satellite* & administered the Holy Communion. My subject was the Lord's Supper.

At one [o'clock] I had a class of young men, the Captain's class, & examined them in scripture. I was greatly pleased. It is indeed a happy thing for these lads to have such a friend as Captain Prevost. I spoke to Nightingale, a Yarmouth man on board. I preached & read prayers at Esquimalt in the afternoon.

On returning I passed the open air mission just as Mr. Garrett had concluded. There was a goodly muster. All varieties of people & all costumes. There were Indians & Chinese as well as miners & labourers & artisans of other nations. Some were sitting, some smoking, some with hats off, some a little way off with ears attentive. The main portion were evidently such as seldom, if ever, would be seen at the House of God.

I preached in the evening at Christ Church. Captain Prevost drank tea with me.

May 14, Monday.

The steamer *Pacific* came in. I was aroused at six o'clock by Mr. Crease who brought a letter from the English Consul in Francisco, relating the elopement of Mrs. Harvey with a Mr. [. . .]. This worthless woman has now clearly proved her character & has deliberately adopted a life of sin. Unhappy creature, may God turn her heart.

Had weekly meeting of clergy. One of the subjects was the devotional meeting for this evening. It was objected to by Mr. Dundas & Mr. Sheepshanks who thought it a departure from church principle.

My own belief & hope is that it will prove a strengthening of the Church, (1) by aiding to promote a more devotional feeling, (2) by leading persons to take especial interest in the work of religion, (3) by meeting a want often felt & expressed by dissenters as a difficulty in their return to the Church of England, [and] (4) by introducing special subjects which the public service forbids.

It may not be the exact [. . .] I should desire, yet it is earnest work & that I must encourage, in whatever shape it be, so long as not inconsistent with principles.

This evening our meeting took place. A few were present. Amongst them a Congregationalist & a Baptist, both these attend church.

Our subject was prayer. I trust it was useful. I was enabled to draw [attention] to the features of our church service & thus made the meeting rather a help than a hindrance in the great work. May God the Holy Spirit, direct & rule all our hearts.

It was a singular circumstance that a Church of England meeting should be held in what was a few weeks back a Congregational place of worship, and on this occasion was a converted Romist priest, Rivieccio, who has joined us having entirely left the errors of Rome.

May 15, Tuesday.

I had a conversation with Mr. Forsyth, a respectable tradesman, an intelligent man, who was present last evening at the devotional meeting. He said the meeting was the subject of conversation in the town & much curiosity was excited. It was a most unusual thing, indeed on his part unheard of, in the Church of England, that people would hardly believe it. He thought it would hasten the day when all would again return to the mother Church of England. He was here at the commencement of the new colonization when the rush of people was great. There was no other church but our own & people of all sorts frequented it & the system was discussed & pronounced antiquated & [not] progressive. But this was quite a new step & met a want which kept many away. He had been brought up at Kidderminster, a Congregationalist. He now attended the church. He was a friend of Mr. Clarke, the Congregational minister who, the day before he left, expressed his pleasure at the prospect of the Church of England having before her here a noble career of usefulness.

May 16, Wednesday.

Making preparation for departure to British Columbia. Mr. Sheepshanks preached a simple evangelical sermon at Christ Church.

May 17, Holy Thursday.

Full service at Christ Church, a goodly number in attendance. Mr. Cridge preached. At one [o' clock] a [meeting of the] committee of the collegiate school. It was resolved to open the boys' school on Monday week. Made preparation for my departure to the mines.

May 18, Friday.

Very busy all day, preparing to go on my visitation to British Columbia.

At eight steamed off in the *Wilson S. Hunt*, an excellent American Boat, accompanied by Rev. Mr. Sheepshanks. At eight next morning we came opposite the wharf at New Westminster.

REVIEW

I have now been four months in my diocese. I have had more vexations & troubles than in all my ministerial life before. Yet God has been merciful & when the trials were most heavy prayer has brought wondrous dispersion of the clouds. I have felt deeply how unequal I am to combat my difficulties & have seen cause to regret in consequence my acceptance of the sacred office I hold. Yet I did object to undertake the work knowing my deficiencies, but I was [overruled] & submitted to the judgement of others. I believed I acted as providence seemed to direct.

If it be the divine will that I should be thus situated & that trials be my path, I trust in his love & mercy that with the trial shall be a way to escape or strength to bear it.

During the four months I have seen the work in Victoria much strengthened. There have been added:

a Sunday evening service

a Wednesday evening service

open air Sunday service

Services established at Soke [Sooke], Saanich, Cedar Plains, Colwood, Craigflower.

A dissenting chapel has been closed & has passed into our hands.

The collegiate school has been announced for opening on Monday week.

The corner stone of St. John's Church has been laid in the presence of a large concourse of people.

The first confirmation has taken place & produced a good impression.

A converted Romist priest has joined us & may be useful for the Italian & French population.

A first step has been taken towards work amongst the Indians.

Four clergy are at work in Victoria & the adjacent districts.

To God be all the glory.

CHAPTER 3

Some things in Columbia I was prepared for
19 May – 8 June

May 19, Saturday.

Reached New Westminster at eight. Considerable increase in buildings was manifest over what existed at my former visit.

There were several steamboats & a bark, the *Perkins* of Francisco. We could not get near the wharf. It was raining hard.

I walked up to the Camp & found the Moodys & the Governor at breakfast. I was kindly & hospitably welcomed.

May 20, Sunday.

I preached three times, in the morning at nine to the soldiers, at eleven at the Court House, at seven at the Camp. I attended also the afternoon service. At this latter [service] were present two young Chinese, three coloured men & others.

The official persons do not set the best example. On this day Mr. Brew, the Judge for Small Debts & the head of police, was walking about near, but entered not the place of prayer, nor ever does. Captain Gossett, the Treasurer, went no where all day & was measuring his land near the treasury with the tape.

May 21, Monday. [No entry in manuscript]

May 22, Tuesday.

LAYING CORNERSTONE OF TRINITY CHURCH
NEW WESTMINSTER

A lovely day. At quarter to twelve, His Excellency the Governor, Colonel Moody & officers walked towards the town from the Camp & were met by the [church] committee & Mr. Sheepshanks & proceeded to the ground.

The site of the new church is a very beautiful one in Victoria Gardens & commands an extensive view & will be a most prominent object from the river to steamers arriving from the sea. At present two deep ravines are on either side. Around it are huge stumps of trees & the ground is entirely unlevelled. Here the frame of the flooring had been laid, being massive sills on thick short columns of wood. Under one of these pinnings, the south east outer corner of the porch, was laid the stone of granite. A bottle with [an] inscription & coins was inserted. The Governor was received by a guard of [Royal] Engineers. There were many persons assembled, about 300. Chinese, Indians & other nations [were] represented. The same service was used as at St. John's, Victoria. The service was commenced by Mr. Sheepshanks. The Bishop then proceeded. The Governor laid the stone. Addresses were delivered by the Governor, the Bishop & Colonel Moody, concluding with the doxology & blessing.

A RESTAURANT IN THE WOODS

Several of us lunched with the Governor at a capital restaurant, kept by a Frenchman. We had soup, salmon, lamb, green peas, omelet, preserved peaches, claret, champagne, etc. This was provided at a short notice.

I went up the Brunette in [a] canoe, the Governor [also]. This is a beautiful stream. The banks were covered with verdure & overhanging trees. Amongst others, a wild apple was in full blossom with white flowers, very like in appearance our Hawthorn or May. The evening was delicious & the whole scene struck a cord of delight such as I had not experienced before, since leaving old England.

May 23, Wednesday.

Rain.

May 24, Thursday.

THE QUEEN'S BIRTHDAY

The Governor invited a large party to spend the day with him in celebration of the Queen's birthday. He chartered a steamer, the *Maria* for an excursion to the head of Pitt Lake by the river of that name. We started at eleven from the [Royal Engineers] Camp wharf. The day was dull. There was some rain but on the whole the weather was good.

The *Maria* is one of those extraordinary vessels, peculiar to America, which combines light draught, ample accommodation, power & speed. Two hundred people might be stowed in her & she would not be two feet in the water. Her wheel was behind.

We passed up the rich & beautiful banks of the Fraser about five miles when we came to several islands, one called Tree Island behind which flowed in the Coquitlam. We took up a settler here & his friend, Mr. Atkins, a fine old Irish gentleman, who driven away by the Incumbered Estates Act, had wandered from Ireland to Australia & from Australia here where he resides upon 400 acres of land with his two sons. He is a communicant. His daughter was confirmed at Victoria recently & his sons are preparing for the same ordinance.

Manson's Island, shortly after, divided the channel of the Fraser & on one side, the north, lay the Pitt River about half a mile wide. This we entered & steamed along a fine reach with meadows on either side. At one point is the farm of Mr. McLean who fired a salute as we passed. Mr. Good, the Governor's Secretary, has a farm also. On this we observed several stacks of hay. After proceeding about twelve or fourteen miles, [and] passing several Indian villages, we came to the entrance of the lake. The scenery had now become mountainous, we were passing through a range called the Coast Range.

The lake now entered was about fifteen miles long. It is exactly like a Scotch lake. I seemed to be in Loch Ness. Captain Spalding whose father, for many years, has lived at Fort Augustin[e] on that lake, expressed the same opinion. The only difference was that the land was more lofty & the lake perhaps broader but it was not above two miles.

At one or two points where the lake turned & where was a view both ways, nothing could exceed the beauty of the scene. Waterfalls came pouring down in a white path down the mountain side, occasionally hidden by the trees & then visible again below. Fir trees lined the sides & summits of the perpendicular heights, to the extent of from 600 to 1500 feet. At three o'clock we reached the head of the lake. Here we anchored & a boat went on to proceed up a snub river.

We turned back at four & sat down in the saloon to an excellent repast. There was salmon & beef & chicken & ham & all sorts of [pastries] & wines, champagne went about in abundance.

The Governor proposed the loyal toasts of the old country, which were drunk with all honours. The bishop & clergy of the diocese were named with much kindness & their healths drunk with, three times three & one cheer more.

Colonel Moody proposed [the toast to] the Governor.

Various other toasts were given. At the Governor's request I proposed the Press, coupling with it the name [of] the editor of the *Westminster Times* who responded. In returning thanks for my own health & that of the clergy I said among other points, we desired to forward, without being politicians, the institutions of the land. I rejoiced that a step toward self-government had been taken in the grant of a municipal council to New Westminster.

The clergy came out to live & die amongst them. We dreamed not of retiring back to our native land. I spoke of course of the glory of England being in her religion & of the blessing it had been to her & might be to this colony. We were an unendowed, a non-established church, but confidently trusted we should find support.

We reached the [Royal Engineers] Camp at eight o'clock after a most agreeable day.

May 25, Friday.

EXCURSION TO LANGLEY — INDIANS FISHING — THE FRASER

The Governor went away from the [Royal Engineers] Camp to Langley. At one, Captain Parsons with a party of Sappers followed. Considering this a good opportunity of seeing the river & that place, I accepted a place in his whale boat. Mr. Sheepshanks accompanied me.

The distance was 17 miles. The stream was very rapid & the pull was a long [...] & hard one. We did not reach Langley till ten o'clock. I took an oar several times to relieve the men.

The day was beautiful & the scenery pleasing. The river varied from half a mile to a mile & [a] quarter in width. We passed several large islands, Tree Island, Manson's [Island] (lately bought by the Governor) & Barriston's. Every now & then we met a canoe with Indians. One was fishing for salmon. We saw the method. There were three in the boat. Two paddled, one at the stem held a pole, at the end of which was a bag net stretched by a [loop]. This he kept down at a certain depth, going down the stream & meeting the fish in their ascent. As soon as he perceived, by the sensation, that a fish was inside, he quickly drew a string which closed the bag, & the fish was caught & brought into the boat. I understand they will catch salmon sometimes as fast as they can lower & pull in the net.

On either side of us was the most luxuriant foliage. Sometimes the interior was dense with wood, at other times a clearance might without difficulty be made & land brought into cultivation. The grouping of the trees & lower underwood was very beautiful. Rising up to majestic heights were pines of different kinds, cedars, the Douglas, the Black Spruce, then the Cotton Tree, a sort of Poplar & the Maple with graceful outspreading branches, the latter with delicate green. Then lower still & filling in at different heights were Alders, a wild apple in full blossom very like our May [tree], in clustered white flowers, Willows, [and] Hazels bowering over the water so that Indian canoes could paddle under them almost unobserved.

Huge trees were frequently met with, which required good steering to avoid as they came rushing down with the current or remained stuck in the river. 'Snags' they are called & are occasions sometimes of injury to boats.

We passed several villages of Indians but did not land. One village was called the Kaetzi [Katzi], these Indians are numerous. Poor creatures they stood on the edge of the water or rather sat or squatted in their peculiar manner watching us intently.

We found the Governor at the Fort. A large hall was the general room in the quaint wooden building which stood at the head of the enclosure of store houses. Pipes & wine & spirits were on the table & we were hospitably received by the Hudson's Bay Company officials. A comfortable tea & cold beef & sardines gratified & satisfied our inner man & a blanket bed upon the floor of an empty room gave abundant opportunity for refreshing sleep.

May 26, Saturday.

FAMILY WORSHIP AT FORT LANGLEY

I rose early. A little before eight the families & guests assembled in the hall & we had family worship. I gave out one of my [cards containing] miners' hymns, read [a] portion of scripture, commented on it & [read] some prayers. Breakfast was then served. We had roast chicken, beef steaks, potatoes cooked thin ways, salmon, butter & cream in perfection amongst other good things.

THE KATZI INDIANS

After breakfast I had an interview with Michelle, the Chief of the Katzi Indians. I asked him of his people. He said they were fewer & fewer. Liquor especially was making sad havoc. He was grieved in heart to see them fading away. He would like to have his children educated. His people knew nothing about the future. They never thought about it. Nobody had come to tell them anything. He thought something himself, but did not know much & would mention to his people what I had said.

Michelle understands a good deal of English & is a well known friend to the white man.

INDIAN UNCERTAINTY

An Indian chief from Harrison River named Seemium agreed to take me in his canoe to New Westminster. We kept him waiting rather longer than he liked & he disappeared. We had agreed for five dollars. These Indians are well paid. I understand at Hope they get four dollars a day (i.e. sixteen shillings). So they are becoming very independent. A couple of years ago they would do anything for a little tobacco. Unless you take them at the moment you want them you may after be disappointed.

LANGLEY TO THE [ROYAL ENGINEERS] CAMP IN A CANOE

We at length found another Indian canoe, paddled by two Indians who agreed for three dollars.

I first inspected the little building at Langley Spit erected by Mr. Crickmer. Twenty feet long by fifteen wide, which he called a district church! Although only a few months since its erection, it is falling to pieces.

I then passed along & visited Lower Langley, etc.

CHURCH AND PARSONAGE—DERBY

Derby. Here the church is in good order. I measured it—

Length about 52 [feet]
Breadth about 22 [feet]

Benches 26 + 2 wall seats = 28 [seats] at 5 sittings each = 140
The parsonage is small, three rooms & a kitchen.

Our two Indians paddled us down the stream in good time. The motion is very delightful. The day was fine, the scenery enlivening.

We reached the [Royal Engineers] Camp at a little before three — having come seventeen miles in rather less than three hours.

Our Indian in command would sometimes stop paddling & point to spots where he & his tribe once roamed in possession. Now a hostile tribe occupied the land of his fathers. He did not speak of the intrusion of the white man. The fact is these tribes have suffered far more from each other than they ever can from the whites.

This Indian belonged to the tribe opposite Langley, the Kortlan or Cartlan [Kwantlen]. Once they dwelt where the [Royal] Engineers Camp is now situated but had long left it, the spot they call Chastless.

May 27, Whitsunday.

I preached three times. At the holy chapel at the [Royal Engineers] Camp, six communicants only, Colonel & Mrs. Moody, Miss Nagle, Captain Prevost & two officers. This is sad. Service in the town was at eleven at the Court House, about twenty people.

May 28, Monday.

COLONEL MOODY'S FARM

Walked with Colonel Moody & Captain Prevost to the farm or clearing belonging to the former, on the way to Burrard's Inlet, about two and a half miles from the [Royal Engineers] Camp. Up to that point all is dense forest. The trail is very rough & not suitable for even a horse, much less a wheel. At the place about seven acres are cleared & a garden made. Pears are growing. Apple trees are planted. The surrounding land has been burned. The forest trees are standing, but dead, the underbrush is gone. One burned & dead tree fell while we were [there].

Two men had been felling. The tree came down with a mighty crash. I measured it & found it 170 feet [long].

Dined today at the [Royal] Engineers mess.

May 29, Tuesday.

A beautiful day. I was engaged in writing letters. Visited the [Royal Engineers] Camp school & had a walk with Colonel Moody & Captain Prevost.

May 30, Wednesday.

Mr. Duncan from Fort Simpson & Mr. Dundas from Victoria arrived to see me. The former [is] not in good health. He has been near three years labouring amongst the Tsimshian Indians till he has obtained a great influence. His accounts are deeply interesting & it is delightful to see the enthusiasm which glows within him for the poor *Sowash* [*Sowash*]. I have arranged that he should come to Victoria & take part in Indian work there. At about half past ten this evening I embarked on board the *Moody* for Hope & Yale. Colonel Moody went at the same time. At half past one we reached Langley where we anchored.

May 31, Thursday.

At half past four we left Langley & steamed on. A few miles on, the river changes its character & becomes bold with rocky heights on either side. [We] reached [the] mouth of [the] Harrison [at] half past twelve, several islands [are] at [the] entrance. The current at [the] junction of Harrison & Fraser [is] very strong. [The] steamer at one point [was] nearly driven on a rock. Her wheel [was] within three feet. [The] Indian village at [the] entrance of the Harrison called Scourlitz, [was] named by Governor [Douglas], Carnarvon. From this to Douglas is 40 miles. We reached the latter at six. The greater part of this lay through a magnificent lake, the Harrison. The water [was] a clear blue of great depth, soundings had not been taken of less than 100 fathoms. The mountains on either side, of considerable height, [were] covered with timber, very rocky, [with] no cultivatable land. Waterfalls & cascades [are] frequent. This lake in all its features is a ditto of the Pitt Lake, only on a double scale.

DOUGLAS

At the head of the lake through a winding channel is the harbour of Douglas with the town at its extremity. It consists at present of a few wooden buildings with an excellent quay.

The Rev. Mr. Gammage met me & I proceeded to his little cottage, the way to which lay across several plank bridges over rushing torrents. Mrs. Gammage was waiting tea for her husband. I sat down with them & we were soon discussing the various spiritual necessities of the place.

Afterwards I visited the ground set apart for a church site & the new road. The latter made by the Royal Engineers is a very creditable work.

MINERS AND THE CHURCH

On my way I was accosted by a miner, 'If you please Sir, how is the church getting on at [New] Westminster?' This was one of the five miners who gave their contribution in labour to clear the site of timber. These five men afterwards presented their log hut to Mr. Sheepshanks & in which he resides.

The other day, it was Sunday, the steamer arrived here bringing miners. Ten miners came in a body, at once, to church. They were Canadians. The Canadians in this matter are a contrast to Americans. The latter, as a body, are not only indifferent but openly abusive of religion. At least their profanity is something horrible. Not so those who have come from our colonies. There is a marked difference. I attribute this respect for religion to the care with which our colonies have of late years been attended to & by the influence under God of the Church of England.

YANKEE PROFANITY AND A YOUNG ENGLISH OFFICER

I was walking with Lieutenant Palmer of the [Royal] Engineers on the upper deck. We were talking of the profanity of Americans. He said it was very painful to hear. He had recently been present when an American was arguing against Christianity. He felt inclined to rebuke him but thought it better not, as a dispute might arise & produce even more profanity. I said I thought he should have borne his testimony. It might have touched others, if not him. He agreed it would have been better to have done so. An hour after, I was walking on the same deck with Mr. O'Reilly, the excellent Magistrate of Hope. We also got upon the topic of the strange opinions that prevailed when he mentioned he had just been present when an American had scoffed at the observance of the Lord's Day, saying, 'he did not want any day of rest & there was no good in keeping Sunday.' Lieutenant Palmer was present & had successfully rebuked the Yankee. Possibly our conversation had prepared him for this opportunity. No doubt he was strengthened himself by the witness he gave. Sin was rebuked & some present at least would lay up the thought in their hearts.

On the way between Langley & Harrison River we had taken up the Governor. He, Colonel Moody, & myself had all gone on shore. After walking about with Mr. Gammage & bidding him & his wife good-bye, I had a cup of tea with Mr. Gaggin the Magistrate & the Governor & Colonel Moody after which, at about half past ten, we all came again on board.

June 1, Friday.

We left Douglas at half past four. Delightful weather. The river [is] very rapid & seems to force itself through a series of mountain gorges, the sides rising to a great height covered with timber. On either bank, however, land [is] suitable for cultivation, the valley varying in breadth from a mile to three or four, exclusive of the river which is from half a mile to three quarters. The Governor today is not well.

Towards the upper river the scenery became more beautiful. The mountains nearer, the river more rapid. About forty miles from the mouth of the Harrison we came upon the mining bars. Hudson's Bar, Last Chance Bar, Blue Nose, Man Hatten [sic], Cornish. Some are sand banks stretching out into the stream covered at the high seasons with the fresh [water], as at present, [and] dry from August to March. Some are the side banks of the river which they dig away, scoop out & extract gold. The upper earth is removed first, then about four feet down is a deposit of black sand in which is the gold. To get this upper earth away the miner brings a stream of water, a method he calls hydraulics, which he plies with a hose in a strong jet & washing away [a] vast quantity in a short time, till he gets to the 'pay dirt.'

The last four miles the stream was so strong that we were two hours in doing the distance.

At length, Hope was reached & the echoes were startled & long & kindly responded to the guns of the fort & the whistle of the steamer which greeted the Governor. It was ten o'clock 'ere we touched the pier. I went on shore & had a lovely stroll by the pale moonlight. The air was balmy & scenery entirely Swiss. You might have believed yourself in Chamouni [Chamonix] or by the upper Rhine, except there are no glaciers shining in the clouds.

STEAMBOATS ON THE FRASER

Some things in Columbia I was prepared for. But I certainly did not expect to see so good accommodation as afforded by the steamboats. The cost of *Moody* was 2000£. It pays the shareholders nearly fifty percent. It could accommodate 300 passengers. I had a cabin the three nights I was on board, superior to that I had on the *La Plata* or *Silent*, ships of the West India Mail Company. Provisions were good & abundant. Thus for dinner the first day, soup, sturgeon, mutton, beef, bacon, potatoes, beans, carrots, apple tart. For breakfast, there was fried sturgeon, bacon, mutton chops, hot rolls, bread, butter, tea, coffee, etc., [and] silver forks & spoons. Everything [was] very clean & well cooked. Prices are high, 4 shillings a meal, besides the passage money. The captain was a Scotchman, the purser an American citizen born in Ireland, the steward an African, the steward's boy a Chinaman, the pilot an American & etc. Such is a Fraser River steamboat.

June 2, Saturday.

I slept on board last night as no provision had been made on shore. Early this morning I turned out & pitched my tent near Mr. Pringle's wooden house before breakfast.

Having done full justice to the cold ham Mrs. Bridgman had put in my basket & to some beef liver & marmalade Mr. Pringle produced, besides making large [inroads] into excellent bread & butter, I went forth to see the place.

I had a walk with the Governor & Chief Justice Begbie & Colonel Moody.

I then went to find out a spot for [a] burial ground with Mr. Pringle & Mr. O'Reilly the Magistrate. Lunched with the Governor, walked with him & Mr. Begbie to the new bridge over the Quecquealla [Coquihalla] a mountain torrent about 200 feet wide, being the road to the Similkameen River where the country is very beautiful & suitable for agriculture, besides being auriferous.

A GENTLEMAN MINER

On returning I met Mr. Pitman in miner's dress with long shaggy hair & bearded face, a young man, some of whose friends I met in England. He had been working on Union Bar. This was his life. I asked if it was not very rough. He said it was more pleasant than people thought.

MINERS

This evening I walked out in the direction of Cornish Bar, down the river. I came to several miners huts. [In] one was a fine young man all the way from Tipperary. His companion boasted of being a Yankee & looked like one. Not much to be done. They were respectful & evidently liked being addressed.

Another miner was sitting with Indians & as an Indian. A fourth was sitting at the door of his log hut reading a Christian Knowledge Society tract [Society for Propagation of Christian Knowledge]. He came from Herefordshire & longed for the old country once more. He seemed intelligent & well disposed & spoke of the absence of the means of grace at the mining bars.

This day a child was buried, belonging to a miner.

June 3, Trinity Sunday.

At eleven we had a good attendance of some forty-five to fifty in Mr. Pringle's room, the Governor, Colonel Moody & Chief Justice [Begbie] present. Preached upon faith in reference to the day. There was [attention]. At the Holy Communion, but five were present.

INDIAN BEAR HUNTER

I had a conversation today with Skiyou a noted bear hunter. He was sent on an expedition to explore a new pass to the Similkameen River. On his way he shot a bear. The animal fell. He went forward to skin it when suddenly it rose up & fought with him. For some time the engagement lasted, leaving Skiyou victor but dreadfully wounded. The bear seized him & mutilated many parts of his person. He bled profusely from his wounds. He nevertheless attempted to crawl home. For ten days he was almost without food. Yet strange to say, he reached Hope at last. Much interest has been felt for him. Today he came to Mr. Pringle's who gave him food. I saw the wounds in his hands & arms caused by the bear's teeth & he explained in a very significant manner how the bear had conducted the fight.

I told him in Chinook of the mercy of his heavenly Father & how much cause he had for thankfulness. He looked thoughtful when he nodded assent but soon passed to other topics. He was more affected when spoken to about his sick child now lying without much hope. He said he was sick, '*tum tum*,' (i.e. heart sick — sad) & Mama also was sick, '*tum tum*.'

INDIAN SAGACITY

The Governor has been occupied yesterday & (today ?), questioning Indians as to the route across to the Similkameen. Some of these Indians show remarkable cleverness in sketching out a map of the route, marking the rivers, mountains, valleys, passes & windings, [and] then describing [them]. The Governor shows immense patience in extracting information.

THE SIMILKAMEEN ROUTE

This route to the Similkameen is important as it opens out to commence the southeastern portion of British Columbia, where are fine rural lands, also a vast region of the United States into which British commerce will find its way from this point on the Fraser. In a military point of view also the route from Hope is important, intercepting any movement of the Americans up into British Columbia gold mines.

This evening, service again was well attended. There could not be less than forty, a great number for Hope. The presence of Americans was evident from the unusual amount of spitting! I preached from Romans 10:13, etc., 'How beautiful,' etc.

Altogether I have enjoyed this Sunday. The fine weather, the exquisite scenery, & the hearty services have combined to invigorate me.

Would that I had more of the power & life of the Holy Spirit within me. Alas, how far far short do I come of the standard it is my duty to set before our congregations.

June 4, Monday.

INDIAN ALLIANCE

Had a conversation with a man name Yates, a servant of the Hudson's Bay Company, eleven years in their employment. [He] speaks the native language, lives with an Indian woman & has a child. [He] is not married, defends the unmarried state as happier. [He] has known instances when men have been married, of unhappiness resulting. A French Canadian, at the instigation of the priest, was married. His wife took advantage of his being bound to her & resorted to many of her own ways which, from fear of dismissal before, she had abstained from. She killed her children, and at length hung herself. He had known other instances. The custom of living with Indian women was universal in the Hudson's Bay Company service.

He came from Orkney, was a Methodist [and] attended the Methodist chapel here. I asked if he would be comfortable to live in an unmarried state in his own country. He said there was a great difference. There were churches in Orkney & white women. I showed him that the sin was the same here as in Britain. He allowed it was not right, but said he had been very comfortable. I explained the subject by the principles of Scripture. I asked if Mr. Robson, the Methodist minister, had spoken to him about the state he was in. He said no but that Mr. Pringle had done so.

INDIAN SCHOOL

Mr. Yates speaks the language well. He said the Indian children would gladly come to schools. There are about fifty here. They had attended well when Mr. Robson (now gone) had held school amongst them. He did not think they needed any other inducement than the desire they had of learning the language of white men.

SPOKAN GARRY

I called at Mr. Gray's, an intelligent American who lives here. He was in Oregon. He remembers Spokan Garry returning from Red River to his tribe & was often in the school he established for his own people. He worked on for some time single handed & unsustained & at length yielded & sunk himself back to all the degradation of heathenism. He is distinguished now from the heathen only by his acquaintance with the English tongue. There was a mission of the American board placed within thirty miles of his school. Application was made to bring it close to Spokan Garry but this was refused. Garry is the chief of his tribe.

TEA MEETING AT HOPE

Mr. Pringle, at my request, gathered a number of his people together to an evening *soirée*. Cups & saucers & candle sticks were levied upon his neighbours. A capital plum cake, bread & butter, tea & coffee were the acceptable & bountiful provision.

Some thirty assembled, amongst them were three Jews & two Roman Catholics. They were principally the traders & merchants, but amongst them were several miners & their wives. Most intelligent men were these latter & highly decked in silks were their better halfs. After discussing the viands & other subjects in a friendly & social way, all very much & not over much at ease, at Mr. Pringle's request I addressed the assembly. I spoke generally of the colony & then of my mission to found churches & schools, to plant clergy & instruct the Indians. I urged pure religion to be the basis & bond of society & pointed out the advantages of the Church of England. I illustrated my remarks with the account of Boston & its ten mile road, Spokan Garry, & an Indian boy who lamented he was not taught religion & concluded with urging them to make provision for Mr. Pringle's comfort. Colonel Moody followed in an excellent speech upon colonial organization & the only basis of society which was religion. We concluded with singing the doxology right heartily & parted about eleven o'clock.

It was an evident pleasure to those present thus to be drawn together. Such a thing had not happened before & both socially & religiously, I believe, through God's blessing will result in much good.

Mr. Hotchins a respectable trader, & a young man, comes from Tattershall in Lincolnshire.

Mr. Marston, a miner whose wife was present & a nice person, comes from Bungay in Suffolk.

The Merritts, miners, [who] have just lost their only child [are] from Cornwall.

Mr. Phillips & his sisters in-law the Ladners, worthy church people, come from Penzance.

June 5, Tuesday.

MEDICINE MAN

I heard strange noises in passing near an Indian hut. When I approached I found it to be that of Skiyou, the Indian bear hunter. His wife had her sick child in her lap. Before her was the medicine man practicing enchantments upon the child. He was a strong featured man of about forty. He repeated over & over a few words with considerable gesture. Occasionally he would stroke the head & stomach of the child. Beside him was a basin of water with some whitening mixture in it. This he would take & rub upon his hands, or he would blow into his hands & upon the child, then burst forth again into his lament & incantations. The mother held her infant towards him & evidently put considerable faith in the enchanter.

A YOUNG CHINESE MINER

I had a conversation with an intelligent young man nineteen years of age—Wong Chan Yun, the latter his personal name. Wong [is] his family or district, from the neighbourhood of Canton. He has been away from China since 1857. [He] came here from California in 1858. He speaks English very fairly & acts as interpreter. I asked if the Chinese here have any worship, he said none, nor a priest. He could not tell if there would be a joss house. In Francisco they had a joss house but it was the wrong god. He could not remember the name, but the true god he worshipped was Shung Ti. He prayed to Shung Ti who was in heaven & would punish the wicked & reward the good. Shung Ti was once a man. He could not tell me all his thoughts about Shung Ti. He did not know enough English. I asked what they did in the joss house, he said they played on the knee with joss sticks.

Only a few of the Chinese thought about such things, the greatest part did not believe.

He had been in Hong Kong & had heard of the Bishop's schools. I asked if he longed to go back. 'O yes, I should like to go back.' 'Have you brothers & sisters?' 'Yes, a sister named Amoy & brothers.' Tears came into his eyes, 'but I have sent them my photograph'!

I asked if he would like to know what the English thought & know about [the] good things of heaven. He said he should. He had heard of Jesus but did not believe in him. He did not know about him. I spoke to him about Jesus Christ & urged him to use his knowledge of English to hear & read of Jesus who had died for our sins. He would be much happier if he knew of Jesus & all he had done for him. He seemed interested & I promised he should have instruction & that Mr. Pringle would help him & give him books to read. He said there were some twelve or fifteen young men who might be got to receive instruction. He does a little with them himself but they find it hard & do not persevere with him.

The Chinese here, he said, have come on their own hook. In California they are bound to some head men who receive part of their earnings.

They live principally upon rice & tea at their three meals, sometimes chicken & pork & potatoes. They send home the bones of their dead. They let the bodies putrefy & the flesh comes off. Then they send home the bones, for the comfort of friends. He knew no other reason.

I was pleased with this youth. There is something engaging & simple & open in his manner.

May this be a commencement of holier thoughts to him & a streak of dawn to his people who are coming over in great multitudes. They seek the gold that persisheth. Let us give them not the stone they blindly ask but the 'living bread which came down from heaven.'

Dined today with Mr. O'Reilly the Magistrate, a truly good man. Shortly before leaving Ireland he left the Roman Catholic religion & joined our church. After dinner we took a delightful walk.

HOPE SCENERY

No spot can be more beautifully situated than Hope. The River Fraser flows past it. The site is on the river bank, on either side are noble mountains opposite an island. To the back mountain scenery, trees from the foot to the summit & deep valleys between through which flow the rapid & beautiful Coquihalla & its tributaries & in which are situated several lakes.

This evening we walked up the Coquihalla, crossed its picturesque bridge, & proceeded along the Brigade trail, a walk winding through trees & flowers & where at times you might fancy yourself in the wilder parts of some cultivated domain in England. The scenery is a combination of Swiss & Scotch. It had been raining & all nature was fresh & lovely & fragrant. About three miles brought us to Dallas Lake, a sweet spot where one felt one could live for ages. 'O Lord how manifold are thy works.'

June 6, Wednesday.

The Governor left early this morning for Yale.

June 7, Thursday.

Had a pleasant ride with Mr. O'Reilly along the Brigade & Boston Bar trails. The path lay along Dallas Lake, to the Coquihalla, through mountain gorges & lovely valleys. Occasionally the ascents & descents were very steep, at other places the road was level & allowed a good gallop. These horses of the country are very sure footed. We had a good six hours spell & I greatly enjoyed both the scenery & the exercise.

CHURCHWARDENS OF HOPE

This evening I had a meeting of the churchwardens (Mr. O'Reilly & Mr. Hotchins), both excellent men & instructed them as to their duty & talked over various matters.

June 8, Friday.

This morning I was to have gone up to Yale. The Indian [whose] canoe was engaged turned out when the time came alas, to be the worse for drink & it was too late as the water was rapid & even dangerous.

I took a walk with Mr. Pringle along a beautiful & romantic trail following a stream & glen to Lake Dallas & then through a gorge into a valley on its northern side where was a stream winding its way to the Fraser. I visited some of the Indian potato grounds in that valley. The soil is very rich. The rows of potatoes were laid with great regularity, indeed in figures [. . .] & patterns such as you see on their basket work. They also 'earth up' at the proper time which shows a more advanced state than I expected.

We ascended a height & upon a rocky, mossy knoll shaded by pines, we had an extensive view of mountain & river scenery. I could have sat there for hours impressed with the grandeur of the works of God. How insignificant the most gigantic accomplishments of man.

We were then on the east side of the Coquihalla. A canoe paddled by an Indian and his squaw brought us quickly down the rapid, rolling, seething Fraser to Hope, for which we paid the sum of a dollar—4/2 for half an hour's paddle. These Indians are well paid.

PURCHASE OF LAND AT HOPE

I this day purchased eighty acres on the Coquihalla from Mr. Donald Chisholm. It would be a beautiful site for a college, or Bishop's residence, a second stream full of trout flows through it.

June 9, Saturday.

At eight a.m. I left Hope in a canoe paddled by three Indians for Yale. The day was fine. The scenery was grand. The mountain sides of the Fraser rose up in towering array. Here & there deep gorges & valleys pouring forth their streams, rushing, roaring down their rocky beds to swell the milky river, now many feet above its winter level, swollen to a mighty, seething, rapid torrent.

The skill of the Indians was tried to the utmost. We crept in close along the shore, even under the branches of the trees to avoid the current. But here at times the rapids were strong. The Indians seemed to love danger & the sight of a breaking, foaming, roaring cascade, up which our frail bark was to ascend, inspired them with ardour. Every nerve was excited, they shouted & pressed the [. . .] [thing], presently it shot past the rocks or snags. Occasionally, so violent was the downward torrent that an eddy was formed which for some way went the contrary direction & drove us upwards. Several times we got out & walked & once the canoe itself was hauled out & carried on land past a dangerous rapid. I could easily understand the fact that in the rush to the mines in 1858 many miners were drowned in endeavouring unassisted to force their way. The difficulty of this portion of the river may be known when [I mention] it took us eight hours to go fifteen miles. On Wednesday when the Governor & Colonel Moody came over the same ground with excellent canoe men they were eleven hours!

Nothing could exceed the picturesque beauty everywhere. The banks were frequently covered with flowers & we actually gathered roses as we went along.

THE MINING BARS

We passed many mining bars. Most of them are just now deserted on account of the rise of the water. A few miners were passed & they were quite ready for a chat. On Puget Sound Bar, on my remarking that the Chinese seemed to be coming into possession, a miner remarked, 'yes we call the country New China.' On Strawberry Island an elderly & respectable man came out & placed an easy chair outside his hut as though he wished us to stop & have a talk. He was reading a newspaper & had on spectacles.

At Hill's Bar two miners were gathering roses & other flowers. Perhaps to adorn their huts for Sunday. Butterflies were abundant. Particularly the [scarce] Swallow Tail & the Painted Lady.

At four o'clock we arrived at Yale & were hospitably received by Mr. Crickmer & his estimable lady.

Excerpt of a letter from Bishop Hills to his sister Caroline Arden, 18 November 1860. This letter accompanied a long handwritten copy of excerpts from Bishop Hills' diary relating his trip to the gold mines in 1860.

ARCHIVES OF THE ECCLESIASTICAL PROVINCE OF
BRITISH COLUMBIA AND YUKON (HEREINAFTER AEPBCY)

Bishop George Hills, n.d., and his signature, G. Columbia.

Kenneth Mackenzie's Lakehill Farm, Victoria, 1867   BCARS PDP 00707

January 19   Visited the farms of the Puget Sound [Agricultural] Company, held by Mr. Skinner, Mackenzie & Langford. Nothing could exceed the romantic beauty of the scenery. . . .

The Puget Sound Agricultural Company was a subsidiary of the Hudson's Bay Company.

Nanaimo Indian Cradle, 1869
BCARS PDP 00945

February 24   There was a baby of about six months old, a fine boy bound to a board hand and foot like a mummy & upon his head the heavy bandage for the flattening process. All seen of the child was its mouth & nose. It was suspended in a horizontal position to the end of a bent stick placed in the ground & was rocked with a string.

The description of the cradle which Bishop Hills saw near New Westminster is similar to the one shown in the 1869 drawing done by artist Vincent Colyer.

Fort Hope Rectory, and explanation of drawing.
Artist A. D. Pringle. BCARS PDP 2123

June 3 We had a good attendance of some forty-five to fifty in Mr. Pringle's room, the Governor, Colonel Moody & Chief Justice [Begbie] present.

Cadboro Bay, near Victoria, Vancouver Island   BCARS 00013
Note reads: see Letter 8, page 232.

Indian Chief's Grave   CITY OF VANCOUVER ARCHIVES IN P. 154 N. 98

July 3   I have passed many Indian burial places. These consist of upright poles, with cross bars upon which are suspended the favourite blankets or portion of dress of the deceased. . . . Beneath are wooden box like tombs upon which are carvings. Usually the figure of a man, dressed in hat, shirt & trousers with hands in his pockets is the principal attraction.

St. John's Church, 1860   BCARS 8143

The prefabricated church was shipped from England. It was built on the corner
of Douglas and Fisgard streets in Victoria. Local people called it it 'Iron Church.'

B.C. Mines (Fraser River). Chinese Emigrants, Gold Mining.
CITY OF VANCOUVER ARCHIVES OUT P. 810 N. 369

June 15   We met many Chinese.... Their dress, for the most part, seems never to have
been changed for they are exact realizations of the pictures [of] old China to which one
has been accustomed from one's youth to see.... They carry everything on two ends of a
pole which rests on the shoulder.

Holy Trinity Church, New Westminster, 1860s   BCARS 8173

The church was designed by a nephew of Bishop Hills' who was a Royal Engineer,
Arthur R. Lempriere.

Colonel Moody's Farm, n.d.   BCARS PDP 05447

May 28   Walked with Colonel Moody & Captain Prevost to the farm, or clearing,
belonging to the former, on the way to Burrard's Inlet, about two and a half miles from the
[Royal Engineers] Camp. . . . At the place about seven acres are cleared & a garden made.

Colonel Moody was the Commander of the Royal Engineers and Chief Commissioner of Lands and
Works in British Columbia.

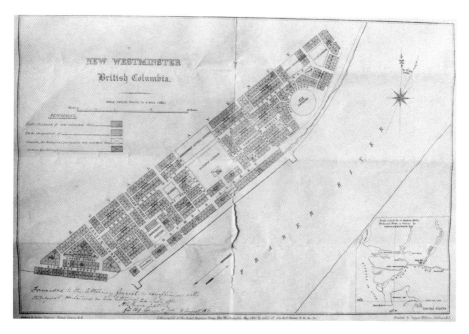

Town lots, New Westminster, as produced by the Royal Engineers, May 1861.
BCARS CM/A164

General view of New Westminster looking east, *ca.* 1859   BCARS 11190

General view of Yale, 1860s.   BCARS 1905

February 4   I received this day a petition from the married people of Yale asking me to supply them with a school & churches. This town is the headquarters of the gold diggings & a few months ago notorious for its proceedings.

Christ Church, Hope, 1978. PHOTO: BARRY DOWNS

Christ Church Hope was constructed in 1861. It was the second Anglican church built in the Colony of British Columbia and the only one that remains from the colonial period.

General view, Fort Hope, 1860. BCARS 9609

June 1 At length, Hope was reached & the echoes were startled & long & kindly responded to the guns of the fort & the whistle of the steamer which greeted the governor.

Bishop's Close   AEPBCY

August 9   Glad to find myself in my iron cottage, thankful for the mercy & loving-kindness that has been vouchsafed during my twelve weeks sojourn in [the Colony of] British Columbia.

The 1913 print shows the original building and a wing that was added sometime prior to 1889. The building was constructed on the site where Christ Church Cathedral now stands.

Legislative Buildings (The Birdcages), Victoria, *ca.* 1867.   BCARS 1996

LADIES' COLLEGE.

OR

FEMALE COLLEGIATE SCHOOL

(*The House lately occupied by Chief Justice Cameron.*)

FOR CHILDREN AND YOUNG PERSONS OF ALL AGES,

VICTORIA, VANCOUVER ISLAND.

It is the object of this Institution to provide careful Religious training, in combination with a solid English Education, and the usual accomplishments.

VISITOR.

THE LORD BISHOP OF BRITISH COLUMBIA AND VANCOUVER ISLAND.

LADY SUPERINTENDENT,

MRS. WOODS.

LADY SUPERINTENDENT, (pro tem.)

MRS. LOWE.

LADIES ASSISTANTS.

MISS PENRICE, MISS A. PENRICE.

THE COURSE OF EDUCATION INCLUDES

Religious and Moral Training in conformity with the principles of the Church of England, and the Protestant Episcopal Church of America.

English in all its branches, including Grammar, Geography, History (Ancient and Modern,) Arithmetic, Mathematics, Natural Philosophy, Latin, Modern Languages, French, German, Spanish and Italian. Music and Singing. Drawing and Painting.

Industrial Classes for instruction in Domestic Economy, Needle work, etc.

Victoria possesses peculiar attractions for an establishment of this kind, being situated near the sea, with a Public Park, in a country unsurpassed for Salubrity of climate and for beauty and grandeur of scenery; there is speedy and direct communication with the Chief Ports on the Pacific, affording an opportunity for a First Class Education to families residing, not only in Victoria and British Columbia, but in more distant places of the Continent.

TERMS.

INCLUSIVE OF FRENCH.

Per month.

Under ten years	$5 00.
Above ten and under fifteen years of age	6 00.
Above fifteen years of age	10 00.

The only extras are

(1) Modern Language
(2) Music and Singing } $2 per month each.
(3) Drawing and Painting

For Terms for Boarders and other particulars apply personally or by letter to the Lady Superintendent at the College.

N. B.—Boys under seven years of age, will be received at the lowest rates mentioned above.

THERE WILL BE TWO VACATIONS IN THE YEAR. ALL FEES TO BE PAID IN ADVANCE.

The school opened on September 3, 1860 in Victoria. It operated in the house that was formerly the residence of Chief Justice David Cameron.   AEPBCY

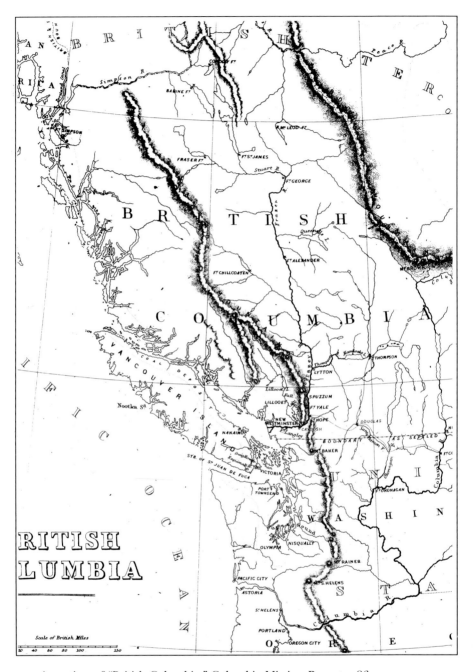

A portion of "British Columbia," Columbia Mission Report, 1860   AEPBCY

The map shows the colonial Diocese of British Columbia which contained both colonies until 1879 when it was divided into three diocese.

Bishop Hills

He named twenty-two sites where gold miners were at work in
1860—SEE INDEX UNDER GOLD MINING BARS.

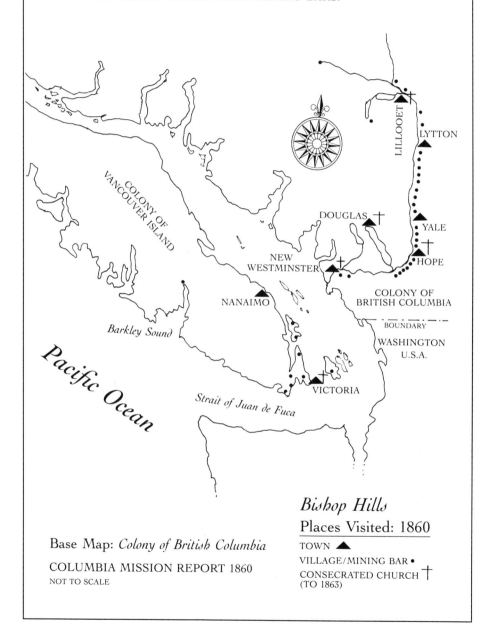

Base Map: *Colony of British Columbia*

COLUMBIA MISSION REPORT 1860

NOT TO SCALE

Bishop Hills
Places Visited: 1860

TOWN ▲
VILLAGE/MINING BAR ●
CONSECRATED CHURCH †
(TO 1863)

CHAPTER 4

*They are then entrusted with the goods
and are never known to betray the trust*

10 June – 24 June

June 10, Sunday.

This was the opening of the temporary church here (at Yale). It is a
small place, formerly a store, fitted up with taste by Mr. Crickmer. He has
a melodeon which the people have purchased. The musical part of the
service was very creditably performed, considering most present had
never before heard chanting. About 40 persons were present, amongst
others the Governor & Colonel Moody. The usual congregation is not
above twelve or fifteen, so this was a large representation. I preached
twice. In the morning a written sermon, 'Draw nigh to God' & in the
evening, extempore, but painful & laboured. There were about twenty-
five present in the evening.

In the afternoon I walked with Mr. Crickmer & visited some Indians &
Chinese. The Holy Communion was celebrated in the morning. There
were but three communicants.

INDIANS AND ROMIST PRIESTS

One of the Indians asked me if I had to do with the priests, making at
the same time the sign of the cross on the breast to make me understand what sort of priest was meant. It was an elderly woman who asked
me. She seemed to ask the question anxiously & with suspicion.

I found out afterwards the people were excited against the Romist
missionaries.

A few weeks since, a priest came round & according to their custom
baptized all [the] children. Some children have since died & the
Indians attribute the disaster to the priest. Several Indians were dis-
patched after him to kill him & he has only escaped by returning
another way, by the Douglas route instead of this.

June 11, Monday.

Rain most of the day. [I] went & looked at sites for [a] burial ground. A
romantic ravine with rolling torrent borders the north part of the town.
It is quite a study, a picturesque bridge crosses the stream at the town
path.

MULES AND PACKHORSES

Near this were mules & horses preparing to pack for the upper country. I spoke to a man who had charge. He was a rough looking bearded young man about thirty. He had been to the mines & had evidently suffered privation. There was something superior & gentle in his voice & manner. I asked him about his present occupation, how the mules were fed, etc. I asked if he observed the Sunday. No difference was made he said. I urged the observance of the Lord's Day on the ground of rest for the body & refreshment for the soul. He received what I said respectfully & even with approval.

SOIRÉE AT YALE PARSONAGE

Mr. Crickmer invited some of the principal people to meet me at tea. It was an opportunity of social intercourse useful to the people, as binding the disjointed elements somewhat together & affording an acquaintance with myself & removing any impression of prejudice against the clergy & the church. Amidst varied conversation many openings were found for the introduction of topics of higher interest. Not being a good converser & wanting alas, the presence of a constant aim to magnify my Saviour, I am painfully conscious of coming far short in using such opportunities as there were. About twenty were present, amongst whom [were] two Romanists, a Jew, Lutherans, Presbyterians, etc. Half were Americans, yet all most friendly & evidently pleased to be asked to the parsonage & to meet the Bishop.

June 12, Tuesday.

It rained all night & until breakfast.

THE CANYON

I went today to see the works being carried on to form a road through the canyon, or a narrow gorge, of the mountain where the Fraser emerges. The object is to get a road for mules round the base of perpendicular rocks. A party of Royal Engineers, assisted by others, are at work blasting the rocks. The work is one of great magnitude, dangerous & arduous of execution. I walked over the narrow ledge round the place at present under the hands of the Sappers. Along this, Indians travel laden with merchandise, packed with 100 pounds [of] weight. The footing in some places was certainly not more than half an inch, in one spot a mere indentation for a naked Indian heel. A slip from this would precipitate a fall down into the abyss of the whirling torrent. It is said many miners lost their lives in forcing their way here. Some hardy men, when they arrived at these points, would cast away in fear all they had in their hands & about them, in order to escape any how with their lives.

One Sapper had been engaged two days in easing the path for the Indians at a point even more difficult than those described. Here the only way of passing had been to bend the back in a particular manner to preserve the balance. A rock was blasted by the Sapper to allow the pass to be made in a straight position. Over two chasms twenty or thirty feet across, a plank was placed in one case; in another, two slender rounded poles tied together. Beneath these bending, slender pathways nothing intervenes to the roaring waters below.

The only other way to pass the range is over the mountain by a dangerous, long & arduous trail. This, in winter, is closed by snow. It is of great moment, therefore, to open a road which shall be short, safe & accessible at all seasons.

The men were pleased at Mr. Crickmer & myself visiting these works & treading the critical footholds. We waited while a blast was fired under shelter of a rock & witnessed the vast fragments hurled up into the air & then dashed around, some into the waters, others upon the rocks while the thunder of the explosion reverberated again & again as though there were many blastings instead of one. The men seemed to regard us with particular care & were evidently gratified by our sharing with them some slight danger. 'Well Sir, we could not get the Colonel [Moody] to come round here,' said one, as though he thought us braver than the colonel. The good colonel of course being quite ready to go anywhere that duty required.

INDIANS GAMBLING

As we went, we passed by a large room in which were many people. I looked in & saw about twenty Indians sitting on the ground playing eagerly at cards. Further on at the Indian camp we passed a similar group. On our return, sometime after, both these parties were still gambling. They had been for hours thus engaged. There was a haggard & anxious look upon them all. This is a great vice amongst them all. The cards are a white man's introduction but in other methods they have long been addicted to it. I met an Indian afterwards whom I knew. He had with him two others. He said these two are from the Similkameen. I asked what they did here. He said, 'they work & when they get money they spend it all in gambling, yes, all goes in cards.' I said this is very wrong. 'Yes,' he said, 'it is not right.'

TEA MEETING AT YALE

This evening a gathering took place of most of the inhabitants to give me an address of welcome. A dollar each (four shillings) was paid for admission so that the compliment was greater. The Chair was taken by Mr. Curtz [Kurtz], an American of German origin. Most of those present were Americans. There were three Romanists & others of various persuasions including Jews, the chairman being a Lutheran. The utmost harmony & good feeling prevailed. I replied to the address. Colonel Moody followed & while speaking of various topics of interest connected with their town, he urged forcibly & with tact, their adhesion to a religious life.

The chairman alluded to the varied nationalities before him, to the gathering of representatives of many sects & urged all to become a unified body & make the Church of England their religion.

The last visit of Colonel Moody had been with an armed force to capture the notorious Ned McGowan. All feeling of disaffection had now vanished. A change had come over Americans & they were valuing more the order & security & genuine freedom of British rule. One of them remarked this to me when I asked him if they all meant to remain & settle down.

One of the ringleaders of the McGowan disturbance was there. He is a fine young man of superior qualifications who had left his home in Boston for the gold mines. On Sunday I observed him in church, one of the most zealous of the choir. Tonight he rose & in a clear, short, well expressed speech proposed a vote of thanks to me for the way I had spoken of the American people & to Colonel Moody for bringing his Sappers, not for war, but for improvement. His name is Kelly. I told him I hope to visit him at the bar. He said, 'you shall have a welcome from all the miners.'

Altogether this occasion was one of deep interest & to be long remembered. In the morning the contract had been signed for making a road, to be the great road to the interior, perhaps to Canada & England. It was a great step in civilization & progress. Fitting was it to solemnize the occasion by expression of respect for religion & for advancing the cause of Christ's church.

June 13, Wednesday.

A fine day.

THE CHINESE

The Chinese are coming up in great numbers & spreading themselves over the bars. They work over again the claims which have already been searched by the European. They are content with a dollar or two dollars a day & will frequently make much more. They have been buying up claims & paying as much as from 500 to 4000 dollars. In California they have not been liked. They are heavily taxed & recently a law has passed which prohibits the arrival of any more.

Whether here we shall find them troublesome remains to be seen. At present they are helping us to develop the land, they are consumers of manufactures, they are cultivating gardens out of barren wastes, & Mr. Perrier, a leading miner on Hill's Bar, told me today he employed them as labourers & preferred them greatly to white men. They worked for two and a half dollars instead of four dollars, worked longer & more obediently, so that their labour was a great saving.

I walked today with Mr. Crickmer in search of a burial ground. We selected a spot westward near two streams. Our ramble was pleasant amidst beautiful scenery & flowers in wondrous profusion. We gathered strawberries.

June 14, Thursday.

HILL'S BAR

I crossed the river opposite Yale & took the trail to Hill's Bar. We walked through groves of young pines. Much of the ground is cleared.

Hill's Bar, about a couple of miles below Yale, was the scene of great excitement in 1858. It was the richest of all the 'diggings.' Thousands flocked to it & thousands of pounds have been extracted from it. It was here that the McGowan riots took place when Colonel Moody marched up his men to capture the rioters, but when he came to the spot, [he] drank champagne with them instead.

The first gold diggings were upon the bank of the river, upon this bank grew giant trees. All these & acres of soil have been swept away, to the depth of some ten or twelve feet.

It is now found that the higher banks, or flats still further from the river, are highly auriferous. These are now being worked.

FLUMING

One of the most interesting things in connection with gold mining is the courage & enterprise of the miner. Water is absolutely necessary for two purposes, washing away the earth above the gold, and washing the earth or 'pay dirt' which contains the gold. For the former work an immense [power] of water is frequently necessary. This is brought from a distance in wooden canals, aquaducts, & courses excavated in the soil or rock & then is made to descend upon the workings & applied by a hose to work away vast masses of earth.

At Hill's Bar I visited today a flume two miles long which had cost 12,000 dollars or £2400. A company [. . .] it in twelve shares, eight of which are held by one man, Mr. Perrier. The miners of the various claims pay for a head of water, five dollars a day. Sometimes there will be forty claims, & the flume will be making, to the proprietors, 200 dollars or £40 a day!

We visited spots where by rockers, without the sluicing power, Chinese were making five dollars a day. The sluice is where the water is brought in a body from the flume & continual shovelling into the sluice boxes of earth produces a large return of gold, because more earth can be washed, and the more earth washed in a given time, the greater the yield. The rocker is by the river side. It is a sort of wheelbarrow on rollers, with a scuttle front. Within is a sieve, beneath which are two blankets, & at the bottom is a copper plate with quicksilver. The pay earth is cast into the sieve & the machine rocked with one hand while the other hand keeps pouring in water. The earth & water pass through the sieve & blankets. The sieve stops the stones & larger particles. The blankets catch other atoms, of gold, etc. & the quicksilver retains the golden dust.

MINERS ON HILL'S BAR

We first came upon a fine young Irishman, well spoken & glad of a chat. He was clearing away the trees from a piece of high ground ready for working. He came from Cork.

A Welshman next attracted our notice. He was in a deep cutting, had been two years on the bar.

I had conversation with many men as we passed through the extensive ground. But seldom could I introduce the subject of religion even indirectly.

On passing a hut we perceived a female inside.

THE MINER'S WIFE

There was an order & neatness. She came out & directed us to a house we sought. I asked a question or two further. She said, 'pray come in.' This young woman was from the North of Ireland. She was a Protestant. She had married in Australia & had been two years here. There was something simple & touching in her [manner]. I entered upon the subject of religion. She loved to attend church, had been piously brought up. Her father used always to have family prayers morning & night. He was still living. She was very lonely & had no female society. One other female there was, but her character was such that she could not associate with her. Her husband, named Bean, was an American. He came in, asked us to excuse him as he was very busy. He seemed a fine young man. When he went out she said, 'you must excuse him he is very rough here, so different from what he was in Melbourne, but this place makes people rough.' She had no Bible or Prayer Book. I read a portion of Scripture, explained it & prayed. She said, 'oh how I remember all that.' On going away she thanked us several times & said, 'I never thought here I should have a reverend gentleman to call upon me.'

MINERS — RESTLESS

I asked one sturdy miner how it was that those like himself who had been out in California & here for ten years had not realized a fortune. He said, 'because Sir the miner is always agitated by any news of richer diggings & frequently gives up good paying claims to follow out some hearsay report, thinking to better himself & frequently spends all & comes back poorer than he went. I myself, if I hear of anything better, cannot keep quiet, I must be off. I once had 6000 dollars, but it all went away.'

The excitement of gold mining is great. The miner never feels tired. There is an interest in the work which always sustains him. Mr. Perrier told me cards & whisky are their bane. They seldom play for money, but for drink, a dollar a game.

A man will go into Yale on Sunday & spend twenty-five to forty dollars in drink & treating others. He does not know any men on temperance principles. There are however many temperate men. He himself, though an old miner, never touches spirit, only porter & ale. He always has a dozen of English porter in his house (on the bar).

June 15, Friday.

Fine day. Colonel Moody left. The Chinese had a grand affair with [fire] crackers in honour of his departure.

A WALK ON THE TRAIL — INDIANS LOADS

At eleven we left Yale for the trail towards the north. It lay over steep hills & rocky paths. We met many Indians whom we [discovered?]. All were pleased at the notice. One family were travelling the same way, [all were] heavily laden, the father, mother & two little girls. The heaviest weight of near 100 pounds was carried by the woman. One little girl carried a very heavy load for a child. They were laden with flour & bread. They carry weights on their back aided by a strap over the forehead.

CHINESE

We met many Chinese. They were coming into the town for provisions. On our way back we met them loaded. They carry everything on two ends of a pole which rests on the shoulder. Their dress, for the most part, seems never to have been changed, for they are exact realizations of the pictures [of] old China to which one has been accustomed from one's youth to see.

A Chinese shop is exactly what is painted. Every Chinaman in it, every attitude is just that quaint reality. Some of the Chinese, after a time, adopt our customs & buy our clothing which improves their appearance. One of those I met today told me he had a wife & children at Canton. I asked why he did not bring [them] here. He said he had no means. Another Chinaman who stood by said, this country was no place for China ladies, their feet were too small, they were too fine for this place.

SCENERY

At the Four Mile House [?] we branched off by the river trail & presently came to a most lovely & most magnificent view. We were upon an eminence 1100 feet above the river which beneath our feet was winding its tumultuous way through mountain passes. The view was exactly similar to that from the Bastei in Saxon, Switzerland where the Elbe passes out of Bohemia into Saxony through the mountains. I have a most vivid recollection of that view & this was the very same, excepting that the mountains were higher & more grand & that the river flowed continuously in the mountains, whereas the view from the Bastei shows the Elbe emerging forth into country less rugged, with lower ranges.

We descended this height of 1100 feet by an almost perpendicular descent & came to a lovely walk along the river. At the foot was a garden, kept by an American, [and] of remarkable fertility. Some radishes we brought home. Further on about a mile & [a] half was a place of call, a wayside house, called Hodges. Here we got some fried bacon & potatoes & coffee. When I proffered payment, they would take none. A booth was erected where on the Fourth of July was to be a gathering of Americans. On our way back we met miners returning from Quesnelle [Quesnel] River. They had not met the success they expected though gold was abundant. They had walked from Quesnel in about fifteen days, 450 miles.

After our walk of some 13 miles over a rough trail we reached home surprised to find how little fatigued we were with our eight hours excursion.

MINERS — THE QUESNEL

The miners from the Quesnel were old hands. They had come away not for the lack of gold but because of the expense of provisions. They would have stayed if they could find a digging yielding twelve dollars a day. This was their aim, (viz. nine months in the year about £500).

They said there was no doubt about the plenty of gold & some miners were doing extremely well. There was more gold than on the lower Fraser and, if provisions were cheaper, in every respect the Alexandria & Quesnel country was preferable, one exception alone being that the winters were more severe. Everywhere, they said, was a magnificent grazing country. You could go up on a hill top & see in all directions, far & near, fine grasslands. One of these men was named Clark. [He was] well known as an early & successful miner near Yale.

June 16, Saturday.

Took a walk with Mr. Crickmer up the Yale Creek. We went a considerable way along this beautiful stream which is a continual torrent, forming at every point a picture, dashing down the mountain gorge, waterfalls & cascades. On either side, the mountains are covered with trees & undergrowth & rise to immense height. There was no road or track. We forced our way through the trees & stumps & tangled underwood & from rock to rock. Frequently but a twig held us on the precipitous side many hundred feet above the torrent which was foaming perpendicularly below. We had repeated falls & our excursion was not without danger. We failed to get far enough to find a lake said to exist, but on the whole had a good afternoon's exercise.

June 17, Sunday. Second after Trinity.

A fine day, two services. I preached in the morning on the observance of the Sunday [and] in the evening on 'the first resurrection' from Colossians 3:1-4.

Congregations were about thirty in the morning & twenty in the evening. This was fair considering all the shops are open & more business [is conducted] on Sunday than any other day, in addition to which boats laden with freight came in from Hope, and many Indians arrived from the upper country, to be packed this evening, ready for a start by daybreak.

Some of the people are desirous a stop should be put to this Sunday traffic. The miners universally make it their business day. They divide their profits or their claims & then come in to the neighbouring stores. It will be difficult no doubt to break with the custom. We must however bear witness to the will of our God, a most merciful will, in giving a day of rest & trust by degrees to obtain a better observance.

There were miners present, both morning & evening. The services were hearty. A melodeon gave spirit. Mr. Crickmer has to go through the town from one end to the other ringing a bell before the service. There is not one resident communicant. Truly it is 'the day of small things.' Yet the Lord surely is with us & will bless without doubt his own means & we shall yet 'return with joy & bring our sheaves with us.'

June 18, Monday.

Visited the trail makers & the blasting operations round the canyons bluff.

INDIANS AND THE PRIESTS

I went into an Indian lodge. There were four resting places or beds, a fire in the midst. Several *squaws* were there, mostly fine young women. I asked about the child of one. She said his name was Paul. I asked if he was baptized. She went to a box & drew out a paper which she handed to me to see. This was a certificate in French that Father Vary, the authorized priest, had baptized the son of Peter, by the name of Paul. The child of another *squaw* had also been baptized, but she had left her paper at Hope, to which place she belonged.

INDIAN REGARD FOR THE ENGLISH

There came in a middle aged Indian man who sat down by an old one eyed *squaw*. He was evidently interested by our presence. I asked him whence he was & his name. He was from Kamloops & Mr. McLean, the head of the Hudson's Bay Company fort there, was a friend of his. He asked who we were. I said we were King George's men, i.e., English, & Clergymen. He rose up, expressed his joy, held out his hand, shook hands & took off his cap in respect.

A ROMAN CATHOLIC — A MINER'S WIFE

I called upon Mrs. McRoberts. Her husband is a miner. They have been in Australia & California. They are natives of Ireland. She is an earnest, worthy, motherly person. I had seen her at church the first Sunday I was here. Her husband is a Presbyterian from the North of Ireland. She is a Romanist. He never misses church & is a superior man, well off & looked up to.

I asked about her religious welfare. She said it was a drawback [that] she had no church of her own. I told her she had better come to us. She said she would do so for she was not strong in her own way. They have a pretty garden, well stocked with vegetables & there was an air of neatness, order & comfort about all their arrangements which betokened superiority. I think she will become a regular attendant at church & we may hope, come to learn & hold the pure truth as it is in Jesus.

I spoke to Mexicans who are the muleteers of the country.

The traffic between Yale & the upper country, (i.e., to Lytton about 80 miles) is carried on the backs of Indians through the winter, and now also in the want of sufficient animals. I met a day or two ago a party of Indians, a family they seemed. They were all loaded [with packs]. I felt the weight of each [pack]. The woman's load must have been at least 80 pounds. A little girl was carrying 40 pounds. Today I was in the store of a tinman, Mr. Griffin, & saw packs made up for Indians to go off with in the morning. They weighed 100 pounds, 120 pounds, & 130 pounds each. The Indians who were to carry them had been [in] & fitted them to their backs & had arranged them for starting. I could hardly lift them. One, a package of long handled mining shovels, was most awkward to carry. Yet these packs were to be carried along precipices, up almost perpendicular heights & for weary mile after mile.

June 19, Tuesday.

Walked to the Indian camp. Witnessed the incantations of a medicine man.

Called upon Mr. Kurtz, an American, well affected towards the church. He gave me information as to the persons likely to be interested & [who] would assist me on the road up the river.

INDIAN FIDELITY

A number of Indians were in Mr. Kurtz's store preparing for their packs to the Upper Country [for] tomorrow. He packed goods to the weight of 100 pounds & upwards. The Indians came & fitted them to their backs. They hold the pack on by a strap which comes round the forehead. They get from sixteen to twenty shillings a day. These Indians had been sent down from the Upper Country, from Lytton, with the order & with the money from the merchant there. They bring the money with great care. It is secreted upon their persons. They come to the supplying merchant. He is strange to them, they have never seen him before. They want to be quite sure if he is the person to whom they must give the money. They hand him the note. They watch his countenance. He says, 'you have money for me.' They say, 'no money.' He says, 'yes, yes.' He tells them exactly how much. They smile, see he is the right party & dive down into the folds of their dress & produce the money. They are then entrusted with the goods & are never known to betray their trust.

June 20, Wednesday.

HOPE

[I] came this day, in a canoe, to Hope. [We] left at quarter past two, [and] reached here in less than two hours. We were eight hours going up. The river is very full & dangerous. During the last few days five canoes have been upset & the freight lost.

COLONIAL CIVILITY

I went into a chemist, [Mr.] Bradshaw, [and] bought a toothbrush. He would not let me pay anything. He never charges, he says, the clergy.

Mr. Crickmer told me he went into a store for a box-plane & they would not let him pay.

June 21, Thursday.

Walked with Mr. Pringle & Crickmer to the bridge & over a hill towards the mouth of Coquihalla where is a lovely view of the [. . .].

WESTERN TRAIL FROM HOPE

Rode out with Mr. O'Reilly and Mr. Charles along the river trail. By this route cattle are brought in from Bellingham Bay. It has been formed without expense to government. It goes through a considerable tract of land, at present altogether uncleared. Logs of wood were frequently in the path which sometimes involved a leap. We had to get off & walk our animals through some rough & steep places. Several [. . .] of water were to be forded, one of which was a considerable ford, being a river called, I think, the Hope Creek. My horse tripped & the water was over his neck. Of course I was saturated so far as the lower portions of the limbs [were] concerned. In coming back Mr. O'Reilly wished me to go over a bridge, a single tree about 150 feet & let him ford the horse. This of course I declined desiring to accustom myself to rough exercise.

On the way we passed Cornish Bar, or Murderer's Bar as it used to be called. Here extensive minings have been carried on. The water being high & covering the claims, not a soul was there. One black cat alone represented life in the midst of unused & desolated huts. Ere long however, as the water subsides, busy life will again be there.

Lower down a large tract of bank was entered upon some months since, but abandoned because water could not be conveniently got for sluicing the [ground]. No doubt all this ground which is highly auriferous will be worked in time.

On the opposite side nearer Hope, or rather in the stream, is an island called Merivale. On it is a settler named Hose. There [are] 80 acres. He wishes the island to be named Cathcart after Lord Cathcart upon whose property his father is tenant.

HUDSON'S BAY COMPANY STORE—THE BRIGADE

I went into the store of the Hudson's Bay Company. The brigade of pack horses bringing the furs is hourly expected. Two brigades arrived in

[this] year. They bring the trade produce from the north, middle & south districts of British Columbia & take back stores of food & clothing & articles of Indian traffic. The three districts are New Caledonia in the north, Thompson River middle, & Colville south. The goods are all made up in packages [reaching weights] from 80 to 100 pounds, two are slung to the sides of each animal. There are some two hundred animals attended by thirty or forty men, principally half breeds & Indians. From the most northern posts the brigade will have been probably two months on the road.

Yesterday, two strange looking Indians came in with letters announcing the approach of the brigade. They are from Fort Colville & [are] more copper coloured than Indians here.

INDIAN NAME FOR HOPE

I asked the Indians who paddled me down from Yale the Indian name for Hope. They said *Tsiltzlitya*.

In my ride today, by the western trail, I saw barley in several spots, in ear.

June 22, Friday.

Walked with Mr. Crickmer & Mr. Pringle. Went round the lake called Dallas, some way. Visited the Indian gardens. Not only have they a large tract sown in potatoes but also turnips, an advance.

I visited also a garden upon land lately belonging to Mr. Chisholm. About two acres have been reclaimed & nothing could exceed the richness of the soil. It is well stocked. The butcher who holds it pays, with the right of run over the entire farm of 85 acres, only 100 dollars. The coloured gardener working there told me 300 dollars would be made out of the cabbages alone. Saw wild thyme & the white 'everlasting flower.'

June 23, Saturday.

This morning very early the steamer *Douglas* arrived at Hope from New Westminster. I got a disappointing letter from Victoria announcing the works on St. John's [Church] suspended. [. . .].

By the boat came Mr. & Mrs. Gammage on their way to Victoria, whither I had requested him to go, to allow Mr. Dundas to relieve Mr. Sheepshanks at New Westminster.

REV. MR. GAMMAGE AND A BEAR

Mr. Gammage informed me he had been walking along the Douglas road when he perceived close to him a bear! The animal was walking with nose on ground. Mr. Gammage instantly beat a retreat.

Mr. Pringle had engaged a canoe & Indians over night. At a quarter before ten we were seated. One Indian had failed, another came in his place. When about to start they said they had had no breakfast, '*no muk muk*,' we were compelled to submit. A quarter of dollar apiece satisfied them. They disappeared & presently returned from the baker with a beautiful loaf of bread each.

Away we went. The water was at least six feet lower than when I went up before & not so difficult now therefore to encounter.

The day was charming. There was sun. There was [fresh] air. Two showers on the way were not inconvenient. There was thunder. I asked what that was in Indian, they said *Sowas* & wished to know what was the English.

Our Indians were three. The canoe [was] about twenty feet in length by three and a half wide, hewn out of a single tree. One Indian had on a bright crimson shirt, another pink, the third blue. So they looked very picturesque.

We passed many boats. One canoe was going down the river at a great rate with eight Indians, some female. One had an orange shirt, another crimson & others of various colours, which with their black flowing hair & handsome painted canoe with rising prow formed a romantic & pleasing sight. This was a party upon a mission of charity. One had been sick & died. They had come from his burial.

INDIAN WOMEN

The Indian women take a full share of labour. Even more is carried by them than by men. They were paddling with as much strength. One woman was steering a canoe & came close to us, indeed we passed it. She had eight silver rings on two fingers of [her] left hand & six bracelets. They have earrings also & sometimes armlets. These ornaments are made out of silver dollars.

CANOE DANGERS

Although the water was lower, all difficulties were not removed. On the contrary, some rapids became more dangerous. We got out several times while the canoe, lightened, was poled through intricacies of the torrent washed rocks. At one of them an accident occurred. We had got out. A dangerous rapid round a succession of rocks was to be passed. It was impossible to paddle or pole against the torrent which was boiling & surging & rushing & foaming round & upon the rocks. The elder Indian took a long rope over the rocks & having reached a certain point gave notice & began to haul, the other men keeping the boat from the rocks with poles & shoving. We stood beside the old Indian. The boat began to appear round the bluff. The force of the torrent meeting her seemed to lift her bows up in the air. Presently, in an instant, back she went & disappeared. It was as if swallowed up. The old man shouted, was frightened & sprang forward shouting & then [ran] over the rocks with alarm upon his countenance. The rope had [broken] & he knew not but his boat had been caught & upset. We too hastened round & looked first in the distance down the torrent expecting under the best circumstances to find it carried far back. Nothing was to be seen. We clambered upon the high cliff rock to look down near the spot we last saw it. There in a retired nook, in a quiet eddy out of the torrent lay the canoe, quite safe, her two Indians sitting laughing as though the danger was a joke. Presently the old man appeared. The delight upon his countenance was that of a child. Again an attempt was made with the mended rope, a second Indian came to the old man's help. The canoe pulled through safely. The rope held & we got in. One of the Indians suggested it was well we had not been killed.

Considering how many canoes have been upset recently, we may indeed be thankful for this day's mercy.

INDIAN CONTEMPT FOR CHINESE

All along the river, at the mining bars & in boats, were Chinese. Our Indians seemed to hold them in great contempt. They called out continually, 'John, John' & having arrested 'John Chinaman's' attention imitated some Chinese expression, sounding [like] *Hah, ah, war.* It was all done in good nature. The Chinese are evidently afraid of the Indians, who regard them with contempt. The Indian certainly compares favourably with the Chinese. The specimens we have of the latter are spare & delicate looking. They no doubt, however, excel the Indian in the arts of life.

June 24, Sunday.

Very warm. Preached twice, [in the] morning [on] 'The Mammon of Unrighteousness,' [in the] evening [on] 'The Hid Treasure.'

The services were fairly attended, & were hearty. The Lord's Day is, however, entirely unobserved here, trade being carried on to a greater extent than on other days.

I walked down the town about half past nine & no shops were closed. Several billiard tables were in full operation, open to the street & the rooms occupied with groups evidently of the miner class.

CHAPTER 5

I have passed many Indian burial places
25 June – 6 July

June 25, Monday.

JOURNEY — YALE TO SPUZZUM

[This is] my day for starting to the Upper Country. I had intended taking Indians to convey my baggage. One is obliged to travel in this country, in its present state, more heavily laden than in an older land. Blankets & tents & provisions are necessary over & above other things.

Indian labour is expensive & sometimes difficult to manage. Mr. Kurtz, a respectable storekeeper in Yale, procured for me two pack-horses & the owner who agreed to take my things to Lytton, 80 miles [away], for sixty dollars. I got an Indian named Sacher besides. When the time came the packer declined to take a portmanteau. I had gone forward & was sent for & had to return. I would not give in & the portmanteau went. We were, however, delayed a couple of hours & left Yale at length at 1:10 P.M.

Our first road lay up a steep mountain, then a ravine to the Four Mile House, a log building kept by an American named Emmerson. This we reached [at] 3:30. On the way we met many Indians, chiefly of the Thompson River tribes who spoke a different language from those of Yale & lower down. From one of these parties we collected the pronunciation of many words among which the numerals [. . .] appear regular & simple.

We met an Australian & Californian miner named Carter. He had just come from the Quesnel mines. He reports favourably, from all his experience that [this] is the country for mining. The gold there, unlike lower down, is coarse. He reported not above 300 miners & 450 packers, shopkeepers & others [are there]. He was an Irishman who had seen the world. In language [he was] civil towards us, profane towards his mules.

After the Four Mile House, the road passes along a ravine widening occasionally towards the proportions of a small valley, till we began a deep descent, the winding path of which was like the winding way of the tower of Babel as shown in Bible pictures. If we chanced to be a little ahead of our animals they appeared like walking on a shelf over our heads.

Here & there we passed the bones of a horse or mule which had dropped down beneath their load.

At the foot of this descent was a fine mountain torrent, foaming & roaring & shiny as it forced its way over rocks & through gorges of the mountain. Over this was a bridge by the side of which [was] a log house. We next commenced a terrible ascent of which it had been remarked, there was no end to it. It seemed ever continuous. At length we did reach the summit, [but] not before one of our packages had fallen over & tumbled a considerable way down the hill. The descent then began & continued for a tedious period.

A ROADSIDE HUT

We left our horses & pressed on to Spuzzum, [to] a roadside hut, where we arrived at 7:15 having accomplished twelve miles. It soon began to rain & darkness came on. Our horses & baggage had not come. Flash after flash of lightning & pouring rain prevented our going out. An Indian was sent, but returned with no tidings. We resolved to remain. An excellent supper was speedily provided, consisting of chicken, from [a] tin, [a] small quantity of mutton, potatoes, oyster soup, tomatoes, capital bread, butter, cheese, cranberry tart, [puckleberries?], pickles, preserved ginger, coffee, etc.

The owner is a respectable American, W.F. Way. Here pass daily, & cross the ferry, travellers & pack animals.

There were several persons. An expressman, a packer, miners, [and] a seemingly worthy woman, a Mrs. Hicks, the wife of a person who held office under our government at Yale & was dismissed. [She] also resided in the house, or near, & did the housekeeping department. She alluded to her husband's defalcations & informed us [that] during his term of office he had made by [. . .] 5000 dollars [or] 1000£, & that had he known all he knew afterwards, he could have made very much more.

Introducing, as I endeavour to do where I can, the subject of religion, she spoke out of her unhappiness as to her own state of life. She once lived, she said, a Christian life & was happy & every day her resolutions were good. She was surrounded by profanity which her heart condemned. She had been a Unitarian. No difference is made by the people on Sunday. They dress no different, all work goes on just the same.

NIGHT SERVICE IN A LOG HUT

Before we retired I proposed we should have a short service. My proposal was received with gladness by Mrs. Hicks & with respectful attention by the rest. A table was placed, [and] on it [were] two candles. The packers & others sat about. I read the parables of the lost sheep & piece of money & explained them, exhorting all present to ponder well their present life & not [allow] the opportunity of the Saviour's mercy [to] pass from them unheeded. We then sang the evening hymn, I offered prayer & we prepared for rest.

A NIGHT ON THE FLOOR OF A LOG HUT

The room in which we slept was on the ground of course, there being not a second storey, nor indeed a second room, a portion only being partitioned off for a small kitchen. There was an out house [or building] called the bakery, where some slept. Our room was that where the liquor was sold, [with a] door opening to the wood & path. My bed consisted of blankets laid upon a mattress on the floor. Near me on one side on the floor was Mr. Crickmer, on the other side of me within arms length was a box filled with a cat & kittens, so I was safe from rats coming to my face. William & three other men were lodged in different parts of the same room.

I confess, tired though I was, I could not sleep much, principally owing to the heat of the room. I would gladly have seen the doorway wide open to the fresh air. It rain[ed] in torrents most of the night & gave our beds some drops of the cool shower.

June 26, Tuesday.

MY BIRTHDAY

God be praised for sparing me to this point of life. How undeserved by me his great mercies. May this new sphere be a means of devoting to him my whole self in a way I have never yet done. Yet how I linger after some thing, I know not what. Would that it were a more constant craving after heavenly things, a greater thirst & hunger for the true righteousness.

On this my forty-fourth birthday I awoke on the floor of a log hut in the wild & almost unaccessible recesses of the Cascade Mountains, the Fraser flowing at my feet. The five other individuals who occupied other parts of the room had been not otherwise than quiet. Sleep however, I had had but little. I rose about half past five. A comfortable breakfast at seven, of tea, coffee, ham, etc., prepared us for the arduous day before us.

Our horses had arrived in the neighbourhood the night before & [at] about eight [o'clock] came up ready equipped.

HOSPITALITY IN A LOG HUT

Nothing could induce the good people of the house to take a single farthing for either supper, lodging or breakfast which they had given to

my party of three. They said they only regretted the accommodation &
the fare had been so poor.

In passing the ferry too, when two Indians were added to my party,
Mr. Way declined to take anything. The fare over, being three shillings
for each person, it was no small attention, in addition to the suppers &
breakfasts.

THE FERRY AT SPUZZUM

The Fraser is about 250 yards [wide] at this point. The current is strong.
A rope is suspended from bank to bank. From this rope is tackle which
works the large punt shaped ferry boat. A most ingenious method, the
current acting as the wind acts upon a sail. The side of the boat being
the sail & kept by the tackle in an inclined position to the stream. The
stronger the current the less inclined need be the boat. Without the
slightest difficulty, the river is thus quickly crossed.

SPUZZUM TO BOSTON BAR

For five miles our route lay along the river till we got to Chapman's Bar.
The trail [was] generally good. You might go at a hard gallop much of
the way. One exception to this was a piece of road to which going up
stairs for a horse was nothing, [when] compared.

On the way were many Chinese, few Englishmen, at one place I
conversed with a French miner.

At Chapman's Bar I found a respectable storekeeper, a young man
named Alexander. He had been a miner, a pleasing person from Indi-
ana. We spoke about the Sunday observance & how a man could be
religious in the midst of wickedness. On Sundays he said the miners
only worked at their chores. They mended their clothes & did other
small jobs. He spoke of the temptation & hardships of the miner's life.
He knew many steady men.

From Chapman's Bar there is a continuous ascent. We had very fine
views of the river as we ascended, also of the mountains & distant [. . .].

Flowers [were] on all sides, amongst which [were] roses, wild pansy,
columbine & other well known plants. Ten miles from Chapman's Bar
the Lake House is situated. It is high up in the mountain near a series of
lakes. We reached [it] at ten minutes past one.

The view of the Fraser, encompassed in mountains from this point, or
rather from a point near, is grand indeed. It is not unlike the view from
the Four Mile House which resembles so much that from the Bastei in
the Saxon, Switzerland, excepting that it is much grander, even terrible
compared with it.

We left the Lake House at three, magnificent views open out occasionally. The road now divides, one for mules & horses twenty miles [long], the other impassable for animals excepting man, ten miles [long]. We, of course for ourselves, chose the latter & having packed upon two Indians sufficient [supplies] for a day away from our horses, we started for Boston Bar.

We continued the ascent for some distance. Impassable indeed, much of it was, for horses & mules, & even for man, not without danger. We must have been at a height of 2500 or 3000 feet. Our pathway lay along the edge of a perpendicular fall of such a height, sometimes along beds of loose rock & most warily must the feet step from stone to stone. A slip would either precipitate [a fall] to the abyss below or cast you into the rocks where a limb might easily be broken. At other times in the descent, the path was nil, the projections for the foot not an inch. It seemed like the crawling of a fly upon the perpendicular wall. This sort of work lasted for hours. It was, however, so absorbing & required the utmost constant stretch of attention for self preservation that the time passed more rapidly than one would have thought. At [these] times the critical character of the operation was such that, though near together, no one spoke. There was a solemnity as if it were realized we were hanging between life & death. Frequently we had to crawl upon [our] hands & knees. It was quite wonderful to see the Indians with their heavy loads pass along. One of ours did fall however, once.

We came occasionally to mountain torrents bringing down the cool water from the snowy heights. At one time we slaked our thirst from the snow itself. At length we had gone over the worst of the lake mountain. The Fraser was again spread out before us. The smoke in the distance pointed out the dwellings upon Boston Bar. We reached our camping ground at eight o'clock, having accomplished twenty miles. Tents pitched, a fire made, we enjoyed a refreshing cup of tea & slices of cold ham. Before retiring to rest, the Indians having had their meal, we sang together the evening hymn & waked the echoes in praises to our merciful God whose gracious protection had been so signally with us during the day.

Thus was passed my birthday. I awoke in a log hut on the floor, I laid down upon the grass at night. I can rejoice my Lord has in his Providence called me to this life wherein he has offered me the opportunity of more self denial & of a higher life than the care & comfort of home, though it is a burden to me continually that I am so unworthy of this sacred office & so weak an instrument of the glorious gospel of my God. I can only trust that he who has called me will aid me & out of weakness show his own strength & power in the progress of his gospel & the conversion of hearts.

June 27, Wednesday.

INTRUDERS

Last night I was attracted by some thing, a person, I thought, prowling near my tent. Presently the tent door opened. I jumped up. It was an Indian dog. The ham in my tent had drawn him. I got my stick & laid it near at hand in case I had another visit.

BOSTON BAR

I visited the village of Boston Bar, which is over the Anderson River which here runs into the Fraser. There are but five houses, two stores, a liquor shop, a restaurant & a blacksmith's, inhabited by eight persons. It is however, the centre of a considerable mining district where the mines have paid well, so that much business is done.

I was struck at once by the gardens which are highly productive & which form a grateful contrast to anything seen before on the river.

We entered the first store. It was that of two Frenchmen. We were civilly received & invited to take a drink. I declined, saying I never took any thing of the sort, [although it was] kindly offered, but would be glad of a glass of water. Raspberry syrup was added & when payment was offered it was steadily declined. I spoke to several miners I found there. A Frenchman, and a Spaniard amongst the rest. They could speak English fairly [well].

The next store was that of a young Frenchman named Brassey. He was very civil, showed us his garden, offered refreshment & insisted upon our taking away some excellent lettuce & radishes. We then went into his restaurant department, carried on by two coloured men whom we talked to.

Our next visit was to the ferryman & liquor house keeper. He insisted upon nothing being paid for passage across the ferry, a saving to us of a dollar each. We afterwards saw the blacksmith & so the whole resident population came under review.

The miners we spoke to all reported good success.

PRICES AT BOSTON BAR JUNE 27, 1860

Flour 18 cents a pound—9 ∂, or 10 shillings, 6 pence
Bacon 3 bits—1 shilling, 6 pence

QUAYOME INDIANS — ILCOCHAN

On return to our camping ground several Indians had assembled, amongst whom were three old men who sat like sages, grave & solemn, watching proceedings, a few others also stood about. There was waiting too, a smart looking middle aged Indian who wished to see me. He had a paper of which he was proud & which he produced from beneath numerous foldings of other paper. It was a certificate by some American to say that the bearer was *Tyhee*, or chief, of the Boston Bar Indians & was worthy. Beneath was written, 'the chief's name is Ilcochan' to which was appended a magnificent red official seal round which was stamped, 'the Seal of the Supreme Court of British Columbia' with 'Matt. B. Begbie' written. These poor people think much of a bit of paper from the whites with something written in their favour. Ilcochan, however, was not the chief of the Boston Bar Indians, nor a chief at all. He was, however, a chief speaker with a magnificent voice.

I proceeded to address the Indians, the three old men in particular. Ilcochan interpreted, that is, he turned my Chinook into the local tongue.

I spoke of the love of God in sending Jesus Christ, showed the Gospel invitation to be for all, gave particulars of the life of Jesus. [I] asked what became of them when they died, explained the spiritual nature of man, pointed out that God punished the evil, & blessed the good, held up the Bible as the word of God to them as well as to us. Ilcochan & Sacher my own Indian, interpreted. Both were at times very excited & seemed fully to enter into the subject. Amongst evil things to put away I had named drink, for whisky is their curse. My interpreters took that up particularly & pointed out for all the lamentable effects so [. . .] to all. After a deeply interesting & touching scene we dismissed the assembly that we might have our meal.

A short time afterwards we heard a loud noise at the Indian camp. We could see it was Ilcochan haranguing the Indians. His loud & clear voice brought echoes from the mountains. We could see his figure standing upon some rising ground & distinctly heard him repeating what I had said.

NIGHT SCENE — PREACHING TO INDIANS

Towards dusk Indians began again to assemble. One Indian brought a present of a salmon, worth, to sell at this time, 10 shillings. Mr. Crickmer & William were gone away across the River Anderson to see if they could find our horses & baggage. I was alone with the Indians who came up one after the other unobserved, except now & then a greater glare from the fire revealed more faces of sitters. The Indian is particularly stealthy in his movements. Amongst others who had come up & taken a more prominent place, but wrapped this time in a blanket, was Ilcochan, whom I did not at first recognize. I took my seat on a tree in front of him. There was now a large gathering. I stood up & commenced to address them. Ilcochan & Sacher interpreted, a good deal was understood, because I spoke in Chinook, which many Indians know, [and] which indeed was the way of reaching my interpreters. Our talk was long. The evening grew darker, the fire blazed brighter. Ilcochan became very excited. He stood up & with great gesticulations interpreted my words in the Quayome tongue. The scene was striking.

Mr. Crickmer & William approached from the distance. The latter had no idea it was our camp but supposed the spot was on the way & that an excitement of Indians was going on. Mr. Crickmer felt alarmed. He knew that our camp was in that spot & that I was alone & thought there must be some trouble. He was relieved to find myself sitting in the midst of the circle, patiently watching Ilcochan. Indeed, I was deeply interested, I may say affected. It was deeply interesting to see the evident impression made upon these poor Indians. I was also interested to mark the pantomime of gesture with which Ilcochan sought to move the spirits of his people. It was a lesson I hoped to profit by. It was affecting to think of the entire darkness which clouds the minds of these people.

NIGHT SCENE—THE CHILDREN OF
THE QUAYOMES BROUGHT TO THE BISHOP

Amongst other subjects, I mentioned my desire to bring education within their reach. After a lengthened talk upon the improvement it would make in their temporal as well as spiritual circumstances, I enquired how many children there [were] in the tribe. It was difficult to make them understand, at length they appeared to catch my meaning. Two young men started up, came forward & offered to go. I supposed they were going to the different houses to find out how many children in each family. Presently they came back. There was a difficulty. Instantly every one shouted to put them on their mettle & not to [see] difficulties. They conferred & then darted off into the darkness.

Presently from all quarters approached more Indians, as they came on the ground they took their seats in rows. I perceived every one had a child. I discovered, to my dismay, that they had misunderstood me & that they were bringing the children themselves, instead of their numbers. It was past ten o'clock. All these poor things had been pulled out of bed, most were naked, some in their cradles. In the midst of my last talk an Indian woman brought a lighted mould candle & set it down near me.

We concluded by singing the evening hymn. A most devotional & deep impression sat upon each & all. When we stopped it was most striking to behold. Reluctantly they took their leave one by one, every one came & shook hands. They came up in file before me & every little child was brought & held out its little hand for my [hand]shake.

June 28, Thursday.

Left Boston Bar & its gardens a little before eight.

REVOLVERS NOT NEEDED IN BRITISH TERRITORY

Overtook a miner from California with a revolver on one side, a Bowie knife on the other. I spoke about the former, he said they were needed in California, but not here.

I have met very few miners with these weapons, once none went without. Things are now as quiet & orderly as possible. All classes are well treated. Chinamen, Indians & blacks have justice as equal as do others. Indeed it is evident that what the Californian looked upon as a sign of high spirit & courage, he is now ashamed of & these terrible weapons are put away.

NICK NAMES

The appellation of all miners is 'boy.' Their chief is 'Cap.' All are called 'Dick, Tom or Henry.' Men are not known by their real names. You inquire, as I have often done, the name of someone. Nobody knows his name, only he is called so & so of such & such a bar.

I was speaking to a miner. He said he had just come from California & with him had come a miner who had sold his claim there for 1800 dollars. I asked what the man's name was. He said he went by a nick name, 'Bam.' He knew not his real name. He had known, in California, instances of considerable difficulty arising from this.

A man came into the country from the eastern states seeking his brother. His enquiries for Thomas McGuire produced no result. He went away back to the states. Yet his brother was known & was working with those who had heard the enquiry, but they had not the least notion their friend who had some opposite nick name was really Thomas McGuire.

THE COUNTRY AFTER BOSTON BAR

The valley of the Fraser [is] in many parts more open & relieved. Still generally high & precipitate sides, yet more frequent openings, beautiful flats, or terraces a mile wide, grassy & thinly wooded, along which for miles a carriage might run. [There is] nothing of this sort before Boston Bar.

VEGETATION

Bunch grass now appears & animals get food in most places. Of this grass are various kinds which are common in England, such as Rye,

Dog's Tail & two others in particular. All grow in bunches which is a form common to all the sorts of grass.

There is now a good deal of timber [that] carpenters call yellow [spruce], also white & red.

SOIL

The soil is somewhat different, perhaps from the presence of a slaty substance which comes from the wet disintegration. A California miner said that [it] put him in the mind of California. Afterwards I saw gravel.

MINING BARS

Visited Paul's Flat, a few miles beyond Boston Bar. Spoke to a Frenchman & an Italian, both civil. These were clearing together twenty dollars a day.

Ensley's Flat. [There a] store [was] kept by a Frenchman. [There are] great preparations for working this flat.

At this place [is] a flume of great extent, several miles [long], at one part of its progress it crosses a ravine & small river 100 feet high. The work which carries the aquaduct is like a spider's web.

We passed Fargo's Bar & after a beautiful walk of eighteen miles, encamped in a park like country at half past four. Near our camp was a delicious stream in which both evening & morning I had a delightful bath.

WAHILAH, CHIEF OF THE QUAYOMES

In the evening I was visited by the Indians of the neighbourhood & amongst others, by Wahilah the Chief of the Indians I had preached to at Boston Bar. He is a fine looking man of about fifty, not, however, an orator. I preached to him & those present. Sacher, my own Indian, interpreted. Long after dark by the fire light I spoke to these people who did not like to go. We concluded with singing the evening hymn.

June 29, Friday.

At half past seven we moved away. About two miles on is the Half Way House. Here we found a butcher's shop. I said, 'If I had known you were so near I should certainly have sent for some of your fresh meat, for we have been on salt provisions for some days.' He said, 'if I had known you had been so near you should certainly have had some, Sir.'

SWEARING REPROVED

At this point, at the door of a log hut in a garden, I accosted a respectable looking miner. He was civil & glad of a talk. He came from

New Brunswick. Upon his interspersing his remarks with profane language, I reproved him. He took it well & said he knew it was wrong, but it was a bad habit he had learned lately.

The Americans are terrible swearers, language is exhausted by them to procure excessive profanity. They all do it.

I met another miner today named Farringdon a young man of about twenty-six [years], six feet four inches high. He sat down & we had a talk. I spoke of his home. He said he did not like the mining life. He said nothing improper. He went into a store where he found out who I was. He affected to be greatly concerned for he had been talking to the Bishop & the Bishop had touched his feelings & made him swear. He professed to be shocked at swearing before a Bishop. The fact was he supposed he had sworn since it was so habitual a thing with him.

CHINESE INGENUITY AND RESPECT FOR THE ENGLISH

Yesterday, at Ensley's Creek, under the flume was a pretty bridge for which, according to a notice, twenty-five cents or one shilling was charged for foot passengers, a dollar for a mule or horse. On the arrival of my party, six on foot & two horses, the Chinaman in charge refuse[d] to take anything. His name was Ah Fah. We had much talk with him. The origin of the bridge was thus. An American had placed over the river two logs & connecting them, had made a sort of bridge. He charged everybody [a] high [price] & when the poor Chinamen came with no money, he would take away their mining implements. Complaint was made to Captain Ball, the Magistrate at Lytton, who advised them to make a bridge for themselves. The American very soon gave way, sold his right & a really beautiful bridge, six feet wide, with tasteful rails, [now] permits not only men but animals to pass over.

Today we came to another bridge, larger in size, being 120 [feet] long, built upon coffer dams & at a cost of 535 dollars or 107£. Here was a Chinaman, named Ah Soo. On our approach he ran forward with cool water to drink & told us we were free of the bridge. No Englishman, he said, pays [to go] over the bridge, & no poor Chinaman. 'Me makee no chargee to de English. Me chargee Boston man (American). Boston man chargee Chinaman very high in Californy. Chinaman now chargee Boston man, ha ha.'

BRITISH SOIL A WELCOME HOME FOR ALL RACES

We meet many Chinese. They are pouring in. There are upon the river from Fort Hope & upwards not less than 3000. (This is the opinion of Mr. Ballard, Chinese merchant at Lytton, & he expects 2000 more this summer.) They are selling out their mining claims in California to come up here & are purchasing claims of the white miners. This very day, said Mr. Ballard, a claim on Foster's Bar was bought by Chinese for 3500 dollars. They are well & equally treated here & are not taxed. In California they are taxed 50 dollars a year.

The Indian race is comparatively happy here. Everywhere King George's men (English) are looked upon as their friends. They come & shake hands & hang about us. What a contrast to the constant massacre in the American Territory.

A third race ill treated by the Americans is the African. Here, everywhere they are treated fairly.

Thus in these three instances is British soil a welcome home. May God grant it may [be] a home blessed to their souls with the light, the peace & the power of the Gospel of Jesus Christ.

THE JACKASS MOUNTAIN

We crossed this famed difficulty without trouble. Our previous experience in hazardous paths has made us insensible to what really probably are dangers. This trail has been much improved & our horses went over, instead of going round. The chief difficulty is an ascent very steep of loose stones, with a precipice 500 feet straight down. The name is derived from the fall & destruction of a mule. Certainly a slip would be destruction. God who has watched over us so far mercifully protected us here.

Owing to having to wait two hours, under the impression our horses were behind, whereas they were before us, we made but twelve miles, & encamped in a lovely spot about half past three. It was a rising ground between two small ravines about 200 feet above the Fraser which flowed at the foot. Trees encompassed our encampment, on either side was park like country, grass & trees. Opposite, in the west over the Fraser, were mountains behind which the sun descended & left us a long & cool evening.

Not far from us our packer & another man were encamped & our Indians made our fire, pitched our tents & then themselves lay down on the ground to rest.

It was a delicious evening. We sat & talked for hours of old England & dear friends & the work of our God, after which we awoke the solitude of nature by the evening hymn in which our Indians devoutly joined.

June 30, Saturday.

Started at half past seven. Our walk has been on the left or east bank since crossing at Spuzzum.

We passed today Kanaka Bar & Hungarian Flat. At the latter place a store is kept by an intelligent Frenchman, Fontaine. He speaks English well. He has been twenty-seven years from home & has an aged mother who writes him long letters. He was born at [Le] Havre.

[At the] next bar or flat, the store [was] kept also by a Frenchman, who could not speak English.

Soon after [we] met two fine looking men, Germans, doing well. I practised German on them. One of them asked if I were a German!

We learned that at Big Bar an ounce a day, to the [man], was being made (16 dollars).

SOIL

We passed numerous blocks of conglomerate of trap & granite, moulded together evidently by action of water.

Arrived at Lytton [at] half past one, pitched tents on a flat over looking the River Fraser & Thompson & looking up the valley of the Fraser.

LYTTON

Lytton (*Koonotchin* in the native) is situated on a bench or flat at the junction or forks of the Fraser & Thompson. The country is more open than lower down & some small farms are here & there to be seen. The valley of the Fraser, looking north as I see from my tent door, reminds me of Wharfdale, on a large scale.

The immediate environs of Lytton are bare & dusty. The Sappers are laying out a town. I was much disappointed at the appearance of it, not a tree near for some hundreds of yards.

VISIT TO THE LYTTONISTS

After our meal we sallied forth. Mr. Crickmer & myself accompanied by Captain Ball the Magistrate. We went into all the stores & restaurants. The people were civil & offered hospitality. There was but one Englishman, of French there were several. Jews & Americans predominate. I spoke to miners & packers also.

A PRODIGAL

One man, the only Englishman I saw, was much excited by my call, or rather talk with him, for I met him in a store. His name is Hill, he was born in Milk Street in London. He spoke of his past life having been very wild. He had been wandering in all parts & living an Indian life. Spoke of having been at sea a good deal. [He] had taken interest in my appointment & had read with eagerness the account of the Mansion

House Meeting, [and] now was overcome with joy to see the man actually at Lytton, who had come over the rugged paths of the mountain trails, whose words he had read as uttered at the Mansion House [in London].

'But Sir,' he continued, 'when I read your speech, I said, how little he knows what he is coming to & the kind of people we are. What a strange thing that a gentleman & a pious man should leave his home comforts & friends in England to come out amongst us, he certainly had better stay there. I thought Sir, you were very foolish & would repent of it & that you [would] much better have left us as we are. But Sir, my heart is full, let me grasp your hand, it's all I can give, but it is a right down welcome, this is the happiest day of my life.'

Mr. Hill has a farm & provided us with abundance of excellent milk & wished us to help ourselves out of his garden to any vegetables we wanted.

TENTS IN DANGER

Lytton is a very windy spot. It blew rather harder than usual. It was with considerable difficulty we fixed our tents & during the night were by no means confident we should not have our encampment razed by the wind. A merciful God, however, protected us & though the storm rages.

ROMIST PRIEST AND INDIAN BAPTISMS

We have several times traced the progress before us of a Romist priest named Charles Vary. He goes to the villages & baptizes the heathen children.

On the road we met a man today, an Indian who asked us if we had to do with a little man who was high up the country riding upon a horse, a *Leplate* [*Le plete*, or priest], for he had been getting much money from the Indians. We understood him that he [the priest] had given the Indians much money, though we could hardly believe it. On enquiry of Captain Ball, he said it was the other way altogether & I, this evening, had a proof.

An Indian named Pallak came up to me & produced a paper, on which was written as follows,

'This Indian is very generous. After having baptized his children he gives to me two dollars.' 'Charles Vary'

I asked Pallak if he knew what was written, his answer was *Halo Kumtax* [*Halo Kumtuks*]. (I do not know).

Mr. Vary's great object appears to be to get as many baptized as possible & money from the Indians as he proceeds. We shall ere long hear that all the natives of British Columbia are baptized converts & that they support with generous liberality their own clergy! Yet, the fact is that the whole mass of the people are in utter darkness, are still bound by their old superstitions, & that the children are brought up heathens like their fathers.

At present the Indians are well paid for labour & being friendly disposed to the whites, may be worked upon by designing persons to give of their money of which they know not the value. The Indians are very fond of having a piece of paper with some recommendation of themselves upon it. They make great efforts to get a paper. It is not at all improbable the poor man may have given the two dollars in order to obtain the paper.

GOLD DUST TAKEN FOR COIN

In all business of trade gold dust is received in payment. This is the case the whole way up from Yale. I saw payments made to the Magistrate at Yale & in stores here. The rate in Yale was sixteen dollars the ounce, some merchants there have refused to receive it except at fifteen [dollars]. Here it is sixteen [dollars].

July 1, Sunday.

SUNDAY AT LYTTON

We had two services at the Court House. They were well attended considering the population & the character of the people as regards nation & creed. There were fourteen in the morning, twenty in the evening. The service was hearty. We had much singing & the cards containing ten hymns [were] distributed, [and] answered well. I preached in the morning upon the happy results of true religion from Romans 10:13-15, & in the evening upon prayer, explaining the Lord's Prayer. There was great attention. In the morning all but three were in shirt sleeves. No one but Captain Ball & my own party had prayer books. We had morning prayer & litany & the evening service. The Venite & Jubilate were chanted. Mr. Crickmer read prayers & led the singing.

A SCOFFER

Previous to the morning service Mr. Crickmer went through the town announcing it. One man asked if we were 'going to stand treat at the end.' Mr. Crickmer did not quite catch what he said & made him repeat it, which the man was rather ashamed to do. He was answered 'there will be a rich treat for those who have the taste to receive it.'

July 2, Monday.

PRICES AT LYTTON

Flour 20 cents a pound (10 shillings or 11 shillings, 8 pence per stone)
Beef 25 cents a pound (12 shillings, a half pence)
Potatoes 20 cents a pound
Preserved meat [in] tins, 2 pounds each, 2 dollars each or 8 shillings, 4 pence

TEMPORAL CONDITION OF THE INDIANS IMPROVED

There is now an abundance of work for the Indians, so much so as to induce many to give up their former method of living & live as the whites.

I was introduced, on Saturday, to two chiefs of the Thompson River Indians. One of them told me, Spintlum, before the whites came there were seasons when the salmon fishing failed & then hundreds & thousands of Indians died of starvation, but now he said, *Hyou Pack [Hyiu Pack], Hyou Chikamen [Hyiu Chickamin], Muck-muck Hyou [Muckamuck Hyiu],* plenty of packing, plenty of money, plenty of food.

PURCHASE OF TWO HORSES AT LYTTON— PREMIUM UPON PAPER MONEY, OR RATHER DRAFTS

At Lytton, I purchased two horses. The same which had faithfully carried out loads from Yale & of whose wonderful sure footedness we were certain. I had proposed obtaining animals here but found prices high. I therefore on the evening of Saturday sent to Mr. Hatch, our packer to learn if he would pack forwards with the same animals. He came to say he had sold them for ninety-five dollars apiece. I said I was sorry & would have given more. He went away & by & by returned to say, the man he sold them to would sell to me, for a profit of twenty dollars. I agreed. I thought, knowing the animals so well it was worth at least the additional sum, & if two packers had agreed to the value, a gentleman might well be satisfied.

I proposed to pay by cheque. Mr. Hatch wished the money in coin. I applied at the stores & found they would give a premium upon the draft, of four dollars upon the 210 dollars. This being an easy mode of their own payments having to pay a premium upon gold dust, etc. On mentioning the circumstance to Hatch, he of course preferred the paper & I doubt not got even a greater advantage by it.

INDIAN NAME FOR LYTTON

The Indian name for Lytton is *Koonotchin.*

July 3, Tuesday.

LYTTON

We left Lytton without regret. It is a cold, windy, unsheltered flat & the people more alien than any place I have been in. Captain Ball, the Magistrate lives with his constables in rough quarters. He seems a kind hearted man but his position cannot be a pleasant [one], except under the feeling that he is doing a duty. There is only one white female, a Mrs. Price, & she a person of ill reputation. Even the Indians were less inclined to visit us here, there were, however, but few to come, being dispersed over the country gathering berries (*Ollays*) [*Ollillie* or berries].

THE FERRY OVER THE THOMPSON

We left our ground about a quarter to eight & crossed [on] the ferry soon after. For my horses & party of five, I paid four dollars and fifty cents, eighteen shillings, a charge rarely made for clergymen.

COUNTRY FROM LYTTON, ORIGIN OF FLATS

The valley becomes wider generally, here & there are narrow gorges, which seem originally to have produced the flats, the river being pent up & raging & eddying up to the edge of the obstruction & depositing sand & gravel & gold upon the benches or flats. In course of time these obstructions were broken down, the pass between them is a canyon & the flats are left high & dry.

The mountain range runs on either side, the whole course of the river. Upon the flats which are wider, [and] thus high, are the spots for vegetation. Some flats are lower than others. There is frequently a double bank, steps as it were. The theory of origin would be quite consistent, in some places a higher portion of the cascade obstruction would go first, then the upper bank would be left & the process of deposit go on at a lower level, by & by another portion of the cascade or rapid would go & a second bench would be left dry. The process is still going on & the bars one day will be left by the river as the obstructions are worn away & the beds [take] a lower & an easier course.

INDIAN BURYING PLACES

I have passed many Indian burial places. These consist of upright poles, with cross bars upon which are suspended the favourite blankets or portion of dress of the deceased. Blankets, red, green, red & blue, we frequently see. These float in the wind above. Beneath are wooden square box like tombs upon which are carvings. Usually the figure of a man, dressed in hat, shirt & trousers with hands in his pockets is the principal attraction. Sometimes this figure has an actual musket in his hand, I saw one with two. He was a sportsman & might[y] hunter. The face is generally well painted (i.e., largely painted). The carving is rude, a favourite animal to delineate is the beaver, sometimes a bird. But nowhere have I seen the slightest trace of religious feeling, or idea of a future state, excepting alone this supply to the deceased of something he was fond of, a canoe for instance. They place the remains sometimes in a box above the surface of the ground, but also dig holes & bury many in the same spot.

At Lytton was a burying place where was the figure of a man, & near him, hanging up, the skin of a horse. This was to represent the son of Spintlum, the Indian Chief & the horse he loved to ride.

SPINTLUM'S FLAT

About ten or twelve miles from Lytton is Spintlum's Flat, a place where mining goes on. I called at a store, the only one, it was kept by a Dane who lives there with an Indian wife. He had been many years in the country. At this place the prices were,

Flour 23 dollars per 100 pounds
(11 shillings, half pence per pound,
13 shillings, 5 pence stone)
Bacon 45 cents per pound

INDIANS BERRY PICKING

We passed today several encampments of Indians. They are dispersed at present, picking berries which they preserve for winter use. We spoke to all. Being the heat of the day they were generally lying, resting in their huts, some [of] the women being busily employed making baskets.

A frequent question to us was, 'Are you Boston men?,' are you Americans that is. This was asked with an anxious look, not well pleased. On our replying we were King George men their faces brightened & all seemed happy. At one place they offered us berries. At one place we explained our desire to give instruction to the children. This they seemed quite to appreciate.

I hope these meetings with Indians in their present 'dispersion' may be a means of commencing a good understanding with them. They will recognize us by & by when we visit them at other seasons in their settled homes.

SCENERY BETWEEN LYTTON AND CAYOOSH

About eighteen miles from Lytton on the right bank is a group of very beautiful mountains. We passed through a region of much grass of the bunch sort, [one] rolling plain after another. Water, however, on our side (the left) [was] not abundant. We stopped at one place & found delicious fruit, a berry now ripe. It grows upon a shrubby tree about ten or twelve feet high, leaf between poplar & barberry, berries in clusters, shape like black current, size rather larger than black current, colour black with blueish tinge. Taste between plum & cherry.

HUMMINGBIRD

I saw today close to me as he settled upon a thistle, or rather hovered at one, a hummingbird. This is the second I have seen.

LOST OUR WAY

We had agreed after lunching at Spintlum's Flat to stop at the first best watering place.

Mr. Crickmer, William & myself were on before, the horses, Mr. Hatch & Sacher in the rear. We walked on a long way in vain trying to find a good spot, at length a trail took us towards the river & we came to a beautiful green place where we lay down waiting for our baggage. Time passed & we began to suspect a mistake. Enquiring of some Chinese, [they] gave us the information that our horses were not on before us on that [trail] but that the right & usual course was above, on the flats some 500 feet over our heads.

We ascended this trackless height & at length found the trail. We determined to hasten & try to overtake our horses which had no doubt passed, thinking we were on before. Whatever came we would push on to Foster's Bar where miners were living, should night [first] come on. After some time, to our joy, we saw a fire & my tent already pitched. I do not think a night was ever more thankfully passed.

Mr. Crickmer had run on before. A beautiful stream of water flowed close past our encampment.

CAMPING FOR THE NIGHT

The first thing done on coming to camping ground is to light a fire. This was done always by our Indian, Sacher. He darts off & returns speedily with just the right sort of wood & the fire is soon blazing. Sometimes from a noble log which lasts the night & next day too. Then the water is put on to boil.

William commences to prepare dinner or supper. Bread is generally one thing to be done, with flour & water & baking powder this operation is soon accomplished. Meanwhile, Sacher is sent forth for tent poles & stakes. He goes off to the thicket & returns with what is wanted. Then all assist in getting up the tents. Mine is generally first erected, so many willing hands engaged in it.

I then unfold my blankets, get the interior arranged & by this time our meal is ready. A tarpaulin or mackintosh is spread on the ground not far from the fire and as the sun sets & the cool air begins to blow we are thankfully drinking our tea & coffee & eating beans & fried bacon. On this journey so far our food has been principally salted provision. At Lytton we had fresh meat. The party sitting or rather lying down at the meal consists of Mr. Crickmer, William, Mr. Hatch the packer & myself. Sacher waits upon us & takes his own meal with great contentment afterwards. He likes coffee & sugar & bacon & bread. After returning thanks, sitting a while, & singing the evening hymn we retire to rest.

We three Englishmen each have our tent & blankets, the earth is our mattress, sheets we dream not of, a pillow is found by rolling up coats & clothing.

Mr. Hatch, a weather beaten American, prepares to sleep with his blankets under a tree without a tent & Sacher takes his single blanket & lies behind a log or where he is sheltered from the wind.

In the morning we rise early, get breakfast at half past six or seven & are off before eight. I have always continued to get a delicious bath before breakfast in the river or some stream near our encampment.

July 4, Wednesday.

INDIAN ATTENTION

On rising this morning I found the old Chief Spintlum & his son waiting to see me. Their encampment was near. He said he understood we were tired from yesterday's long walk & he hoped I would ride one of his horses to Cayoosh. Mr. Crickmer might have another. He suited his action to the word for the two horses were caught and fastened close to us during breakfast. I was certainly footsore, yet I was anxious to accomplish the journey on foot, especially as we all could not have horses & so I declined.

Last night when our packer & the Indians came to a stand, finding from the Indians [that] we had not passed, it was Spintlum's son who mounted his steed & flew away like the wind to scour the country for us, going more particularly to the lower trail Mr. Crickmer & I had got in. He overtook William & offered him his horse, to bring him in to the camp. There seemed to be in these acts a genuine feeling of kindness.

About midday we stopped to lunch beside a brook & under trees. Presently we heard shouts & on the hill, down which we had come, we saw two mounted Indians tearing down a most steep descent as if mad, shouting & singing. They were dressed fantastically in varied colours. It was old Spintlum & his son, the latter armed with a musket. They dashed up to us, got off & sat awhile. Then they bid us good-bye, shouted & tore away up a steep hill on before us. I think they had come to see if we were going on well & did not need their help.

MINERS FROM QUESNEL — SWEARING

[We] met three miners, [and] had [a] talk, one used oaths continually. I reproved him. He said it was enough to make a man swear to be disappointed after going a great distance. He took the reproof, however, good naturedly.

COUNTRY FROM FOSTER'S BAR

A fine succession of grassy flats, with, however, but few streams, except of course the river, not a mile off [in] any part. Towards Cayoosh there is a contraction of the [country].

THE SLIDE

We had far away heard of the slide. We were told we should have to go round by the Fountain, an extra distance of twelve miles in order to avoid this dangerous route. The path lay down the side of a mountain. At a point where the footing is narrow & when the descent is at once perpendicular on the inner side is a jutting rock. If an animal hits his pack against this he loses his footing & must go over & be lost, down to the depths. The packers therefore avoid this. The chief difficulty is the impossibility of recovery of footing if once off balance & certain destruction of [the] animal. Mules not infrequently lose their footing & roll over & down but then they pick themselves up again & are not killed. Here the risk is great, the destruction in case of [a] slip, certain. We, however, risked this formidable spot & our faithful beasts came safely through.

CATTLE

Towards Cayoosh we were gladdened by the sight of cattle, & even cows in milk. Horses too were browsing upon the grass.

July 5, Thursday.

Visited by Mr. A. MacDonald, [the] Hudson's Bay Company agent, & his brother who keeps the ferry. Also [visited] by Mr. Elwyn, the Magistrate of Cayoosh.

It had rained in the night. I dined with Mr. Elwyn & Mr. Crickmer at a restaurant in Cayoosh where we had green peas & salad, a pleasing change.

Mr. Elwyn tells me of a murder at Alexandria. An Irishman had been 'charging' about that place several days when he attacked a Frenchman & after one or two shots he killed him. The storekeeper took him into custody but, there being no one in authority & no assurance of their expenses being repaid, they let him go. Mr. Elwyn, as soon as he heard, having application from them, sent a constable who would find the man gone. The place is not, however, within his jurisdiction & not long since he was reproved for doing duty in that direction.

One man came 200 miles to record a claim.

At Quesnel gambling goes on to a fearful extent.

INDIANS ON HORSEBACK

This evening a party of equestrian Indians rode up to my camp. Two females, very plain young women, & two young men. The ladies were riding as men. Their dresses were gay, European manufacture, bright colours. Their horses had bells. They came up at full gallop & they tore away in like style.

July 6, Friday.

I was occupied the greater part of this day in writing.

CHAPTER 6

They said they meant to settle in this country
7 July – 22 July

July 7, Saturday.

[I] crossed over & met Mr. Sheepshanks, arranged for services tomorrow on both sides of the river [and] changed my camp to the Cayoosh side. Visited people.

VISIT TO MINERS—READINESS TO ATTEND SERVICE

I went to Canada Flat, where amongst others, is a company of seven Englishmen. They live in two log huts. An elderly man named Martin is their captain. They greatly welcomed me. Several came from Cornwall. They had all worked in California. When I spoke about the service for tomorrow they expressed pleasure & said earnestly 'it is fourteen years since some of us have attended service.' Another miner told Mr. Elwyn, when he mentioned the service, that he had not been in a place of worship for ten years & that he would gladly come. One of these miners on Canada Flat is named Barker, he comes from Norfolk & used to ply on the river between Cambridgeshire & Lynn. The railway sent him, he says, to America. He was very glad to talk about old England. I knew, of course well, some of the places he most fondly remembered. He had not written for years & no letters now came to him. Yet, he has a daughter whom he had not seen since she was two years old. That was fourteen years ago. I urged him to write. He said he would. He hope[s] yet to go back to the old country.

All these men were at service the following day.

CAYOOSH

This point of the Fraser is a wide plateau of benches, however, rising like steps up the river, but each covered with grass. Here is an entrance from a lower part of the Fraser through the Cascade range on the right bank. Two small streams called Lillooet & Cayoosh fall into the main stream from that opening. A chain of lakes connects with the Harrison River.

This junction of two main routes, the only known opening at present into the upper country, renders Cayoosh of importance. There is also much mining in the neighbourhood.

179

The scenery is very beautiful, the view from Cayoosh down the river with mountains on one side & green slopes & trees & the plateau which looks like a park on the other, [is] particularly pleasing.

The soil is better than it is lower down, gardens flourish. Oats & barley are [. . .] in full ear. It does not pay however, to grow these for the grain, but only for the hay, [the] expense of threshing etc. being too great.

ORIGIN OF THE NAME CAYOOSH

A packer named Hutchinson lost some Cayoosh horses in the stream falling in here. He named it Cayoosh. Cayoosh is a district on the river Columbia in American territory. The little stream has since gone by that name & probably the namers of the new town, supposing it the Indian name for the locality, considered it appropriate.

INDIAN NAMES FOR CAYOOSH LOCALITY

The Indian name for the spot where now stands,

Cayoosh is	*Schadtk*
For the opposite side	*Nikokomanna*
Cayoosh River	*Tsammuk*
Lillooet River	*Skumkain*

July 8, Sunday.

SUNDAY AT CAYOOSH—INDIANS AT SERVICE—CHILHOVSELS

In the morning we had divine service in an upper room of a new store belonging to a Frenchman & a Romanist. The room was well filled, principally by miners. The prayers were read by Mr. Sheepshanks. I preached from Matthew 13, on 'The Hid Treasure.' There was much attention. The door was glorified with Indians. Amongst others [there] came in a remarkably fine Indian. He was the chief of the tribes hereabout, more particularly of the Fountain Indians. He was dressed in crimson & black. His fine flowing black hair hung over his shoulders. He stood up & faced me with great intelligence the whole time. After service he & other Indians remained. He shook hands & said in the Chinook, 'good, good,' pointed to Mr. Sheepshanks & then to me & repeated, 'good, good.' I asked him if he knew what we had been doing. He said yes & pointed upwards, saying *Sackally Tyhee Papa* [*Saghalie Tyee Papa*, Oh Mighty Great Chief Father]. He also crossed himself. The Romanists have from time to time visited these Indians. I showed him the Bible & told him it was the word, the *wahweh* of the *Saghalie Tyee*

Papa. As far as I can trace yet with these poor people, though they have gained an idea of the supreme being, or perhaps have never lost that, they know nothing of Jesus Christ and the Bible. These two are new topics. Rome having taught them no doubt of the Virgin.

Chilhovsels (the chief's name) asked if we were going to have service again. We told him, yes, on the other side in the evening. He said he should come. In the evening, as we were waiting by the river for the boat, we heard a loud & wild shout far up on the mountain, over our head[s]. I looked & there on a point overhanging the precipice was Chilhovsels on horseback. He waved his [plumed] cap & shouted & disappeared. By & by he was with us in the boat, pulling an oar over the dangerous current. He went with us to the service, which was held in a saloon kept by a person named Boyle.

We had a goodly attendance. There were several Indians. I preached upon the 'power of the gospel to elevate the character of man' from Colossians 3:1 & 'If ye then be risen with Christ.'

Chilhovsels lingered at the door & bid us goodbye.

After service, Mr. Neufelder, a German, a respectable storekeeper expressed himself much pleased. He has been formerly, if not now, a Jew. He thought a deep impression had been made.

I asked Mr. Boyle, the keeper of the saloon, if he could without inconvenience allow the room for Sunday next. 'I shall be delighted, Sir. I only wish you were going to be here many Sundays.'

July 9, Monday.

CAYOOSH — GARDENS AND FIELDS

I visited excellent gardens in great fertility, potatoes remarkably luxuriant, also cabbages, tomatoes, carrots, turnips, onions & indeed all vegetables.

Several fields also of barley & oats, also Indian corn.

SETON LAKE

I rode out this evening with Mr. Elwyn & Mr. Sheepshanks to Seton Lake. The way to it is along a valley of two small rivers called Lillooet & Cayoosh, but more properly *Skumkain* & *Tsammuk*. On either side the mountain heights rose up in picturesque grandeur. Green foliage lined the banks of the rivers which flowed parallel to each other, the water was of the clearest conceivable. The lake is eighteen miles long. We rode to the head. It is severe in scenery. A steamboat run plies daily upon this portion of the route from Douglas. The evening was lovely.

July 10, Tuesday.

I was visited in my tent by Indians. They like a chat but never have an idea of going away. An elderly man & his nephew were my first visitors. I got words from them, for instance the numerals of the dialect of this place. They differ considerably from the numerals of the Komtchin [Kumcheen] & Quayome Indians, although [they are] sufficiently similar to prove the two dialects to be the same language.

Numbers:

2	[in] Kumcheen	[is]	*Shayah,*	[in] Cayoosh	[is]	*Auneras*
4	"		*Mosh*	"		*Khogin*
9	"		*Tempspayah*	"		*Kumpalaman*
10	"		*Sperraxh*	"		*Kump*

whereas

1	[in] Kumcheen	[is]	*Payah*	[in] Cayoosh	[is]	*Palah*
3	"		*Kartlash*	"		*Kartlosh*
5	"		*Cheixt*	"		*chelixt*
6	"		*Clarkamuset*	"		*Clarkamuset*
7	"		*Chulekah*	"		*Chutelakah*
8	"		*Peops*	"		*Pelopest*

I next received a visit from Chilhovsels, the chief of the Fountain Indians. He is a fine Indian, the same who came to our services on Sunday. I got from him the Indian name for God, that is, it was Indian for *Saghalie Tyee Papa,* the Chinook for the Almighty. *Skatzalkeetlah,* was above, was great, was good, saw us, but we could not see him. I have yet to find out what their ideas & traditions are on this subject.

The chief sat with me some time & expressed his great delight & hoped I should come again & others come too. I am sure his ideas were reverent & that he recognized that a mission of higher good had come to his people.

We had fixed this evening for a meeting of the Indians of this place. At half past six they began to assemble. As they came up all advanced to shake hands & many of them made the sign of the cross on the face & breast. The children too were brought & their little hands were all held out to be touched.

They then seated themselves in a ring round Mr. Sheepshanks & myself. Every now & then one would start up & shout towards the village for some stray Indian that had not yet come & once an Indian darted off & returned with several [others].

There was one very old man with silvery hair. He was the village chief. His name was Tsualtoc. Two others were prominent in repeating what was said & interpreting.

I addressed them, told them who I was, why I had come, showed them the Bible, [and] told them it was the word of God. We knew what it contained, they did not. There was a message of love to them as well as to us. We wished them to know [the] message from their heavenly Father. There were many friends of the Indian in King George land, who wished the Indians to know the love of their God & to understand his word. I then spoke to them of God, of his attributes. I pointed out that all were sinners & that our good God was justly angry & then told of the love & work of Christ. They must accept the mercy of God in Christ. They must repent. They must be good, else after death the wicked would be punished. Jesus Christ invited all to come to Him, Indians, King George men, Boston men. He loved all. He died for all. I showed them of the death & resurrection & ascension of Christ & that he is alone our friend & has provided a place for the righteous.

Two points I especially pressed which they might remember as distinctive of our visit, in contrast to Roman [Catholic] teaching. I spoke much of Christ, made them repeat over & over the name of Jesus, Jesus is their friend, & secondly, I held up to them, in my hand, the Bible, the word of God & by sign & language expressed the value with which we hold it.

These poor people frequently became much moved, discussed vehemently what was said, so I had occasionally to pause & I believe [they] received true impressions notwithstanding our stammering lips.

Mr. Sheepshanks followed & made an effective address, after which I again spoke to them & repeated the Lord's Prayer which I had translated into Chinook & which they repeated after me. I also spoke about the education of their children. We then sang the evening hymn, which always impresses them & in which tonight they mingled their voices.

Some of the town's people came & listened & were interested. Miners stopped as they passed & Chinese had an opportunity of being reminded there was a God.

For two hours the interest did not for an instant flag. None moved till we suggested it was time to go to rest. Then, one by one, all came & shook hands & still lingered round till we ourselves left the spot.

July 11, Wednesday.

[I] rode to Bridge River about four miles up. This stream flows into the Fraser on the right bank. It differs from all other streams I have seen which flow into the Fraser by being thick & milky. The Thompson & others are singularly clear & transparent.

The Indian name for Bridge River is *Hoichton.* We visited the Indians there & found them intelligent. Here, as elsewhere at present, they are engaged picking the service berry. These they dry over a fire & form them into cakes which they preserve for winter food. We had rain in the evening.

At Bridge River the store is kept by a German.

July 12, Thursday.

THE FOUNTAIN — HOSPITALITY OF AN INDIAN

At twelve-thirty started for the Fountain. This spot on the river about seven miles north on the left bank is where the road from Lytton joins that from Cayoosh for the upper country. The Fountain (so called from a Frenchman) is an open plain. Here were three houses. One [was] a store kept by an Italian named Lorenzo Littora. Mr. Elwyn & Mr. Sheepshanks accompanied me. Lorenzo gave us luncheon, bread, cheese, radishes, raisins, [and] claret and would make no charge.

SPOKAN GARRY'S HORSE

I have before mentioned this Indian. Curious enough, I, this day, rode one of his horses. Mr. Dallas, of the Hudson's Bay Company, recently visited Colville. In that neighbourhood are the Spokan, or Spogan Indians of whom Spokan Garry is chief. The latter desired to make a present to Mr. Dallas & bid him select one of the best of his horses. The fleetest was chosen. Mr. Dallas brought him this far & could not bring him on, so sold him to Mr. McDonald who this day allowed me the use of him.

PACKERS

Packing is one of the most lucrative employments. A train of twelve or eighteen horses, or mules, very soon pays the expenses of first cost & then great profits are made. The packers are principally Mexicans. There are, however, many Americans.

I met this day a train under the conduct of a very old looking dust begrimed packer. He had a broken in, slouched, wide awake [manner?]. I was introduced to him. His speech showed him to be an educated English gentleman. A few years since he was a smart officer with his regiment in Canada. He came to California where he followed packing. He now packs on British soil with the best horse pack in the colony. Mr. Elwyn told me the train was purchased a few months since, he has an interest in the concern himself. It has already realized its original cost.

184

With Mr. Meason is Mr. Hankin, a fine young man, well educated from the neighbourhood of [. . .].

ROMIST PRIESTS AND BAPTISM

I have mentioned that Romist Priests go about baptizing the children of the heathen. Mr. MacDonald of the ferry here told me today that the French Priest, [named] Vary, who was lately here, spoke of his anxiety to baptize all the children. There was one in particular, the parents were not willing he should do so. He was scheming how he could contrive to get hold of the child by any means & in talking of it said with much anxiety, 'You know if I do not baptize it, it will go to hell.'

Much rain at night.

July 13, Friday.

INDIANS AT CAYOOSH

Most of the morning I have had Indians at my tent. Two women complained of the treatment they receive from Americans. They say the evil men come & steal away even the wives in the face of their husbands, for evil purposes. They struggle & they cry but frequently it is of no avail. I told them to appeal to the English Magistrate. He would be their friend & not allow such conduct. They said they knew he was their friend.

INDIAN IDEAS OF GOD—THE SUN

Most of the Indians profess to [know] of the *Saghalie Tyee Papa*, they point upwards. They say he sees all, is all wise & strong & good & never dies. I found out today from two Indians of this place [that] *Skatzalkeetlah* is all the same as *Squagash Snokum*, or the sun. The sun is the *Saghalie Tyee Papa. Klanamton*, the moon, is his wife & the stars their children.

Two Indians of the Shuswap tribe also visited me. Their word for the *Saghalie Tyee* is *Kardchicht*. They also said that was all the same for the sun—viz *Squilqualt*.

INDIAN IDEAS AS TO THE DEAD

One woman had lost her father & mother & children. They were dead & in the earth. I asked where they were. Did she know whither they were gone? She did not know, only they were gone *kukkow*, very far.

INTEMPERANCE

A good deal of the talk of my two female friends was about husbands beating & killing their wives. They said whisky was the great cause. One of them, however, was a good husband, his name was 'James.'

'Boston man, very bad. They work the river & then no salmon & no food for Indians.' I said further down was plenty of work for Indians, 'plenty money, plenty food.' It was not so here they said.

DISLIKE OF INDIAN WOMEN TO POLYGAMY

My two visitors were very full of their grievances as to polygamy. They said nothing came of it but fight, fight & sometimes murder.

I visited in the afternoon & evening various people, a Jew, a Swede, a German, & discoursed with many.

July 14, Saturday.

Engaged most of the day in writing, weather fine, slight shower.

July 15, Sunday.

SECOND SUNDAY AT CAYOOSH

Divine service [was held] in a saloon at Nikokomanna [Nicoamen], the opposite side of the river to Cayoosh, or as it is called by Americans, Parsonsville from an American storekeeper who built the first house. We had a fair attendance, though not so good as the Sunday before when the service was in the evening. One only of the female sex attended, the only white person in fact living there, a nice person, Mrs. Neufelder. The only other [woman] lived at a little distance. Her husband was present. There were, however, Indian women as well as Indian men. This is the case with all our services.

In the evening we had a good attendance at Cayoosh. Every seat was occupied, some stood & some sat on the ground. It was held in a large upper room. The singing was shared by a greater number than last Sunday. There was no female. The men were mostly miners & their attention was great. I took for my subject prayer & explained the Lord's Prayer (Matthew 6:9, etc.). In the morning I preached from I Corinthians 15:55, etc. [on] death, sin & victory.

THE FOUNTAIN INDIANS — PREACHING AT NICOAMEN

After divine service in the morning, Chilhovsels, his wives & other Indians desired us to speak to them. They had come on purpose to meet us. We also expected Indians from another direction, led by an Indian named McKenzie.

Bye & bye all were assembled. It was under a tree on rising ground. They took their seats in a circle. One spread a blanket in the midst, for us to sit upon. Chilhovsels dressed picturesquely in scarlet & black, sat in a prominent place opposite.

We commenced by singing two verses of the Hundredth Psalm. I explained first the nature of the act. I then offered up a prayer that our Heavenly Father would look with blessing upon our feeble efforts, & overrule our stammering speech to convey some leading points of saving truth to these benighted children & draw them to his dear son through our ministry. At the close a beautiful & deep impression rested upon the assembled multitude. Every eye was closed, as in prayer & so continued until we spoke.

I then addressed them. I told them who I was, [and about] my mission. I showed them of their Heavenly Father, that 'in him they live & move' & have all things, that he made the sun, the moon, the stars, the mountains, the water & all men. That man is sinful, that God in mercy sent his son who died to save us, of that blessed one, his coming, his death, his resurrection, ascension, his present interest in us, his invitation & love & all. I showed sins must be put away, spoke of the dead, & the judgement.

Mr. Sheepshanks also addressed them & I concluded by a sort of summing up & all present one by one, children & elders, men & women repeated Jesus *ammah nsugua*, 'Jesus the good friend.' Then all repeated it together & they shouted, *ammah ammah-kloshe kloshe*, 'good good.' I then addressed the Chief Chilhovsels, very solemnly & said, 'all these people are your children, you call all the tribe your children. I want you & all these to become the children of Jesus. You are their earthly chief & father, be you & they, the loving & obedient children of Jesus your heavenly chief & father. Mr. Sheepshanks & I look to Jesus, we are his children, be you his children too. Then one day we shall all dwell together in heaven & there will be only one language.'

I am sure our addresses made an impression upon these interesting people, especially upon the thoughtful Chilhovsels. I wish indeed I had a missionary to leave amongst them. The example of the white men amongst them is sad & they need every help. They are a simple people as yet, but the youth alas are growing up, of both sexes, precocious in vice.

EXPLAINING THE ECLIPSE TO INDIANS

We were with the Indians several hours. In the course of the afternoon I explained to them the eclipse of the sun which is to take place on Wednesday. Great discussion ensued. One old chief, LeCrow, from Kamloops of the Shuswap tribes, was very eloquent & exhibited fine gesture. He spoke another language but many present understood him. I also had got a few words in [stock].

Of course we directed them from nature up to nature's God, & while showing our superior knowledge pointed out the blessings of the knowledge of God which we also possessed. I shall be curious to see how the Indians receive the eclipse.

July 16, Monday.

Indians visited my tent today & I got more words. [The] express came in, [I] received letters from England. Rode in the evening with Mr. Elwyn, Mr. Trutch & Mr. Sheepshanks. Afterwards [I] walked to the mouth of the Cayoosh.

July 17, Tuesday.

Visited the Indian village of Shadtke. The Indians were drying their service berries. A woman brought us a plate full of excellent raspberries. All came & shook hands.

PURCHASE OF TWO HORSES AT CAYOOSH

Mr. Elwyn very kindly undertook to buy me two horses. A cream & a chestnut were the result of the transaction, at 100 dollars the former, 70 dollars the latter.

LIVERPOOL JACK

A man of notorious character, a miner, of the nickname of Liverpool Jack was firing gunpowder in honour of the fourth of July. He rammed powder into a tree, stopped it with a plug & then recklessly fired it with his cigar. The plug struck him & knocked him down. It was thought his skull was fractured. To the astonishment of everybody poor Jack began to pray earnestly to God, to have mercy upon his soul & to pardon his many sins. The fervour with which this prodigal in his distress turned to his God appears to have made an impression. I enquired after him hoping to see him, but he was gone to [New] Westminster where he might be able to get good medical advice. I trust we may yet recover him & that this incident may bring him humbled & a penitent to his Saviour.

FRENCH MINERS

I visited Canada Bar[Flat]. [In the] first cabin, two Frenchmen [were] reading French newspapers outside their door. They placed seats for Mr. Sheepshanks & myself. They said they meant to settle in this country. They were Catholics R[oman] but no priest had ever visited them. We spoke of the cutting off from religion which was incidental to the miners' life. They received our remarks with respect. My belief is many of these French & others from R[oman] Catholic countries might be won to pure Christianity by a faithful & vigorous ministry.

MINERS OFFERING TO SUPPORT A MINISTER

I next visited a company of Englishmen. They are fine fellows. They had attended the service at Cayoosh. They had been in California & when they were in the mines had had no means of grace. I spoke of my desire to send a clergyman. They said they truly wished I might do so. The miners generally would be glad & they would willingly help towards his support. One man said, 'yes if we had a minister the place would look more like home.' Tears filled his eyes when he talked of home. When I bid them goodbye they said, 'we hope Sir you will send us a minister & we will all help to support him.'

These hearty fellows were about to sit down to supper after a hard day's work. The weather had been hot & they looked fagged. Yet they would have us wait & talk & pressed us much to have some supper with them.

CHILHOVSELS

On our way to the mining bars this evening we met three horsemen coming towards Cayoosh at a tearing pace. They were Indians. Two who came on first at once pulled up & greeted us with enthusiasm. One we knew, the other was a fine boy of about thirteen. The latter told us he was the son of Chilhovsels to whom he pointed as coming up on the third horse. Chilhovsels took off his cap & greeted us affectionately. The happiness of these three Indians in meeting us was remarkable. The boy was especially interesting, as though Chilhovsels had told his children & friends to regard us highly. As we parted the Chief said his heart went with us & hoped our heart would follow him.

There is something striking in Chilhovsels. He is thoughtful & benign in countenance. Two Indians were with me yesterday who [were] full of the good points of this chief. 'Other chiefs often got angry, there was Swegels, the Chief of the Hoichton Indians, who beat & sometimes killed his people, but Chilhovsels was never angry & prayed often to the Almighty Father.'

July 18, Wednesday.

LEAVE TAKING BY INDIANS AT CAYOOSH

My camp this morning was surrounded with Indians come to see me off. A party of four equestrians came several miles for the same purpose. For two or three hours they waited & came down to the water side & wished us goodbye. There were women also & children. These went away first. One man came to my tent door & said the women were going away & wished to see me. They had been there, I should [think] three hours. I shook hands with all. They brought also their children & held them up for me to shake their little hands. We crossed the ferry. Our horses had

189

been swum [across] earlier. Here was Chilhovsels waiting to say good-bye. After packing & saddling our four horses I found also the wives & children of Chilhovsels also waiting. These had all come some distance & had given up work for the time, which was of consequence to them.

ACCIDENT IN PACKING HORSES

All merchandise is carried here upon pack horses. The only exception being that Indians also carry goods. Pack mules carry the heaviest loads. I saw mules today packed with nearly 400 pounds of goods. There is great art in packing. Bulk is the thing to avoid. If a pack is in small compass, much more can be carried than when the contrary. My packer on this occasion was a young man not very well up to the art. Several experienced packers were engaged at the ferry packing their own animals & two very kindly & disinterestedly gave my man very valuable aid & hints. One of them was pulling a rope with all his might, attached to the pack of one of my horses, when it broke, & he was precipitated back under the feet of another of my animals which, frightened, started & kicked. The kick was with great force, but happily it missed the head & struck the back, the shoulder of the worthy packer. I felt much grieved. I left him sitting down. I spoke to him of the narrow escape he had had; for had the blow struck the head, a fractured skull must have resulted & how thankful, therefore, we should be to Almighty God. He was manly & patient. I could not help, however, thinking much about him all day. How near we continually are to eternity. Yet how continually is the gracious hand & care of our heavenly Father ready to avert from us many an evil.

We did not get clear away till two o'clock. The weather was very hot & at about five we reached a camping ground on the river where we settled for the night.

A MINER AND THE MEANS OF GRACE

As I was breaking up camp, amongst others who drew near was a gold miner. He was well spoken & friendly. He came to say he wished me all success. This was said heartily. He told me that the sermon on Sunday was the first he had heard for ten years. I said, 'I am sure you felt the occasion one deeply interesting to you.' He said, 'indeed sir it was.' I spoke about sending a clergyman. He said there ought to be one amongst them & he should rejoice to see him.

July 19, Thursday.

BREAKING UP CAMP

Camp life is peculiar. Early hours is our order of the day. Our rule is to endeavour to have breakfast at six & to get away about seven in order to have cool hours for travelling. As we always camp by a stream, one of the first comforts of the day to me is a bathe. Our Indian makes the fire. The packer looks after the horses. This morning we had a difficulty. One of our horses refused to be caught, so we had to hunt him with the lasso. Our Indian, Inlasket, at length caught him & rode him into the camp in triumph. William cooks & attends to the provisions & such important matters. My Chaplain & I take down the tents, strap & tie up the blankets, tents, [and] baggage in their respective wrappers. Then, while the packer & the Indian [are] arranging the pack horses, we saddle the others & fit on saddle bags & such like accoutrements. Then a walk round to see that nothing be left & we are off, a few Indians generally wishing us goodbye.

We left our ground today about eight. It was the same road I had recently passed. We came to the famous 'slide.' The terror of packers, who usually avoid it, & prefer a round of twelve miles by the Fountain rather than risk the loss of a mule. We stopped to dine about twelve at a refreshing creek beyond the slide, & camped about six. Weather fine, but warm.

July 20, Friday.

Left our camp at eight. Stopped for dinner at one [o'clock], at a creek beyond Spintlum's Flat, [then at] the Ten Mile House & next, after the rocky ridge. At a half past three, we left this spot & reached Lytton at about seven.

PACK HORSE RUNNING OFF

One of our pack horses, having been passed by an Indian who was going at a canter, took to the same speed, his load notwithstanding. A very delicate bit of path was no hinderance. Though there was hardly footing, in some places not six inches & this upon a moving & loose precipitous side of a mountain, he galloped as though upon a broad road. As was to be expected, he lost his footing & went down the side. The packer expected to see him roll over & packs & all to be dashed in atoms. Marvellous to say he recovered himself & pack & all regained the narrow ledge upon which he again proceeded to canter. I was on before [him]. He came up to me. I was asked to stop him. I did this by filling up the path with my horse & he came to a stand & we thought all was right. Presently, however, he jumped on the bank above & darted ahead. Later on he set off in full gallop. Again, [the pack horse] came in contact with a tree which knocked his load & scattered provisions, carpet bags & pots & pans on the way & then continued for some distance where we found him quietly feeding. He allowed himself to be caught, ridden back, packed again &, with some care on our part, came safely on the rest of the way.

PLANTS

I regret much my ignorance of botany. Amongst other plants & shrubs we have seen, clematis, michaelmas daisy, a [. . .] daisy, cactus, syringa. The service berry has been plentiful, also I have had brought me excellent raspberries. There is also a small wild cherry & gooseberry. On our road & at Cayoosh prices of most things have been high. At Cayoosh,

Bacon	45 & 50 cents per pound
Flour	16 cents per pound
Coffee	50 cents per pound
Sugar	37½ cents per pound
Beef	20 to 25 cents per pound
Milk	12½ cents per pint

Yet all this is considered cheap, considering what prices were.

ROMIST BAPTISMS OF HEATHEN CHILDREN

At Cayoosh (east side) I saw a little girl about eight years old whose parent showed me a certificate of her Baptism, 'Rosalie, Baptized May 18, 1860 by C. Vary.' So not only infants, but quick children, are baptized without preparation beforehand or care that they be brought up Christians.

LYTTON—JULY 20, 1860

Soon after our arrival Captain Ball, the Magistrate [of Lytton], & Mr. Elwyn, the Magistrate of Cayoosh, now on a visit, came to see us & helped to put up my tent. It was late before we were fairly encamped & took our evening meal. We felt thankful, however, for the mercy we had experienced in the journey & having sung the evening hymn retired gladly to rest.

July 21, Saturday.

I had a delicious bathe in the clear waters of the Thompson. I, at the same time, washed several articles of clothing, for in starting before [. . .] this [journey] I had disencumbered myself of every piece of clothing I could possibly dispense with & consequently require the employment of my skill in the ablutionary art the oftener.

The morning was very hot & the only refuge, & that but slight, from the heat & where most air could be got was [at] my tent door. I sat in the tent door in the heat of the day. So did Abraham in a strange land far from the house of his birth. How great the honour to be called in the Providence of God to the work of the ministry in this distant land. Yet how utterly insufficient are we for the work. As I sit in my tent door I see souls immortal pass before me. There is a pathway leading to the ferry. By far the greater number are Chinese, at least 100 have passed by this morning, then Indians, then miners of all nations. That which all are least disposed to listen to is the [purport?] of my mission. Then the variety of language increases the difficulty. [. . .] believing [. . .] religion can never flourish here. The Lord will never establish his kingdom here, so Abraham might have argued. It is the same faith which sustained him that alone can sustain us. So that our earnest prayer must be, 'Lord increase my faith.' Then in due time the mountains of difficulty shall vanish & 'a highway shall be made' for the Lord & His Christ.

BIRDS SEEN

Columbia does not abound in the feathered tribe. I have seen, however, eagles, hawks, rooks, jays, grouse, duck, loons, robins (as large as blackbirds & good eating) & hummingbirds.

LIBERAL ROMANIST

At Cayoosh our service was held in the house of a French Roman Catholic. It was just built, but not yet occupied. The place was a large upper room, unfurnished. I thanked him afterwards & he said he was very happy to have been able to accommodate me.

INDIAN RELICS

Captain Ball presented to me two curiosities. An Indian God & an instrument of war, both of stone. I asked an Indian what they were. He said one was the *Tyee* above, pointing upwards. The other was used formerly by the Thompson or Kumcheen Indians in warfare against the Lillooet Indians when the latter came against them. These two relics were found down the river about eight miles hence.

PRICE OF BEEF, ETC. [AT LYTTON]

Beef is sold here at 25 cents [per] pound. A fat ox, or rather an ox sufficiently fat to kill, is sold here at 40 dollars weighing 400 pounds, having been driven from Oregon.

Flour	19 cents [per] pound
Bacon	45 cents [per] pound
Sugar	[omitted]
Milk	12½ cents [per] pint

It is difficult to get an Indian, at this time, to work at any price. This is their berry season, with which the country abounds. Salmon too is beginning to come in. Before I started, a number of Indians were about at the ferry at Cayoosh, but none would go. At length, a youth would go, for five dollars & his food, to Lytton. This was 8/- a day, & food!

July 22, Sunday.

Very hot. Ninety-four [degrees] in [the] shade. Service [was held] at [the] Court House [in the] morning at ten thirty, about ten present. Mr. Sheepshanks read prayers, morning prayer, second lesson, litany. I preached from Luke 16:9. Evening service [was] at eight, but a very small congregation indeed.

CHINESE ON SUNDAYS

I observed today the Chinese generally at work on the bars. I had not seen this at Cayoosh. I understand, from a Chinese merchant, an American, that they only work when very hard set for money to buy food with.

MURDERS AMONGST MINERS

At Alexandria recently a gold miner having had success was some days 'charging about,' as the cant expression is, when he quarrelled with a Frenchman & after two or three shots wounded him severely. He was taken into custody but let off, there being no magistrate or constable, & the storekeepers did not wish to be responsible. This occurred a week or two since.

Last week up the Thompson forty miles, two friends were at work, partners in a gold claim. They quarrelled, one took out a knife, another a revolver. Barr was killed by Patten's revolver & the latter has escaped.

QUESNEL MINES — CARIBOO

Mr. David Potts, now at Lytton states he has part of a claim at Cariboo. He & three others took out in one day forty-three ounces. This was the best day they had. They frequently took out two ounces to the man. Captain Ball says he can be relied on.

CHAPTER 7

*Nothing would have opened this tract
except its mineral produce. It would drive back
the sturdiest traveller*

23 July – 8 August

July 23, Monday.

[We] rose at half past three. Left Lytton at six-thirty, got on but slowly [and] dined about one [o'clock], at a spot by a considerable creek, about seven miles from Lytton.

Mr. Sheepshanks & I pushed on with one of the pack animals. After proceeding some distance, we perceived a horse galloping after us. It was our other pack horse. He had run off, not liking to be separated from his companion. The ropes were hanging to him but his burden had been knocked away.

CHINESE AND INDIANS

While we waited for the reloading of our runaway pack we entered into conversation with Indians who came forth to greet us as chiefs & ministers of God. There were two old men & some little children. A Chinaman came up. He could speak a little English & said he was a headman. There was something more pleasing about him than usual with the Chinese & this notwithstanding his tartar countenance. The Indians look upon him with an evident sense of their own superiority. It was amusing to see their patronizing manner when they spoke to 'John Chinaman.' It is true they have the Chinese in great contempt. Both races, however, respect ourselves. It was an interesting circumstance that missionaries from the Church of England should be sitting in the midst of Chinese & Indians in that wild spot, seeking an entrance within their hearts for the saving faith of Jesus. How much, on such occasions, can one realize the one love of God for all & the bond of union for time & eternity. Christ is unto all nations.

We camped at night on the same spot I had occupied on the twenty-ninth of June. It came on to rain & poured heavily during the night. There was thunder & a great wind. Our merciful God preserved us safe.

July 24, Tuesday.

Rose at half past four. Off at eight. Crossed the Jackass Mountain by the summit. I had gone round before & intended to do so again though pack animals do not usually take that route, which is dangerous. Not being up with the rest when the road diverged, my packer took the safer trail & mounted the summit, by which however we were delayed in our progress. We dined at Ah Soo's bridge & stayed from one to four. The weather was very hot.

HALFWAY HOUSE

At the Halfway House the people received us kindly. There are several houses, & mining flats with houses also, gardens too, [and] a butcher's shop. We got meat & vegetables.

AN ASSURING REMARK

Our animals were frequently admired. Today the butcher particularly notice[d] the 'rigging.' 'Sir, do you mean to say you travel without revolvers?' 'Oh yes,' said I. 'Sir, I consider that very rash.'

STOREKEEPER AT THE HALFWAY HOUSE

One of the storekeepers is a young man of pleasing manner. He told me Mr. Crickmer, in passing back, had given them a service which was highly appreciated & attended by some twenty men. He said he always liked to attend such opportunities & was much pleased at the discourse. He is an American & I should think would always help us & give notice of services, if we at any time could let him know when about to pass that way.

We camped about two miles further on, at our old ground where our conference took place with Wahilah, Chief of the Quayomes.

INDIANS AT KPALTHOO

I had a talk with Indians here. This is the spot where I met Wahilah. One worthy Indian when he heard we wanted salmon went & fetched some, refusing to take money for it. His mother came also & presented a basket of berries. I had met this Indian before. He is a friend of Sacher.

AN AWKWARD SURPRISE

During the evening I went out to bathe. The spot was a lovely one. As I was sitting upon the brink of the stream I looked up & there stood before me a sinister looking Indian with a brandished large knife in his hand. He stood there & watched my proceedings. I was considerably startled, but concealed my surprise as well as I could, & told him who I was & particularly that I was a King George man. He was very black & I told him I thought it would be a very good thing if he were to wash a little oftener in the pure stream, pointing at the same time to thick coats of dirt upon his skin. He said he washed at home. I gave him some odd pieces of soap with which he was pleased & I was glad to [see] my dark friend take himself off.

July 25, Wednesday.

Left camp at eight. Passed an Indian encampment.

INDIANS OF SOWANNA — CARD PLAYING

We passed an Indian encampment. There were about ten men, no women. They were playing cards. The cards seemed a new pack. The game was a simple one. Every card is of equal value. They deal out the pack. Each player takes up three & never holds more in his hand. When his turn to play comes he must throw down a card, if there is one of the same number or picture, he takes it & a second & a third if the numbers correspond & he supplies his hand with enough to make up three again from his deal. Whoever, at the end, has taken up most cards wins. Gambling has always been a propensity of these Indians. They will sit for hours & gamble away everything they possess, even to the last article of clothing.

INDIAN ANXIETY

A Chinese has lately been murdered. The Chinese are angry & lay the crime to the charge of the Indians. At Kpaltkoo, the Indians very anxiously asked us if it were true that the Indians were to be murdered because of that Chinaman's death. They said that Chinese in large parties had been to them, charging them with the murder & saying they should soon be very numerous & then they would kill all the Indians. I explained to them that in British territory no one could take the law into his own hands. I said the law was equal against all & for all. For a murder, death was the punishment. The Most High has said that his will was that 'whosoever sheddeth man's blood, by man shall his blood be shed' & that it was all the same whether King George man, Boston man, China-man, [or] *Siwash* were guilty. The murderer must suffer death. I said it was wrong to charge the Indians with this murder unless there was proof & they might rest assured that so long as they obeyed the laws & did right, they would have no hurt & no one should touch them with impunity. They were much pleased with this assurance & I trust the feeling that was rising would be allayed.

INDIAN UNTRUSTFULNESS

The Sowanna Indians who were engaged in gambling did not seem friendly. I asked them about the Chinese murder. They said they knew nothing about it. I asked if they had caught any salmon. They said, *halo salmon* [no salmon]. This was false, for a fine salmon was hanging up over their heads. To this I pointed & they laughed. There was something mysterious about this party of Indians, [there were] no women. [They were] all stout & warlike. I cannot help thinking the impression was upon them that the Chinese meditated revenge & that they were prepared to resist. I could not however gather this from them.

A MURDERED CHINAMAN

On coming within six or seven miles of Boston Bar, we passed a tree on which a paper was affixed with the following writing:

> A few yards from this place is the body of a dead Chinaman under the hill. He appears to have been murdered.
>
> Discovered by R. P. Smith
T. W. Argles

July 18, 1860

I found out the body. It was doubled up & thrust under the roots of a tree in the bank. It was evidently that of a murdered man, a young man. He had no boots or stockings on & decomposition had offensively commenced. He might have been dead ten days.

MINERS

I visited Rough Flat. A miner told me some were making an ounce a day per man.

BOSTON BAR

I reached Boston Bar at five & [was] met, as before, with a kind reception. Mr. Wetherall, the ferryman, gave us milk & a supply of new potatoes.

We had an excellent dinner at a restaurant kept by a coloured man. We replenished our exhausted stock of provisions from the store of Mr. Brassey a young Frenchman, a Roman Catholic.

WAHILAH AND WHISKY

Here I met Wahilah again, the Chief of the Indians of this place. I had talked much to him when last this way, meeting him at Kpaltkoo. He had then promised me he would do all he could to stop his people from drinking whisky. He told me today his great grief was that many of his people transgressed in this matter notwithstanding all his exertions.

In a shed near the store of Mr. Brassey I observed two fine youths busily engaged playing cards.

At seven o'clock, we left Boston Bar intending to camp a few miles out on the way.

A very steep mountain over, we reached our ground & the moon enabled us to see to put up our tents. Mosquitoes were more numerous here than in any spot I have visited yet. We believed this place to be called Mud [Sperry], which may account for the mosquitoes.

July 26, Thursday.

Left camp at eight. We have found plenty of grass. Our route lay over several ridges [running] parallel to each other towards the River Anderson which river we at length reached, at about twelve miles from Boston Bar. Here we dined & camped. It is a pleasing spot, close to the first crossing. The water is clear, sparkling & rapid. I had two delightful bathes.

CAMP IN A STRAWBERRY BED

I pitched my camp in the midst of strawberries & other fruit. After dinner I gathered strawberries which had an excellent flavour, also service berries & from a tree overhanging my tent I could get a dish full of nuts.

Mr. Langvoydt [Landvoight] of Hope rode up on his way to Boston Bar. He very kindly gave me what barley he had left. Another party, including Mr. Mcarthy, who had been at our services at Cayoosh & Lytton, also passed us. They were bound to Yale.

July 27, Friday.

Left [the camp] ground at six-thirty. Rode across the Anderson on a single tree. About two miles on are the forks of the trail. We turned up the wrong way, that to Yale & on discovering our mistake fixed up a notice that others might [not] go astray. About two miles on we recrossed the Anderson, fording it with our animals. We now followed the valley of the Anderson in an easterly direction, passing several creeks and good camping grounds, though not much grass. It rained most of the morning & the wet trees through which we passed added to the discomfort. We stopped to lunch by the river at a place about ten miles from our morning camp where is plenty of a kind of vetch. Mr. Landvoight called it clover. Our horses, however, did not relish it. We made a good [fire] before some trees under which we had shelter & got our wet clothing well dried. Along the valley of the Anderson we proceeded at a great height on flats, crossing occasionally several creeks & at length one considerable one, after which [we went] up a narrow ridge to a flat of firs dressed in grey mossy tresses which had a strange appearance. Then we came to a flat of burned firs which stood up like pale & wan spectres, the remains of the charring being very slight. Beneath was [abortive] small firs struggling to rise, & in the midst, huge granite boulders, white & shining, while above towering overhead was a granite & trap mountain, with three peaks, with [a] face as though cut down with a knife & from which the vast isolated portions mentioned had fallen. There was [such] a strange & unearthly gloominess seeming to pervade this region that we called it the Valley of Desolation.

A short time after, the scene again changed & we were upon a flat of almost tropical luxuriance. Fruits & flowers & rich foliage enclosed our path, after which we entered the forest, continually ascending till we reached the snow. Here we touched the river Anderson again, at this high level, drew our water for tea & camped upon the damp swamp. We had difficulty in making a fire owing to the wet which saturated every thing around. However, a journey of twenty miles had rendered rest agreeable & notwithstanding, rain, damp & mosquitoes, all slept soundly & I trust awoke thankfully. [I] saw a raccoon.

July 28, Saturday.

I was up at a quarter to four. It was raining hard. We had breakfast & Mr. Sheepshanks & myself got away (the former, however, following me at an interval) about half past five. We had to ride over the mountain thirty miles to Hope. I passed packers asleep on the other side of the Anderson which I now crossed for the last time. The ascent was very gradual & at seven o'clock I came to an encampment of workmen engaged upon the trail. They told me, to my surprise & pleasure, that I was some way past the summit. In about an hour I came up with a train of mules & horses & passed them in a short time. The trail being only wide enough for one animal, it is difficult to get past a train.

For about ten miles the trail was bad, i.e., soft & muddy owing to the foundation being of rotten wood. It was a succession of holes, [with] roots of trees intersecting the path, which made it very dangerous, except at a walking pace.

Towards the foot of the mountain I saw some beautiful cascades, some I suppose not less than 100 to 150 feet in fall. At length, in four hours from starting, I reached [the] river on this side of the mountain & entered the picturesque valley of the Coquihalla which flows into Hope. A region of magnificent timber was now entered & the trail lay along the river, diverging now & then to gain a higher flat so to avoid a canyon, or to save distance.

At twelve, I stopped to luncheon & to rest my horse. I had been here three quarters of an hour when Mr. Sheepshanks joined me. We stopped a like additional period & then went, the trail being for the most very good & affording frequent opportunity for a canter.

We met a pack train with barley & purchased a feed for our two horses on the spot. We came gently along at the last & reached Hope at eight. The day cleared up early & the evening was [. . .].

BOSTON BAR AND HOPE TRAIL

The trail I consider to be full of interest. It is new & therefore, at present, imperfect. It has no steep ascents or stony slides, or dangerous pitches. It is, on the whole, level & easy in grade. It may be divided thus, [in miles]:

Boston Bar to the foot of the mountain, being the valley of the Anderson.	32
The foot of the mountain where the Anderson is left, over the summit to the valley of the Coquihalla.	10
The foot of the mountain, along the valley of the Coquihalla to Hope.	20
Total	62

The two valleys have much beautiful scenery. The mountain region is striking.

One day this will be a favourite ride to the upper country.

The difficulty is the want of food for thirty miles between the foot by the Anderson [River] & Hope.

BRIDGES OF A SINGLE TREE

It will afford some idea of the size of timber, when I state that, in the above distance, I rode over three rivers on bridges of a single tree.

July 29, Sunday.

Morning services: I preached in the morning on the observance of the Sabbath, Mr. Pringle read morning prayer, Mr. Sheepshanks the litany. The attendance was not so good as it ought to be, but was fair. I dined between the services with the Moodys.

July 30, Monday.

My two pack horses having arrived yesterday I went to my tent today. Mr. Pringle having hospitably housed me for two nights.

Most people have expressed their opinion that I am looking altered from the effects of this journey. I certainly have had a rougher time than I ever experienced & I have had to do some amount of hard physical labour. My dress has become tattered, my shoes worn out & my appearance anything but clerical. As I entered Hope near the bridge, Mr. Hotchins said, 'why Sir you look like a miner.' I was in a coloured woolen shirt, no waistcoat, no neckcloth & my coat was in holes. Yet I have enjoyed my journey much. I thank my heavenly Father for his care & protection over me & I feel my gratitude for the opportunity he has given me, for the honour he has conferred upon me of speaking in his name & in seeking the souls of my fellow sinners. But, oh my God, how deeply do I deplore my shortcomings & deficiencies. How much have I lacked the love of souls in my heart & how faint has been the dedication of myself to him who died for me. Grant me thy abundant grace in the future, that all these precious occasions of good may be duly improved by me, to thy great & all due glory, to the welfare of immortal souls, & to the blessing of my own weak, helpless, & sin laden self.

This evening I drank tea with the Moodys & discussed the plan for a church for Hope.

I met during the day Mr. Ogden who is the Hudson's Bay Company agent at Fort James, Stewart Lake. He has been many years there, living amongst the Indians & comes away but once a year with the brigade.

I met also a promising young man Mr. Saunders, also in the Hudson's Bay Company employ, going to take charge of their fort at Alexandria. Also Mr. McKay going to Cayoosh & Kamloops with his young wife. These two last, I trust & believe, will in their respective districts do all they can for the progress of religion & the Church of England in particular.

July 31, Tuesday.

I was writing in my tent all the early part of the day, also I had several little jobs of mending my clothes.

About four o'clock a storm of heavy rain & thunder & lightning came on which lasted till seven.

I walked out afterwards. Met & talked with a Mexican, with Indians, and with a respectable man who had just arrived after a hard tramp from Rock Creek, whereabouts, he said, are some 300 miners doing well.

August 1, Wednesday.

A cloudy & rainy day. Spent most of the morning writing & mending my clothes. In the afternoon [I] looked at the church lots with Mr. Pringle who dined with me in my tent. Mr. Gray, an American & Presbyterian, came to press me to take a room in his house. His kind hospitality I declined, but felt gratified. In the evening Mr. Pringle & I nearly lost ourselves in the woods close by the town. We escaped, however, before the darkness closed in upon us.

August 2, Thursday.

Rain. Heard from Mr. Garrett that Mr. Rivieccio had returned to Francisco.

August 3, Friday.

Wrote to Mr. [Thrau?] of Francisco about Mr. Rivieccio.

INDIAN VISIT—TASCHELAK AND HIS WIVES

Taschelak came to see me, showed [me] a paper in which he promises to be sober.

I got from him many words, found the numerals quite different from those above, [on July 10].

August 4, Saturday.

Taschelak came today again & brought his two wives, Tsahtsalote (youngest) and Khalowit & his two boys Malasleton & Karkaywill. One wife looked a dozen years older than the other, the elder had eleven rings, the younger [had] ten rings on the hands. He had had eight children by his two wives, had lost six. Khalowit had lost five, the other [wife] one. Each had one left.

I showed him the Kompchin idol. He said Port Hope Indians had none of those, but he understood what it meant.

He told me he endeavoured to train up his children peaceably & would not let them steal. He said he never got angry & gave himself otherwise an excellent character, with which his wives agreed. He concluded by asking for a bit of paper with some writing upon it. The two women were extremely well behaved. Their heads were nicely covered & their hair braided. They had on each a comfortable English shawl & were dressed in coloured linen gowns, as country people in England. Taschelak said he should be very glad if his children could be instructed. I spoke to them about God & the work of Christ.

This evening Mr. Pringle, Mr. Dundas & myself rode out by the lake to the canyon of the Coquihalla. The scenery was beautiful & the weather pleasant after the rain.

August 5, Sunday.

VISIT FROM AN INDIAN CHIEF — PAHALLAK

Before church Pahallak, the Chief of the Hope Indians & a great chief upon the river, came with my friend of yesterday, Taschelak, to see me. They came twice last evening but I was out. Pahallak is an old man in full vigour & of considerable influence. He has a thoughtful & benign countenance. He was dressed well & wore gloves which he pulled off to shake hands. I arranged with him to meet his tribe today & to speak to them about sacred things.

I afterwards went to his house & saw his wife & daughter & a son about sixteen, a very fine youth & a favourite evidently with his father. He came to the service in the afternoon dressed in a coat of many colours & was remarkable for his devout attention. I thought of Joseph & 'his coat of many colours.' This youth's name is Povhallak.

PREACHING TO INDIANS AT HOPE

At about half past three, Indians began to assemble and soon filled the place, a large store. Several white men also came in. Old Pahallak was in his place. I explained, to the white persons present, my desire to instruct the Indians & leave an impression of one or two chief points. I asked their sympathy. We then [sang] two verses of the Hundredth Psalm. I then offered a prayer, seeking the blessing of our heavenly Father upon our imperfect efforts & [to] overrule our stammering lips, to direct some gleams of light to enter the hearts of some of these poor Indians, that a way might be made for their acceptance of Christ, their Saviour.

I then addressed the Indians. Many of them knew the Thompson dialect. So with Chinook, with Kookptchin, with Lillooet, & some Cowichan I managed to speak to them for near an hour. There was much attention. Occasionally, some would repeat to others, in their own words, what I said. I showed them we possessed the word of God, in which are glad tidings to the Indians as well as to others, & that this is to them a Saviour, Christ the Lord. I explained the requirements of God, our failure & condemnation, Christ's love & work. In conclusion the doxology was sung & the grace pronounced. After which all came up, one by one, & shook hands & departed.

Our two services were fairly attended, morning & evening. I preached twice upon 'Christ as the door' in the morning & our stewardship, being the gospel for the day [and] Luke 16:1 in the evening. Mr. Dundas led the singing & the services were hearty. The holy communion was administered in the morning. There were but five communicants. Mr. Dundas went in the afternoon to Union Bar where he preached & said litany to miners.

ROMIST MISSIONARIES

There are two Romist missionaries at present encamped here. I was fearful they might have hindered our gathering of Indians. If, however, they attempted to do so, they signally failed.

As I was returning to my camp this evening I saw them smoking pipes near their tent. They are about to establish a mission here & have been negotiating for land.

August 6, Monday.

SIMILKAMEEN EXCITEMENT AT HOPE

The town of Hope was excited today by [the] arrival of miners about to go to Similkameen & Rock Creek. I saw a party start. They were in high [spirits]. This is the gold miner's delight, to go forth on some new enterprise, full of expectation leaving probably good paying claims. Many miners have spoken to me of their restless spirits. I have talked to men doing well who have confessed that if news of rich digging were to arrive they must go, though doomed, as they had often been, to disappointment, for in these matters it never happens that all are equally fortunate.

ROCK CREEK GOLD

I saw today a quantity of Rock Creek gold. It was shown me by Mr. Landvoight. It is coarse, flaky gold, no dust.

COMPETITION WITH AMERICANS

Hope is destined to supply the new miners with goods. Yet the Americans are pushing in from other parts. Thus, I am told by Mr. Landvoight of 130 mules, on their way from Seattle, in [Puget] Sound.

Steamboats, they say, can run up to Colville which is not far from the Similkameen.

August 7, Tuesday.

Left Hope by the steamer, *Colonel Moody.* Reached New Westminster at half past two.

MINERS RETURNING HOME

On board were two respectable looking men. They were American miners returning home with a comfortable 'pile.' They both acknowledged this. I asked what was considered a 'pile.' 'From three to five thousand dollars' was the reply. This was the result of two years mining in British Columbia.

One of these men was a young man. He was returning to his home in Ohio, at the solicitation of his father, who said 'come home at any cost. If you have only enough to bring you half way, I will pay the rest.' He was the youngest of three. He had been away from home six years. He had come out by the toilsome route across the plains but was now going home by 'Panama' to New York. 'How do you get on there?' 'By a railroad Sir which goes within a half mile of my father's [house].' 'Would you yet feel a throbbing when the whistle sounds, as you are approaching that station?' Tears jumped up into his eyes. 'Oh yes Sir, how I wish I was there'!

CHARACTER OF MINERS GIVEN BY ONE OF THEMSELVES

This miner said he had never seen so dissolute a class as the miners in British Columbia. Drink & gambling was their chief pleasure. Large fortunes were continually squandered by them.

VISIT TO THE NEW CHURCH AT [NEW] WESTMINSTER

I was much struck, on approaching the town by the river, at the new church. It stands well & comes out in good proportions. I visited it. It is roofed, & the work is well done. It reflects credit upon Captain Lempriere, who designed it.

I dined at the Camp.

August 8, Wednesday.

Made calls. Left at half past two for Victoria. We had a pleasant passage in the *Hunt* & were safely housed by ten o'clock. Mr. Dundas was my companion.

REFLECTIONS UPON THE WORK AND JOURNEY

Thankfulness

I am thankful to have been able thus early to traverse the principal inhabited portions of my diocese. It has pleased God to give me health, strength & protection during the last three months in journeyings & [. . .] by land & by water, amidst a strangely mixed & peculiar population.

Impressions of the Country

My belief in the progress of the colony has been confirmed. There is no doubt now upon any single mind as to the vast resources & attractions in mineral wealth. There is considerable agricultural land in the lower portion of the Fraser. That is to say, along the river up to Hope. On either side large tracts invite the farmer, more especially about the Chilliwack, the Pitt River & Hope, to a fair return of capital & labour.

Above this point, the country is difficult of access, rough & mountainous, until you get some fifty miles through the Cascade Range. Nothing would have opened this tract except its mineral produce. It would drive back the sturdiest traveller. It has sent back thousands in poverty & despair. Beyond this difficult tract, beginning at Boston Bar, there is again invitation for the farmer. Extensive flats now open out on either side of the river, covered with a nutritious bunch grass. Our horses were never without abundance of food in that district. Cattle fatten upon it, even when the summer heat has turned it into hay as it grows. But even this country is not at present accessible. The mountains frequently close in upon it, or ravines separate one portion from another, and the river is in no part navigable, but a furious & dangerous torrent, at least in the summer portion of the year. Beyond Cayoosh I did not go, but at that point some 250 miles up the Fraser, the country is more open, the flats large, the grass more abundant & judging from several fields of barley & oats which I saw, sufficiently rich to produce grain. I was told, however, the season had been unusually favourable from the rain that had fallen at intervals.

The Upper Country, I was told by many persons, was very suitable for farming operations on a large scale. Cayoosh being the termination, or nearly so, of the mountain region.

Difficulties may be Removed

I have little doubt these difficulties of access will be removed by the formation of roads. Already something has been done & miners at Cayoosh were rejoicing in July that flour was cheap, i.e., was 16 cents a pound or 9 shillings, 4 pence a stone, as we should say in England. It had been more than double that sum. This month, through road making & competition it has fallen to 12 cents, i.e., 7 shillings a stone. In course of time, ravines will be bridged & obstructive rocks blasted & both time & toil saved.

Prospects of the Country

The auriferous character of the country being now established & the salubrity of the climate undoubted, it only remains for population & capital to develop it. This, we desire, should come from England. It follows, there must be made, any day, discoveries of rich quartz, the source of the gold which is found in its disintegrated state so widely.

Other metallic wealth is known to exist. Probably from this time a steady increase of population will take place & a few years will see [the colony of] British Columbia a flourishing representative of Britain on the Pacific Coast.

It is most probable that the first successes will be reaped by our enterprising American friends who will pour in & use their California experience to good purpose. We trust, however, Englishmen will come & share the advantage, bring capital & improve it & aid to establish the constitution of England in all its security, fair dealing & purity, as well as freedom.

As a gold country advances, capital for mining becomes absolutely necessary.

Religion and Morals

In every spot but one & that the capital, I have found no religious efforts but such as are made by the Church of England. It is indeed a cause of thankfulness that we are enabled thus to enter upon a field so manifestly & so urgently calling for religious means. Happy, I am sure, will our dear friends in England, who have stirred themselves so nobly, be, to find that they have been most opportune in their aid & have caused the gospel to be preached where no witness for Christ was heard & have, moreover, caused that at least the reproach of neglect & late & tardy aid shall not rest, in this diocese, upon the mother Church of England.

The state of religion is as low as it can possibly be amongst civilized people. There is no recognition of it. The Sunday is a day of business & pleasure & revelling. Most of the mining class are open profaners of the name of God & many are what are called 'free thinkers.' Morals, I fear, are as far from what is right as [is] the case of religion. Some have acknowledged to me their dislike of the ungodly & immoral life which they, in common with those around them, are leading. With others, sin is a matter of indifference. They will speak of their acts & disparage religion with the most unblushing boldness & without an effort. It has often struck me that amongst a large class who have been trained under the American system, faith & shame have departed utterly from them. We complain, in England, of the little hold religion has upon many of the artisan class in our large towns, but I never met with anything at all approaching to the calculating & matter of course infidelity which prevails amongst many who have been trained in America. They seemed to have had full licence to pursue every unfaithful thought & seem [not] to have been reached by any witness or influence of truth. Literally, multitudes live without God in the world! Yet with all this, there is a kindness & even polish in the American miner which is a great contrast to anything amongst Englishmen.

I was everywhere kindly received & in some cases I believe welcomed for religion's sake. Allowance must be made, no doubt, for the frontier life which many of these have led & the absence of all opportunities of grace. But the state of religion is nevertheless a phase of work before us which is not to be seen elsewhere in a British territory & which calls for special exertion, patience & prayer.

Difficulties—Variety of Race and Religion

Variety of race is a remarkable feature & a difficulty in dealing with the population in this country. The Christianity of England is the least known even amongst those who would not pay disrespect to religion. French, Spaniards, Italians, Mexicans & some Germans & Irish are mostly Roman Catholic. They bring their own base ideas of Sunday. Then Germans, most Americans, & Scotch are Presbyterian or Congregational, or Unitarian.

How earnest, how persuasive, how clear must be our teaching & ministry to impress and win to our church & its pure & simple truth & unite in one such hostile & discordant elements. Yet, they are the bulk of the people. We shall be nowhere if we do not win these to the pure faith of Jesus & blend them together in the fold of the [. . .] church. The difficulty is great. We need, with the divine help, men of special gifts & zeal.

The unsettled character of the mining class is another difficulty. They are restless. They feel no spot their home, even for a while. Hence, they will not identify themselves with institutions of the neighbourhood so readily. Then we have Indians & increasing bands of Chinese.

The expense of living is great. During my journey I frequently paid nineteen cents a pound for flour (i.e., eleven shillings, one pence a stone), forty-five & fifty cents a pound for bacon (i.e., two shillings a pound). Fresh meat, milk, [and] potatoes [were] frequently not to be had, except at very high prices. The labour for building is very high, carpenters getting £1 a day & even Indians expecting six shillings & ten shillings a day. Sawn timber [is] very high. These matters will improve no doubt, but for the present the expense will be a considerable difficulty & press heavily upon our funds.

Distance Travelled and Experience Gained

I have travelled during the twelve weeks upwards of 800 miles in steamboat, canoe, horseback & on foot. I am thankful for the experience gained. I have found myself able to walk my twenty miles a day. I have learned to sleep as soundly upon the floor of a log hut, or on the ground, as in a bed & to rise refreshed & thankful, to clean my own shoes, wash my clothes, make my bed, attend to horses, pitch [a] tent & all such matters have become easy duties.

There is no merit in doing this. Everybody here does such things. I wrote this down in order to record my thankfulness at finding myself permitted, with so little difficulty, to take this necessary part in furtherance of my ministry. May God grant me of his love & mercy to spend & be spent in a true spirit of devotedness to my Saviour who has sent me to preach the gospel & bring in sinners to his cross.

Encouragements

I have had encouragements. I have spoken publicly & privately to many: I have discoursed to my fellow sinners in the store, the hut, & by the wayside. I have often seen the glistening tear fill the eye at the sounds of the tidings of a Saviour's love. I have seen the sigh of smitten conscience manifested in the flushed look of the rough & hardy miner.

I have been wished God speed on my work in accents which left no doubt of sincerity. I have still sounding in my ears, the last words from a miner's party, 'be sure Sir & send us a minister & we will support him,' words which at the moment drew tears to my own eyes & I have the fullest persuasion, did not God give such encouragements, that his word spoken even by such feeble lips as ours cannot 'go forth & return void but will accomplish that where unto it has been sent.' One case I may have mentioned.

In my journal, of the twenty-ninth of June, I have noted an instance of reproof to a swearer. The Rev. Mr. Crickmer, one of my most zealous & useful clergy was with me. He afterwards returned alone the same way. An interesting letter from him gives me an account of his journey & the happy opportunities he had of holding services. He says, 'one case especially I must adduce which showed the good resulting from my going over the ground so soon again. Your Lordship reproved a man for swearing, [a man with] an impudent, but pleasant sort of face. It wonderfully struck him. It gave me a good opportunity in conversation to follow up the wound, he came to the service. Next day when I got to Ensley's Flat, there was the man again. His countenance was changed, his eye sank before mine, not with a cowed, but with a subdued look which told [me] that some chord had been struck when that man was reproved for swearing, which promised under God's blessing to produce no small change in the mind, and may be under future providence, life.'

I had the gratification also to find that, after my visit & by the zealous efforts of Mr. Pringle & Mr. Crickmer in the two towns of Hope & Yale, steps had been taken to lessen the Sunday desecration.

So that in the midst of some trials & difficulties we are not left without encouragement. May we more & more be stimulated by the principle & the promise of the apostle: 'Be ye steadfast, unmoveable, always abounding in the work of the Lord, forasmuch as ye know that your labour is not in vain in the Lord.'

Distance Travelled May 18—August 8, 1860

Victoria to New Westminster	60
Pitt Lake & back	70
[New] West[minster] to Douglas & Hope	135
Cornish Bar & back	12
Yale	15
Hill's Bar & back	6
Hope & back from Yale	30
Hodges & back	10
Yale to Cayoosh	137
Fountain & back	14
Bridge River & back	8
Seton Lake & back	6
Cayoosh to Boston Bar	84
Boston Bar to Hope	60
Hope to [New] Westminster	85
[New] Westminister to Victoria	60
	792
Langley & back to [New] Westminster	34
	826

Excursion from Hope
[ditto] about Yale

CHAPTER 8

There is no better land in British Columbia that I have seen, nor in Vancouver Island

9 August – 11 September

August 9, Thursday.

Glad to find myself in my iron cottage, thankful for the mercy & loving-kindness that has been vouchsafed during my twelve weeks sojourn in [the colony of] British Columbia.

The steamer *Oregon* from California has brought out the Rev. L. Tugwell, missionary of the Church Missionary Society, from England.

Many letters also await my return.

August 10, Friday.

Visited the Indian school, a result of our Indian Improvement Committee's work & the meeting held in my absence.

NEW MISSIONARY OF CHURCH MISSIONARY SOCIETY

I was glad to be able to receive into my house today Mr. Tugwell & his young wife. He is a promising young clergyman, of a right spirit & ready to devote himself to the work of the Lord. She is a truly devoted spirit & bears her part with him nobly.

Mr. Cridge & Mr. Garrett dined with me today, Mr. Duncan the catechist, came in the evening, also Captain Gossett.

August 11, Saturday.

Much rain. Visited Indians in the evening.

August 12, Sunday.

Preached twice in Christ Church on 'Indifference' in the morning, 'Work of the Spirit in Conversion,' in the evening.

PREACHING TO THE TSIMSHIAN INDIANS

At three o'clock the Tsimshian & some few other Indians were gathered in their new school room for a service. There were about 100 present.

We began by Mr. Duncan giving out & then singing a hymn in the Tsimshian tongue. A hymn was also sung in English. All joined & it was delightful to hear the beautiful voices of these simple people.

I then offered a prayer in English, which Mr. Duncan explained & afterwards [I] spoke to them in Chinook which many understood but which Mr. Duncan more fully interpreted in Tsimshian.

My points were: the attributes of our heavenly Father,

His love in sending Jesus Christ.
The work of Christ.
The message of the Father—Isaiah 60:1-3
The Covenant of Jesus—Matthew 28:19-20

In obedience to that will of God the Father & our Lord Jesus Christ, we missionaries had come to them. If they listen to the word of God & put away sin & trust in Jesus, they may be happy forever.

Mr. Duncan having explained my sermon at intervals, now examined them in the catechism, a simple one of his own compiling. He then gave a lesson on Belshazzar, we sang & concluded.

The people sat all on the ground in semi-circular rows. There were many faces which would not have looked out of place in any gathering of peasantry in old England. All looked bright & attentive. Their attention had flagged in no degree when we closed at half past four.

They asked if the great chief was coming to teach them every Sunday.

On Friday evening, when [I was] at the Haida camp, they remarked how pleased they were to see the great chief laugh. They knew he would not be angry with them or be a feared chief because he laughed with them. I suppose in speaking to them I had smiled. How simple minded all this is, yet alas how soon will corruption destroy it all. Even alas this very gathering gave proofs of corruption. There were some of the young women decked out in every sort of vulgar finery, even to the wearing of crinoline & hoops. They were the unmarried wives of white men, & worse instances were there than even this.

August 13, Monday.

DEVOTIONAL MEETING

Mr. & Mrs. Tugwell left me for Fort Simpson. They had to take six months provisions. Mrs. Tugwell had a couple of canaries & also two goats for milk.

I attended the devotional meeting attached to Christ Church. I was sorry to see it had not increased, but the contrary. Our subject was 'The Sabbath.' This is not the most usual way perhaps of a church devotional meeting. Some object that it is not in accordance with our order.

Perhaps I might myself, as a parochial minister, not adopt this particular mode. I am, however, quite sure it is allowable. It cannot be otherwise than allowable for a pastor to gather his people, a few of his people [to] read the Scripture & teach, [and] there in the midst offer up his own fervent prayer for their special needs & for the special object they had met to [. . .]. I feel it right, as Bishop, to allow much latitude in this respect & to encourage in my clergy anything earnest. Rather let us have a [. . .] meeting & warm & devoted hearts than cold & unfruitful formality.

August 14, Tuesday.

Beautiful weather.

August 15, Wednesday.

Busy unpacking my library. Preached in the evening at Christ Church. Thin attendance.

August 16, Thursday.

Day warm.

August 17, Friday. [No entry in manuscript]

August 18, Saturday.

FAST IN A SWAMP, BREAKING DOWN A FENCE

Mr. Garrett & myself went this evening to Cedar Plains to visit the people & acquaint them with notice of service tomorrow.

We got into a wood out of which we thought it [. . .] before escaping. We visited several families. At one house, Irvings, they said they were glad we had called, as there was a child to christen & the parents would like to come. Last Sunday three children were baptized. A fine boy on horseback, the son here, offered to go & let them know. Another person, he said, would like to know at the farm furthest off, so away he went, dash[ed] as it was, to let these different people know.

On our way home about eight o'clock we came to a high fence right across the road. It often happens that paths & roads are stopped up in an unsurveyed country. We followed the fence & came to a bog, through it we pushed, until our horses stuck fast in the mud up to their middle. We had to dismount & extricate them how[ever] we could. No opening being apparent, we proceeded to make a way by pulling down the fence. We succeeded in getting through & were replacing the logs when a figure stood near us. It was a man. I hailed him. He wanted to know what we were about & disappeared. Presently three others came in consider-able anger. It was dark. There was no way over there, had we gone on two other fences would have obstructed us. After much grumbling the men put the fence again into order. We had first retraced our steps & then we were led to the road some distance from us. The farmer, a French Canadian became civil. He told us the Governor had recently been thrown from his horse in that same swamp & had lost his way.

We reached home about nine o'clock.

August 19, Sunday.

Preached twice at Christ Church.

MEETING OF TSIMSHIAN INDIANS

In the afternoon I had a gathering of Tsimshians at the Indian school. I instructed them in a few elementary points respecting God and Jesus Christ. I spoke only in Chinook which most of those present knew & which those who knew best interpreted into Chinook [Tsimshian?]. A young merchant, Mr. MacDonald, M.P. for Sooke, went with me & assisted me. He speaks Chinook perfectly having been nine years in the country.

We sang several hymns. The voices of these people are good & they readily joined in such tunes as the Old Hundred, Bedford & the Evening Hymn.

THE SONGHEE AND TSIMSHIAN

There is much jealousy between different tribes. Our Indian school is constructed with a view of uniting different tribes. The Songhees are jealous of the special attention which has been paid recently to the Tsimshian. There were two Songhees present today. I spoke to them after the service. They said those Tsimshian would go away & not understand what they had heard, but that if the Songhees were in-structed they would understand all that was said. I said, well, then we will try the Songhee next Sunday. So we are to have a gathering of that tribe the next time. There is some truth in what they said, as no doubt the Songhees do understand the Chinook better than the Tsimshians.

HEATHEN DEEDS OF CRUELTY

Acts of warfare accompanied by bloodshed & even death had taken place so frequently amongst the various tribes at Victoria recently that the authorities have disarmed the stranger Indians, that is, more partic-ularly the Haidas or Queen Charlotte Islanders. On Friday, a Haida woman was passing through the Cowichan camp when a man of the latter tribe deliberately levelled his gun at her & lodged two bullets, one smashing her elbow & the other entering her side. She lies today in a state bordering on death. The man has been captured & identified.

At the sessions just over, a Tsimshian was found guilty of the murder of a coloured man. The latter was in the Tsimshian camp & in the act of stooping to kiss a child. The Tsimshian deliberately took a knife & stabbed the unfortunate man in the back, from which he died.

A few weeks since, a number of Fort Rupert Indians were returning from Victoria in their canoes when on their way they landed amongst the Cowichans, made an onslaught upon them & murdered about a dozen & having disemboweled them, left their bodies exposed & mutilated.

We see how much there is yet to counteract. Their habitations are full of cruelty as ever has been wherever man is found unenlightened by the gospel. What suffering, what misery may be averted through the gospel. If the divine precepts of love & peace prevail, then such deeds will cease. They will cease at least in their present aspect of atrocity & frequency. Exactly in proportion as the fear of God & a regard for their souls & Christian influences prevail, so must such evil deeds of darkness cease to be perpetrated.

Oh Lord hasten the day when these poor creatures shall be delivered from this bondage of Satan. Bring thy light to dispel their darkness & let thy Holy Spirit sanctify, renew & strengthen them for thy service, in peace & love & holiness. Happy day. Lord hasten it.

August 20, Monday.

VISIT FROM A JEW

A Jew came to ask the loan of the school. I refused on the ground that we never allow our educational or religious buildings to be used for any religious objects not in connection with the Church of England. We had a long talk. He says there are twenty families here. Their cemetery, with fencing, cost them 500 dollars. He expects when the world has lasted 6000 years then their Jehovah will come. 'Messiah' is anyone who comes to their refuge. He is dying & coming every day. All will one day agree to believe in the one God. They expect to be gathered to Jerusalem. None but traitors & hypocrites leave their persuasion. They keep no [holy] days here but two, the New Year and the Day of Atonement. He said circumcision was to be a covenant for ever & ever, therefore, Christians must be wrong. I asked how the Scripture was explained which foretold upon the throne of David there should be a king forever (Isaiah 9:7). He could not explain it. I showed him that we could explain [it] & that the covenant was confirmed in Christ & continues, which once was marked with the outward sign but now 'with the circumcision made without hands' & that Christ is our King upon the throne of the Israel of God.

He had the usual arguments of the unreasonableness of our believing that a man could be God & that there are three persons 'gods,' he said. That we had got the commandments from the Jews, etc.

NEGLECT CONFESSED

A Mr. Doran, an Irish Presbyterian, lately engaged in the *Colonist* newspaper called. He had been long from the old country & lived in California. He had neglected all outward expression of religion for some years. He knew it was wrong & had lately resolved to do differently. I urged this upon him. He has travelled much & lived some weeks in the Salt Lake City amongst the Mormons. His belief is that many would be only too thankful to escape. He lodged with a baker named Golightly who had two wives. He heard instances of wives going insane when a second was taken. The last wife always ruled the household.

He is thinking of getting up a paper at Esquimalt. The expense is not more than 30 dollars weekly, about 1000 dollars required for printing press, etc.

ANOTHER CASE OF NEGLECT CONFIRMED

I called at Rowlands, the builder. His wife told me she was distressed in mind. She had been brought up in the Church of England at Manchester. So had her husband. She married him in America. There he had become neglectful & had ceased to pray on his knees. She had before been most happy as a communicant. Gradually she had fallen away & in America had done as others did & the Sunday was profaned instead of being hallowed. She had even lost her interest in religion. But recently God had afflicted her in her child & she felt how sinful she was & wished to change. They now both attend Church. How great a snare is America. Considering, at least amongst working men, how wide spread is open profanity, it is [rare that] any escape the snare.

DEVOTIONAL MEETING

This evening there were rather more than last Sunday. Our subject was the 'Ministry.' We took it in three points: (1) the institution & requirements in ministers, (2) the part of the faithful laity towards the ministry [and] (3) the blessings resulting from a faithful ministry. I illustrated [the] two first [points] from Matthew 10, Mr. Garrett the third [point], from Ephesians 4.

A Tsimshian named Alatche was condemned at the recent assizes to be executed for the murder of a coloured man named Brown. I was asked today to sign a petition for a respite & mitigation. I assented on the following grounds,

1. The petition was signed in the first place by Mr. Skinner the foreman of the Grand Jury. All the circumstances had come before him. His view therefore inclined to more lenient sentence. I act on the side of mercy by aiding to give the Indian the benefit of the doubt.

2. He was undefended. I cannot think he had every benefit of the law. A prisoner tried for life surely ought to have counsel awarded him if too poor to procure one. They say extenuating circumstances would have been proved.

3. He was intoxicated. This plea should not shelter a white man, but an Indian when intoxicated becomes insane. The drink was given him by white men. [It is] hard that we should make him mad & then punish [him] for the deeds done in madness.

4. It is said that Brown was there, in the Indian camp, for improper purposes & that this was a provocation to the Indian.

I should be sorry to impede the course of justice but this is a case, I think, in which a leaning may be excusable on the side of mercy in saving the life of [a] fellow creature.

August 21, Tuesday.

A WEDDING

I performed today the wedding ceremony of Mr. Doughty, with a daughter of our Chief Justice Cameron. The Church had a goodly attendance & a beautiful day shed brightness over the scene.

Miss Cameron is a niece of the Governor's & was lately confirmed. She is but seventeen & the Bridegroom but nineteen. He was a midshipman in the *Ganges* & is owner, when of age, of property near [. . .] in Suffolk, Theberton. It seems some romance is connected with this union. Two years ago, when a midshipman, he was a favourite of Mrs. Cameron. He proposed for the daughter. Mrs. Cameron reasoned with him upon the youth of both & bid him think no more about it. He said he quite allowed they were both too young to marry at present but he could assure Mrs. Cameron the attachment was no boyish fancy & that in a few years they might marry. He went home & left the service. A short time since the young lady wrote to England to say they had been very young when the engagement was made & that she would release him. He instantly set off & in six weeks was here pressing his suit. The Chief Justice would not permit the marriage to be at present, [but] he persevered, gained his point & his bride in a fortnight. He seems an estimable young man & she is a pleasing & well principled young woman.

We wished them all happiness at the breakfast & their prospect is good.

August [22], Wednesday.

Called upon Lieutenant Helby commanding the *Grappler*, he seems a good man, also upon Captain Hall of the *Termagant*. Dined & stayed on board the *Ganges* with Admiral Sir Lambert R. Baynes.

August [23], Thursday.

The mission party arrived from England in the *Cortez*: Reverends Woods, Glover, Brown, Mrs. Pringle, & the Miss Penrices. This I humbly believe will be a large accession of strength.

I took in the Woods & Penrices.

August [24], Friday.

Called upon the Colonial Secretary as to sites the Imperial Government had sanctioned, grants for religious purposes & had left responsibility with the Governor to take care property should not be misapplied. He thought the trust would be 'the Bishop & Governor.' I objected on the ground of the seeming countenances of the friction of state connection. We should be attacked for the alliance & get all the odium & no advantage, but a chain & a drag.

He said the Governor had asked to be allowed to grant 100 acres of land to any denomination. This [the] Duke of Newcastle declined. [The] Governor then sent [a] dispatch well describing the wants of [the Colony of British] Columbia & proposing grants of 100£ in order to enable 'sects' to purchase land, which government would help select.

August 25, Saturday. [No entry in manuscript]

August 26, Sunday.

I preached in the morning at Christ Church. There were present six clergy including myself, viz. Mr. Cridge, Mr. Pringle, Mr. Woods, Mr. Brown, Mr. Glover. The mission party returned thanks for safe voyage.

THE SONGHEE INDIANS

On Sunday last, two Songhee Indians were at the Tsimshian service in our new school room. They remarked that a gathering of Songhees would be much more satisfactory as they understand better than the

Tsimshian. I took them at their word and fixed for a Songhee gathering today. They came & an interesting occasion it was. Together with the two chiefs 'Freesy' & 'Jim' & adults were about thirty fine children & some very intelligent lads. I explained to them our plans for their improvement & Mr. Pemberton reminded them of a visit I paid with him & Mr. Cridge soon after my arrival, promising them a school. We were now ready to begin. They expressed themselves much pleased.

We sang hymns. I addressed them. Two points I endeavoured to impress: (1) that we had the word of God, (2) that Christ had died for them.

We shall have I suppose more difficulty with these than with others, from their having been the longest subject to the moral contamination of the whites. Yet, there was a good feeling amongst them which I hope we may improve.

I introduced to them Mr. Garrett, who has undertaken to be their minister.

August 27, 1860, Monday.

Rode out with Mr. Glover to Cedar Plains, a delightful afternoon.

August 28, Tuesday.

FIRST EXAMINATION OF THE COLLEGIATE SCHOOL

At three o'clock was the first examination of this institution. It was 'the day of small things.' There were but eleven boys. They were examined by Mr. Garrett in Scripture, Mathematics, Latin, Geography, etc. There was much interest shown by the boys. The school having been but three months in existence could not of course show much result.

A mistake was made in giving too many prizes. These I distributed, addressed the boys & parents & then introduced Mr. Woods & Mr. Glover.

AN AMERICAN AT DINNER

Amongst others who dined with me today was Captain Hunt of the American army. This gentleman was quartered at San Juan under the pacific measures of General Scott. General Harney removed him in order to place there someone who would carry out his own plans. Captain Hunt is one of those Americans who condemns the [...] of his countrymen & takes a sober view of most matters.

Mr. Justice Begbie called today.

THE FEMALE COLLEGIATE SCHOOL

A first step has this day been taken by obtaining possession of the house in which we propose to commence the school, that lately occupied by Judge Cameron.

August 29, Wednesday.

Called upon Admiral Baynes in the *Ganges*. Rode with Mr. Garrett & Mr. Brown, arranged program of [the] Female Institution.

August 30, Thursday.

Mr. & Mrs. Trutch & Mr. Trutch Junior, Mr. & Mrs. Crease, Mr. & Mrs. Lowe, Mr. Woods, [&] the [two] Miss Penrices dined with me today.

August 31, [Friday].

Rain in torrents from early morning until twelve o'clock, showery during the day & at night. Cold & chilly.

September 1, Saturday.

Raining. The [two] Miss Penrices went into the Female Collegiate school. The Lowes and Mr. Woods having gone three days before.

September 2, Sunday.

Fine day. I preached morning & evening at Christ Church. Mr. Garrett had a good gathering of Indians (some eighty) at the Indian school.

September 3, Monday.

EDITOR OF A NEWSPAPER

Mr. Neas, editor of the *Victoria Gazette* called on me on Friday. I spoke of the poor character of his paper & suggested that it would not be difficult to get up a good paper. I had observed that no care was taken to cull from other papers, the *Times* for instance, discussions in Parliament directly affecting this place & America, subjects interesting to all. He said, 'Sir, I rarely see the *Times* newspaper. Sometimes my mother sends me a copy but it is generally an old one'! What a confession for an editor.

OPENING OF THE FEMALE COLLEGIATE SCHOOL

For a long time people have been crying out for a school for girls of the middle & upper sort. There was certainly a necessity, for the Romanists were in the field & young persons whose parents attend [our] church were duly in attendance upon the Sisters of Saint Ann. The arrival of the [two] Miss Penrices happily enabled us to open our Female Institution without delay. This we did today under Mrs. Lowe and the two Miss Penrices. The attendance was twelve. Of these, several had come from the school of the Romist sisters.

CHAPTER [MEETING]

Being Monday we had the usual meeting of Clergy, at which we numbered, including myself, eight. We discussed various matters such as the consecration services & [the] week's proceedings at Saint John's, the formation of a Church Society, the establishment of a church newspaper, etc.

EVENING DEVOTIONAL MEETING

I attended. The subject was the education of the young. Mr. Cridge, Mr. Garrett & I took part. The attendance was very small indeed.

September 4, Tuesday.

A meeting again of Chapter, eight present, various matters settled, Collegiate school prospectus, Church Society, Church Newspaper, etc.

September 5, Wednesday.

A WEDDING

At half past ten I rode out to Hillside to perform the marriage ceremony for a daughter of Mr. Work, a member of the Council, Miss Mary Work to Mr. J.A. Graham. There was a large assemblage. It took place at the house, by the express wish of the family for special reasons, though against my own feelings in some respect. But in these countries while roads are difficult of passage & conveyances are scarce, there must be exceptions made to the rule which would have marriage in the church & sustain the solemn character of the ordinance.

I was not able to stay [for the wedding] breakfast owing to having to start by the *Forward*, H.M. Gunboat at twelve, for Admiral Island [Salt Spring Island] & Nanaimo.

VOYAGE TO ADMIRAL ISLAND AND NANAIMO

Admiral Sir Lambert Baynes very kindly placed the Gunboat, *Forward* at my service. We left the harbour of Victoria about twelve. I found several canoes of Haida Indians about the ship. They wanted protection past the Cowichan. We took them in tow. There were four canoes, with about fifteen to nineteen in each, returning to their home for the winter, having been to Victoria to trade.

The day was lovely & the passage up the Haro Strait & through the many islands was most pleasing. At half past six we came to anchor in Ganges Harbour. I immediately went on shore with Mr. Smith, one of the officers and the Rev. Mr. Lowe.

SETTLEMENT GANGES HARBOUR — EVENING SERVICE IN A LOG HUT

It was dusk & soon became dark but I was anxious to visit at once some of the people. We pulled up to the head of the harbour & walked up a winding trail through a deserted Indian village to a log hut. This was the house of Mr. Lenaker [Lineker] the principal settler. We found himself, a most respectable man who had been a merchant, and his wife the daughter of a clergyman, with their children. In the corner was stored away [many] chickens & little pigs, in addition to the younger branch of the family. After a good deal of talk & having fixed for a service to be held the next day, we had prayers. I read a few lines of Matthew 6 & explained & we concluded with the evening hymn. They expressed their thanks & said they certainly never should have expected the Lord Bishop to visit [an] out of the way settlement like that. 'Oh,' I said, 'if the Bishop is spared, you will, I trust, often see him in such places & much delighted am I to come'!

Mr. Lineker lighted us back to our boat & we pulled again through the quiet & placid water in which the phosphoric light was stirred by the oars & by the fish which we could see darting away in all directions beneath the boat.

EVENING PRAYERS IN THE CAPTAIN'S CABIN

Before retiring to our berths we had prayers. I read a portion of Scripture & offered prayers. It is a comfort to be in a vessel so well ordained & with so good a man as Captain Robson.

September 6, Thursday.

MORNING PRAYERS — THE FORWARD

At nine the crew were mustered as usual. I read a portion of Scripture, John 8:31, etc., 'Sons & Slaves' & explained, [and] then prayers. After breakfast we went on shore. Mr. Lineker was waiting. Captain Robson went out with his gun & shot three grouse. Rev. Mr. Lowe & myself went with Mr. Lineker & Mr. Richardson, a coloured person, to visit the different clearings.

GANGES HARBOUR SETTLEMENT

The plots are laid out in oblongs of 200 acres each. In the whole island some 8000 acres are taken up, about half are on this side. Although hardly a year has elapsed, yet much has been cleared. A log barn has been built upon each. Some three or four acres have been brought under cultivation in each lot. Garden produce of all sorts is to be seen. Cabbages, potatoes, beetroot, onions, tomatoes, peas, cucumbers, watermelons, carrots, etc., & wheat & oats, [also] pigs, poultry & calves.

The soil is good generally, a light kind, some very good black loam, a great deal of this latter principally in the valleys. I should say there is no better land in British Columbia that I have seen, nor in Vancouver Island. There is considerable wood to be cleared, but extensive open ground [is] covered with fern. The timber is not heavy or thick. There is good water from wells. Grouse are to be had. Deer in abundance & good. Fish plentiful. Miss Lineker today was at the water's edge raking in smelts. We had some for dinner & capital they were. In winter wild fowl are abundant. Mr. Lineker told me he could come down & shoot as many as he wanted whenever he liked. The settlers complain of the hawks, the chicken hawks who pounce upon the chickens at the very door of the house.

CANADIAN SETTLER

I visited Mr. Booth's farm. He was busy clearing. I asked how he liked the place, he said very well, it was much better than Canada, from the winter being so mild.

YOUNG MEN FROM ENGLAND

Two fine young fellows from the old country, Despard & Andrews, have a farm. They have just finished their log hut. They came late. They have been unfortunate. A cow got into their potatoes & destroyed all the first fruits of their labours. A sow had a litter but all the little pigs were killed. They were not in good heart, I endeavoured to cheer them up.

COLOURED PEOPLE

I visited the farm of Mr. Richardson, a coloured person. He has shown great diligence & is successfully overcoming the land. Several acres showed abundant crops. I visited Mr. Moore, a coloured preacher, he too has a farm. There are a good many coloured people. Their clearings bear comparison with those of others.

THE LAKE

There is a beautiful lake about three miles from the landing place. Fish & wild fowl abound in it.

DIVINE SERVICE

At three thirty the people gathered at Mr. Lineker's. We had the litany & hymns. I preached from Second Corinthians 4:10-31 [?] & showed the motives, guide, power & fruit of a Christian life. After service, Mr. Lineker expressed the thanks of the settlers for my visit, hoped I should come again & trusted that I [should] be able to send them a clergyman. I replied I was glad to be amongst them & would do all I can.

They came down with me in a body to the boat. We shook hands & parted.

THE SETTLER'S WIFE — AN INDIAN FIGHT

Mrs. Lineker is the daughter of a clergyman in Australia, Sydney, the Rev. Mr. Vincent. Her father was one of the first clergy out there. She knew intimately the well known Samuel Marsden who had often driven her, when a child, in his gig. She used to stay for weeks at his house.

Sometimes the life [here] is one of fear to her. She dreads the Indians. Six weeks ago there was a fight of Indians in the harbour close to their dwelling. A canoe of Haida Indians came in. The Cowichans owed them a grudge for some injury done years ago. Some fifty Cowichan set upon their canoe. They fired at them from behind trees. First, one Haida fell & then another. At length most were killed & one woman taken prisoner. Some escaped a little way but were intercepted & shot down. Ten were thus killed. Mrs. Lineker was much alarmed. She ran with her child to the woods.

A RESCUE

Shortly after, the *Satellite* came into the harbour & succeeded in rescuing the [Indian] woman. She was brought to Victoria. When they arrived one Haida had reached [Victoria] also, the only survivor of the massacre. It turned out he was husband to the woman who was rescued. Their joy may be conceived, each supposing the other murdered.

EVENING SERVICE ON BOARD THE FORWARD

This evening at seven we had evening service. Mr. Lowe read prayers. I read lessons & preached upon the 'Lord's Prayer.' We had a hearty service & plenty of singing. The men seemed to enjoy the service & were very attentive. I trust a blessing was left upon some.

September 7, Friday.

This morning about six we moved round to the settlement on the northeast side of Admiral Island. This we had approached yesterday at the lake. We were two hours steaming round. At nine I read prayers & spoke a few words to the men from the 139th Psalm.

At half past ten went on shore.

NORTHEAST SETTLEMENT ON ADMIRAL ISLAND

Mr. Lowe accompanied me on shore. Several settlers met us. I visited most of the log houses which are built on each lot. The land is much more open than on the other side which we visited yesterday. It is quite park like & the soil is sometimes rich black loam, at other times a marly & not rich kind. There is plenty of fine grass. There are sixteen settlers, mostly young men. Nearly all are living with Indian women.

I visited, amongst others, the farm of Elliot. He was blacksmith at Nanaimo for some years. He has a good log house. He had built extensive accommodation for fattening pigs. He was roofing a cattle house. Several acres were sown with potatoes, etc.

Another farm was that of Mills. He has fenced twenty five acres & plowed them. About three acres were growing potatoes. He has fifty pigs, two cows, & two oxen, [. . .] calves & poultry. He comes from Ethan in Kent.

Another farm was that of Mr. Beggs who understands nursery grounds. He has about four acres under cultivation. He has planted an orchard. His vegetables are excellent. The soil is a rich black loam. He says it is all he could wish. He proposes laying out his ground as a nursery & I doubt not will find a market in the growing requirements of the colonies.

Mills had an ox house, a store barn, in which hay & pea [. . .] were stored & [he] had just completed seven excellent log pens for pigs. All animals at this time live & thrive upon what can be obtained in the bush. Pigs root up 'pig-nuts' & the [. . .]. In the winter stock will be fed upon hay, peas & potatoes. Fish are plentiful. Deer in abundance. You can get a deer weighing eighty pounds for one dollar. A fine buck of 120 pounds for one and a half dollars.

SERVICE AT NORTHEAST SETTLEMENT

At one o'clock I held service, about nine were present. I read litany. We had three hymns. The singing was excellent. The cards which have ten hymns answer well. These I distribute beforehand & gather them in afterwards.

Our service was in the log house of Geary, whose substitute Landers [Lauten] was present & very glad to have the service. I observed several joined as though the words were familiar. I preached from the 'Prodigal Son.' They were attentive. I instanced cases I knew of, in the misery of young men who go to the mines & spend all in riotous living. Some had been to the mines. One told Captain Franklin afterwards, 'Sir, I know many cases exactly as that gentleman described.' I exhorted them to reflect upon their lives. [I] spoke of home & the heavenly home, invited them to the loving & merciful Saviour & trust the word spoken, though feebly, will not be without fruit.

The settlers expressed their desire for a clergyman. I hope we may be able to help them & yet I hardly know how. They accompanied me down to the boat.

GROUSE AT ADMIRAL ISLAND

Captain Robson yesterday shot three [and] today he has bagged a brace of grouse. They are called partridges, but are of the grouse kind, though somewhat larger. They are excellent eating.

INDIANS AT ADMIRAL ISLAND

An old chief came on board this morning. He brought berries & wanted powder which the Captain kindly gave him. He had a chain round his neck to which was appended a crucifix. He had a roll of paper which he prized, amongst which were some scripture cards. We trust somehow they may be [. . .] to the influences of R[omanist] priests. He attended our service on shore & it was interesting to hear him join in the singing. He had been at our prayers on board ship in the morning. I asked if he knew what it meant. He said he did & that God had taught him to be good. He told me that their head chief was anxious to see me. I wish I had something to give these poor creatures which would be prized instead of Romist toys, and yet how much better to give them the 'treasure which rust & moth do not corrupt,' but they are like children & Rome deals with them as such.

September 8, Saturday.

NANAIMO

We reached Nanaimo last evening, at half past seven. The passage was beautiful, a fine day & lovely scenery. By the route we came, Nanaimo is about fifty miles from Victoria, the outside route is seventy-two [miles].

This morning at ten I went ashore. The *Otter* was at the wharf with Mr. Dallas, Mr. Fraser & Mr. McTarvish. I walked about with Mr. Franklin [Franklyn] & Mr. Nichol. Inspected the Methodist meeting house nearly finished. It is to cost 950 dollars. Went into a coal pit. Dined with Mr. Nichols [Nichol], met Dr. Benson, Captain Franklin & Captain Robson, besides Mr. Lowe.

September 9, Sunday.

SUNDAY AT NANAIMO

Service on Board Ship

At nine the crew were mustered under an awning on the deck. Mr. Lowe read the morning prayer. We had three hymns & I preached from Saint Matthew 14:22-23, 'Jesus walking on the sea.' The sailors were particularly attentive & I [felt] the occasion happy & profitable. I could see groups of persons on the shore listening to our hymns. How fitting is such a sight. Too often a British ship is connected with revelling & debauchery & is in no sense a bearer of holy influences to a foreign land. Here within a stone's throw almost, of the Indian village, were going up & around the accents of prayer & the melody of Christian hymns.

Service at Nanaimo

The Methodists had given up the school & had waived their services this day. So we had the ground to ourselves. The Methodist minister, Mr. Robson, however, & all his people were present & seemed to enter heartily into the service. There were many others who usually go nowhere. The room was crowded both morning & evening. We had morning prayer & liturgy in the morning, & evening prayer at half past six. The children knew the chants for the canticles. So we had hearty singing. I preached in the morning from Isaiah 58:13-14 on 'The Sabbath' in the evening from Romans 10:13-15, 'The beautiful results of the Gospel.'

I had, in the evening, a baptism. The people were Church of England & had kept back their child till our arrival. Two others of their children had been baptized by Methodists because they had no one else. I believe many will at once join us.

Address to Children

I invited parents to send their children this afternoon that I might address them, about forty attended. They, most of them go to the Wesleyan Sunday School. In the morning I gave out [that] I did not intend to intrude upon the Sunday School & proposed a quarter past two [to meet], as the Wesleyan School began, I understood, at three. After my sermon, the Wesleyan Minister came up & said I was welcome to come at anytime & that their school began at two. I fixed [to go] then. I spoke of the interest I felt in them, of the system of instruction we should pursue, of Baptism, Confirmation, the Lord's Table, & exhorted them to devote themselves to doing good. I instanced Eleanor [. . .] &

young Balfour. All seemed attentive & [I] trust this part of the day may have been blessed.

VISIT TO INDIANS — THE CATHOLIC LADDER

Mr. Lowe accompanied Dr. Benson & myself to the Indian camp. In one of these lodges is a huge figure of wood. Against this they had hung mats & laid mats down in front. Upon the mat suspended were pictures of the Crucifixion & Christ with the disciples of Emmaus.

There was also what is called *L'échelle Catholique*, 'The Catholic Ladder.' This was a representation of events of the Bible & the church beginning with the creation to the time of the priests visiting these Indians. It represents the Creation & Flood & giving of the land, & the Temple, etc., by [bullet] & circular marks. Each 100 years had its mark as the vertebra of a spine & on either side were the events. At the period of the Reformation was a branch off of heretics & then blocks designated to Luther, Calvin, & Henry VIII all going in the way of destruction.

Two Indians were taught to go through these events. On Sundays they have their services. They ring bells. They kneel down on mats. The old man had been preaching in the morning & the young man was to preach in the afternoon! I examined them as to their knowledge. They knew some events. They knew Mohammed was bad. I asked what they knew of Luther. They would not say. They said Americans all went to the flames, but King George men went the right road. This they evidently said to please us. The priests who came to them once a month are French.

There was another representation, sketched with a pair of heretics going into hell & Catholics to heaven. Purgatory was a by place off the road to heaven, limbo a retreat short of hell.

[Diagram]

September 10, Monday.

Breakfasted with Mr. Nichol. Morning wet. At eleven went out to ride, rode along the Millstone River to Pearse's plains. Here is some good land. Had some interesting conversation on the subject of the bearing of science upon religion.

VISIT TO THE PEOPLE OF NANAIMO

I went with Mr. Lowe & Dr. Benson to the school, examined the children in reading & spelling. The school is old fashioned & inferior. I visited afterwards one by one each family, in number twenty-two, having amongst them about sixty children. I was pleased with some. They are mostly from Staffordshire. The greater part are church people, though

The Catholic Ladder

September 9   There was also what is called *L'échelle catholique*, the
'Catholic ladder.' This was a representation of events of the Bible & the
church, beginning with the creation, to the time of the priests visiting
these Indians.

Hills' rough sketch illustrates an early version of the "Catholic Ladder," a visual
catechism for natives.

The Catholic Ladder

This was a visual catechism for natives, devised in 1839 by Fr. Francis Norbert Blanchet (1795-1883). It was widely used in the Pacific Northwest and Bishop Demers used it in British Columbia. Bishop Hills' rough sketch illustrates an early version. Later versions of the Ladder were more complex.

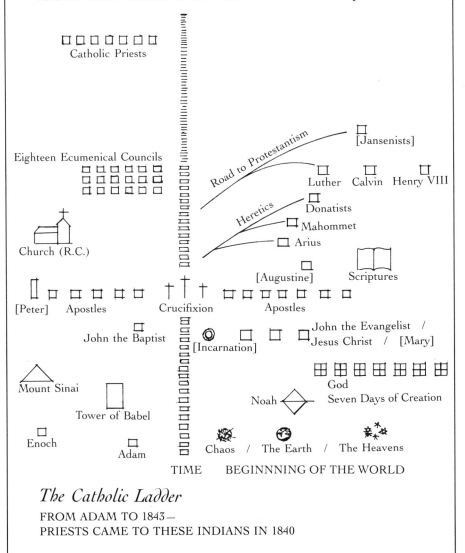

The Catholic Ladder

FROM ADAM TO 1843 —
PRIESTS CAME TO THESE INDIANS IN 1840

from there being no [Anglican] church they have hitherto attended the Methodists. One man called Dick Richardson, once a bad character, now reformed, a Methodist, said he understood we were going to build a church. He wished to subscribe ten dollars. He told me of an apparition he had seen of his father.

There were some nice children.

Captain Robson yesterday caught about a dozen trout in the Millstone River. Today he went out & shot three brace of grouse. Mr. Nichol told me deer are plentiful. The other day, near where we rode, he startled three.

September 11, Tuesday.

We left Nanaimo at half past four. The Captain received on board a dissenting minister & his wife, Mr. & Mrs. Robson. The latter being ill & wishing a passage to Victoria. We also had a daughter of Captain Franklyn.

FULFORD HARBOUR SETTLEMENT

At eleven we reached Fulford Harbour. Captain & myself went on shore. A neat cut road led up to the dwelling of four Germans. These industrious men are occupied in cutting shingles for roofing & staves for salmon casks from the cedar. They are friends who came out from Germany together, who lived at the mines in California together & who have come here & intend to remain. They are Roman Catholics, one [is] a Protestant. They appear quiet & respectable. I spoke of the obligations of religion. They said, when a man had opportunity, it was a disgrace not to go to church. The chief speaker was a fine young man who unhappily, several times, took the name of God in vain.

They have no land yet under cultivation. They take their work to Victoria & bring back food. They clear three and a half dollars on the 1000 shingles. They have a constant supply of venison. A deer just killed was hanging up. Abundance of deer skins showed how good their supply was. They have also grouse.

The spot is pleasant. Some Englishmen lived a short distance off but have left for a while. I should think good land might be found in the west side of the harbour. A small stream runs into the sea, which flows from a lake three miles up.

We reached Victoria at half past six. I found my American guests had arrived. The Reverend Mr. Kendig & wife from the Fort Steelacom, & the Reverend Mr. Willis, from Olympia. Bishop Scott was prevented from coming.

CHAPTER 9

The Colonist newspaper has an attack upon me today
12 September – 18 October

September 12, Wednesday.

Preparation for tomorrow. Reverend W[illiam] Crickmer arrived. I this evening stood for the little girl of Mr. & Mrs. Cridge which was baptized as Mary Hills.

September 13, Thursday.

CONSECRATION OF ST. JOHN'S VICTORIA

The day dawned brightly. The service was at eleven. There were twelve clergy including myself. A good congregation filled the building. A voluntary choir of some twenty-five persons had practised & [sang] admirably. Mr. Slater acted as Registrar. Mr. Cridge as Commissary. I preached from St. Matthew 26:8-10. We had the Holy Communion to about forty [people]. Nothing went amiss. I never was present at a consecration which passed off so smoothly. It brought home old England most vividly. The church arrangements are all correct. The organ most sweet. The Psalms were chanted. The lessons were read by Mr. Crickmer & Mr. Woods. The Epistle & Gospel by Mr. Willis of Olympia & Mr. Sheepshanks, Mr. Cridge took the [. . .] Mr. Dundas [read the] Prayers. I felt most thankful that in five months from the laying [of] the [corner]stone this goodly edifice should be reared. It will, I am sure, revive religion amongst us.

LUNCHEON

I invited the clergy, the committee, the American visitors, the Naval Commanders, the council, & a few others to luncheon, amongst them two coloured gentlemen. We assembled at three. Number present: 50. After our repast I gave the following toasts,

The Queen
The President of the U.S., responded to by Major Tilton.
The Army & Navy, [responded to by] Honorable Captain Spencer, who proposed my health.
The Governor & Deputy Governor, [responded to by] Mr. Finlayson.

Bishop Scott & the Clergy of Oregon & Washington, [responded to by] Reverend Mr. Kendig.

The Committee, [responded to by] Mr. Burnaby who proposed Mr. Dundas' health.

The Architect, [responded to by] Mr. Cockrane.

I trust a good feeling was promoted & something done towards cementing the friendship of the two great nations & above all I trust we advanced the great cause of religion & bound ourselves to an increased exertion. In the evening Mr. Willis preached. It was rainy, yet a fair congregation [attended]. Mrs. Lowe played the organ & most touchingly brought out the Hallelujah Chorus. It was truly exciting & brought one back to [loved] times of old England.

The collections were	356	in the morning
	58	in the evening
Total	414	dollars

September 14, Friday.

Much rain. Services continued at St. John's [Church].

Preacher in the morning, Reverend C. T. Woods, evening Reverend. W. Crickmer.

In the evening after tea we had interesting conversation upon the work of God & the progress of the church. Our party were my four guests, the Kendigs, Messrs. Willis & Crickmer & myself.

September 15, Saturday.

Day fine. Rode out with Mr. Crickmer. Visited Cadboro Bay.

A BACKWOODSMAN

We rode through the bush. We came to a fence, over which our horses leapt. In the midst of the wood we found a man loading a cart with timber. We stopped. He seemed pleased to see us, as though [he was] not a stranger. In the course of conversation he spoke of the great change taking place by the enclosure of land & improvements. He came out in 1853. 'Why then Sir, I seemed as if I could apply the words of Alexander Selkirk, "I seemed to be lord of all I surveyed," lonely indeed was life here then.' I remarked 'yet though apart from men & the world's hum, no one is alone.' 'Yes sir, I know providence is ever watchful. How wonderful is providence. Years back there was Mr. Yale, who lived thirty-five years at Langley trying without success to burn down the forest & clear the land. He could make no impression, the forest was too moist. Yet when the providence of God marked out the time, then the gold was discovered, the crowds of men came & the forest was in a blaze & soon gave way.'

'I suppose, Sir, St. John's is to be opened tomorrow.' 'There are special services tomorrow. The Consecration was on Thursday. Do you think of coming in?' 'Yes Sir I always come in on a Sunday & frequently go to church.' 'That's well.'

In addition to my guests staying in my house, the [two] Miss Penrices, Mr. Lowe, Mr. Pemberton & Captain Robson dined with me. We had a pleasant evening.

September 16, Sunday.

INDIAN SCHOOL

Preached, [in the] morning at St. John's [Church], [in the] evening at Christ Church. In [the] afternoon, [I] visited the Indian school on the reserve. There were 120 present, of all ages & of three different tribes, the Haidas, the Tsimshians, & Songhees. Freesy, Chief of the Songhees asked me to preach to them. Mr. Garrett has made great progress in Chinook & has already established an influence which I trust may turn out to the good of these poor Indians.

Several white people were present. Amongst them a Jew who expressed great interest. Three sisters & the husband of one, all good Chinook speakers were kindly lending their aid.

September 17, Monday.

Licenced to be missionary clergy the Reverends C. T. Woods, L. Brown, O. Glover, A. C. Garrett, W. Crickmer, [and] as Rectors of Christ Church & St. John's, Reverend E. Cridge & Reverend J. R. Dundas.

Yesterday (Sunday) the Rev. J. Chittender from Francisco came to be a candidate for priests orders. [Several persons] dined with me today, besides my guests, Mr. Chittender, Mr. Dundas, & Mr. & Mrs. Wood (banker).

September 18, Tuesday.

My American guests left me this morning. They expressed themselves much gratified by their visit. I rode out with Mr. Crickmer & Mr. Pemberton. Today Mr. Brown left for Douglas & Cayoosh. Mr. Crickmer also departed.

At the evening service at St. John's the Rev. Mr. Chittender preached an excellent sermon.

September 19, Wednesday.

Preached at Christ Church.

September 20, Thursday.

BOYS COLLEGIATE SCHOOL

The numbers are greater than we expected at first. Today thirty-three are in attendance. Several have come from the Roman Catholic School.

JEWISH CHILDREN AT THE COLLEGIATE SCHOOL

There are many Jews in Victoria. Indeed all along the Pacific Coast they abound, in California especially. They are anxious about education. Several have been sent to us. The Reverend Mr. Glover, who obtained at Cambridge the Tynhitt Hebrew Prize, enabled us to promise an efficient instruction in Hebrew. A Hebrew class has been at once formed, the Jews being anxious their children should be instructed. How interesting that the Israelites should be placing their children under a Christian minister and that they should together be reading the Word of God in the ancient language. Who can tell what light & blessing may dawn upon them through this means!

PRINCE LOT KAMEHAMEHA

Yesterday, [there] arrived a beautiful schooner from Honolulu with Prince Lot, brother to the King of the Sandwich Islands, & his suite. I called upon him today. He is a tall stout man of about thirty. His complexion is that of a mulatto, approaching olive. He speaks English perfectly & his manners are good. He is intelligent & fully conversant with the topics of the day. I spoke of the interest we felt in the Sandwich Islands & of the prospect of increased commerce as this British possession opened out its resources & advanced in population. I said their constitution was similar to that of England. I also alluded to the desire which I believe was felt for an Episcopal Clergyman at Honolulu.

He reciprocated the interest we felt & thought increased commerce would benefit England as well as them. Their constitution was partly after England, partly after America. He thought the government by Kings, Lords & Commons more consistent with the order of Providence than the attempt at equality. With regard to the Episcopal Clergyman, he & his brother, the King, had moved in the matter & were anxious about it. There were many Episcopalians there & many who at present went nowhere because they had no church of their own. He said he believed Victoria would become as large as Francisco. He had been to Francisco when it was first occupied & now he was in Victoria under the same circumstances.

September 21, Friday. [No entry in manuscript]

236

September 22, Saturday.

The Reverend J. Chittender took the oaths of allegiance & supremacy & made the submission to the [Thirty-Nine] Articles preparatory to being ordained priest tomorrow.

September 23, Sunday. Sixteenth After Trinity.

FIRST ORDINATION

This Sunday was a memorable day in the annals of this infant diocese. The Reverend J. Chittender wrote to me from Francisco to ordain him priest in the absence of Bishop Kip. Being an Englishman & purposing return to England, he was anxious also to obtain priests orders through a colonial bishop. I replied, if Bishop Kip, or the Standing Committee would give him Letters Dismissory, I would ordain him. Accordingly he came. The form of letters not being as ours, Dismissory, but rather transferring him for the time to my diocese with letters recommendatory & affirmatory of his having passed the necessary examination for the priesthood.

At St. John's Church today the solemn & interesting ceremony took place. I preached the sermon upon the words of ordination, St. John 20:21-23. The Reverends E. Cridge, R. Dundas, C. T. Woods joined in the laying on of hands. The congregation, a considerable one, chiefly of men, seemed much impressed. I must think good will result from thus early showing the solemnity of ordination. I am sure the clergy all deeply felt the occasion. To myself it was almost overpowering. My first ordination, the responsibility of transmitting the commission of the priesthood, the candidate being much older than myself, the words of ordination, all combined to make me feel deeply how insufficient I am for these things, & how entirely I must lean upon the grace & mercy of my heavenly Father for strength & wisdom & confidence in so great & holy a work.

The promise of Christ, our head, is on such occasions most precious to realize, 'Lo, I am with you always even to the end of the world.'

A MISSION STATION

I rode out this afternoon to Cedar Plains & held service in the house of a worthy Presbyterian. There was a smaller attendance than usual owing to several families being absent. Round about this spot are a number of small farmers, each owning land & gradually bringing their acres into subjection, most of them have only been [here] a year or so. By & by this wilderness will become a fruitful garden, these poor men will be substantial landowners, & we hope the Church of England, thus the first to follow them into the bush, will be their adopted mother & the village church & school and pastor will find from them a willing support.

I preached this evening at Christ Church. I was glad to see a fair attendance even though the attraction of St. John's is great. There can be no doubt from the size now of these two congregations that a considerable increase of the church going people has already resulted from the opening of St. John's.

September 24, Monday.

Held a Chapter [meeting] at half past three.

INDIAN WOMEN

At our Chapter [meeting] today the subject of the profligate condition of the population was brought forward. The road to Esquimalt, on Sunday, is lined with the poor Indian women offering to sell themselves to the white men, passers by & instances are to be seen of open bargaining. Mr. Garrett mentioned that there are houses in town where girls of not more than twelve are taken in at night & turned out in the morning, like cattle. What awful hindrances to our work of improvement when our own race are known to these poor Indians by such glaring vices. Surely the profligacy exceeds the degradation of heathendom itself.

DEVOTIONAL MEETING

This evening the usual meeting took place. The subject was 'Praise,' which I illustrated.

September 25, Tuesday.

QUICKNESS OF INDIAN CHILDREN

The Rev. J. Chittender, head of Francisco College, called this morning. He went yesterday to our Indian Mission. He was much struck. He told me he gave a little girl about nine years old some strokes to copy on a slate. He had not left her long before she was pulling his sleeve for something else. She had filled the slate. He gave her 'O's [to write]. She soon did them. He then gave her the vowels, one after another. She copied them well & before he had done she could say them & point to any one he called for. So that in the short space of about an hour & a half, this child had learned to read & to write & to say the English vowels. He said in all his experience he never knew an English child to apprehend so quickly & to make such rapid progress.

Another instance struck him. A diagram of small words in capitals & letter writing with illustration was set up. The word to copy was 'pig.'

There was also a picture of a pig. The class was told to copy the letters. In an incredible short space [of time] an Indian youth held up his slate. He had copied the capitals & the italics & had also produced a most respectable drawing of a pig!

Mr. Chittender, Mr. Woods, Mr. Anderson, Mr. Cridge & the ladies of the Female School dined with me.

September 26, Wednesday.

Rev. Mr. Lowe came down from Nanaimo.

September 27, Thursday.

A FUGITIVE SLAVE [Nothing further in this entry]

September 28, Friday.

[A FUGITIVE SLAVE]

Last night there was a great noise near my residence. Drumming was kept up till past twelve. It was rejoicing at the deliverance of a slave. A youth, brought as a slave to the neighbouring territory by Major Tilton, made his escape on board the *E. Anderson*. Being an American vessel, they confined him while in this harbour. A writ of habeas [corpus] produced him. The Supreme Court yesterday morning declared him free.

Curious enough, his owner was my guest at the consecration of St. John's. Mrs. Tilton the boy's mistress is an excellent churchwoman! How strange to our ears!

Today Mr. Nichol of Nanaimo called.

September 29, Saturday.

Had a long conversation with Rev. C. T. Woods. He agrees to pay all expenses of the school except salaries on consideration of taking one fourth of the receipts, thus having an interest financially in the numbers.

Mr. W. W. Feer, a gentlemanly young man called. Recently from England, [he] was in the bank where he knew my brother.

COLOURED AMBITION

We announce instruction in music on our Ladies College Prospectus. Two well grown worthy 'daughters of Ham' presented themselves to Mrs. Lowe, the Lady Superintendent & requested to be admitted pupils of the piano. They enquired the terms, 'Seven dollars a month' (twenty-eight shilling/2 pence). 'Oh we are quite willing to pay that.' 'Are you fond of music?' 'Oh passionately,' says one, 'I does play the guitar,' said the other looking languishly.

INDIAN REPROOF

An officer (Lieutenant Mayne) of the Navy informed me today that the Indians at Fort Rupert were much excited, on the return of a number of their tribe, by the news that one of their body had been killed by the Songhee Indians at Victoria. They had a gathering & resolved upon an expedition to revenge themselves by an indiscriminate [murder] of every Songhee man, woman, or child they could find. The officers spoke to them & explained that the murderer of their tribesmen would be killed by the authority of the law, that the laws of England did not allow people to kill each other & that if they now went & did what they proposed, they would be taken & hung themselves. These practices must now all be done away.

With difficulty were they pacified & when told of the excellence of the English laws, they spoke long & loud in reproof & wonder because King George men had not come & taught them. 'Why do you not send teachers to us, if what you say is true & right, why do you leave us thus neglected? You have sent a teacher to the Tsimshians. We are ashamed when we stand with the Tsimshians. You have taught them to read & to write & why will you not send us teachers & then we shall know & do right.'

STEWARD OF CHURCH LANDS

I appointed Mr. J. J. Cockrane today to be Steward of Church Lands for Vancouver Island & the District of New Westminster. He is to have three percent upon all transactions, & to discharge duties according to the terms laid down in a letter from him to me of the twenty-seventh inst[ant].

Lieutenant Mayne of the *Plumper* called today & gave me an account of his explorations.

September 30, Sunday.

Stormy & rainy during the night, cessation during morning service. Incessant rain till eight o'clock. Preached at Christ Church in the morning & St. John's in the evening, afternoon at the hospital.

HOSPITAL INMATES

One of the inmates of the hospital was Colonel Singleton, a member of a good family in Ireland. Drink & gambling have been his ruin. I spoke to him seriously about his [. . .]. He professes regret & promises amendment. I advised him to abstain entirely from all intoxicating drink. Then his friends would believe him in earnest. I also spoke of the most vital safeguard of all & urged him to serious repentance. He affected to respond.

Another inmate is a fine youth whose countenance brightened up when I approached his bed, a young [man] who met with an accident on board an Australian ship which arrived here. He is the son of a clergyman in Yorkshire of the name of Close. His eyes glistened with tears at the mention of his family. I bid [him] come & see me when he gets out.

October 1, Monday.

This evening after the Devotional Meeting a Chapter [meeting] was held, at which the Reverend J. Chittender of Francisco was present. Amongst other subjects those of marriages between professed Christians & heathens, discipline of the church, [and] the burial service were discussed. A very strong feeling was manifested, also with reference to the state of morals between the Indians & whites here in Victoria. It was resolved to prepare a memorial on the subject.

October 2, Tuesday.

Mr. Atkins, a settler from the Coquitlam River called upon me & lunched. He is a communicant & an intelligent man.

There dined with me today eleven persons. Reverends Mr. Garrett, Mr. Lowe & their wives, the [two] Miss Penrices, Captain Nichol, Lieutenant Mayne, Lieutenant Commander Helby, Mr. Pemberton, Mr. W. W. Feer. Mr. Mayne stayed.

October 3, Wednesday.

Captain Nicol came to stay. [I] Preached at Christ Church.

October 4, Thursday.

Rode to Cedar Plains with Captain Nicol, Miss Douglas, Miss Franklin, & Reverend Mr. Lowe. Dined with Mr. & Mrs. Lowe at the Female Collegiate School. Had a conversation about the formation of a College Institute with reading room, lectures, book club, etc. Captain Nicol, Mr. Pemberton, Mr. Woods, Mr. Garrett, etc., took part, & the scheme seems to take.

THE COLOUR QUESTION

Mr. Dundas informed me that some respectable trader named Fellowes had not subscribed to St. John's Church. After the consecration a subscription [for funds] was sent. On his calling to thank them, Mr. Fellowes said the cause of his [not] sending a subscription was that he heard that the Bishop had invited Mr. Lester (a coloured gentleman) to luncheon on the day of consecration.

October 5, Friday.

The *Colonist* newspaper has an attack upon me today in reference to certain extracts from my private letters published in an *Occasional Paper* [published by the Columbia Mission in England]. A few of them are certainly somewhat injudiciously selected for publication such as those which would tend to stir up the Americans & the Roman Catholics against us. Otherwise the attack I think will draw attention to important subjects good for reflection both by our own people & those who neglect all religious means.

October 6, Saturday.

Governor returned.

October 7, Sunday.

The mail [ship] (*Brother Jonathan*) arrived at seven this morning. I rejoice to hear of another clergyman, Mr. [J. B.] Good, coming out.

    Preached today at Christ Church, Cedar Plains & St. John's. Mr. Nicol rode with me to Cedar Plains where was a little gathering of some fifteen souls.

October 8, Monday. [No entry in manuscript]

October 9, Tuesday.

Married (in conjunction with Mr. Cridge) two couples, Lieutenant & Mrs. Mowat [and] Mr. & Mrs. Coles.

    Called upon the Governor.

    Captain Robson, Mr. Nicol, Mr. Dundas, & Mr. Good dined with me.

October 10, Wednesday.

The *Brother Jonathan* left for Francisco.

VISIT TO SAN JUAN

I was offered kindly, by Captain Robson & accepted, a passage to San Juan [Island] in H.M.G.B. *Forward.* We left Esquimalt at eight, and reached the encampment of the Royal Marines at twelve. The day was fine & the track through the windings of the islands, as usual, pleasing to the eye.

The encampment is on the northwestern point in a returned bay, picturesque & serene. A parade ground, block house, pier, store & on the other side of a hill, overlooking the Bell tents & log cabins of the men, the officers quarters & mess room constituted the buildings & establishment for this detachment of some [. . .] men.

It will be remembered that the first solution of the question, which nearly had serious consequences last year between the United States & ourselves, was accomplished by the agreement for a joint occupation of the island. Hence, here are the Royal Marines & about fifteen miles off on the southern side are a similar body of American troops under Captain Pickett.

Captain Bazalgette & three other officers are here in charge. With the former, I walked round to see the economy of the arrangements. I was struck with the richness of the soil & the abundant fruitfulness of the vegetables which filled the gardens. Game of several sorts is plentiful. Deer can be had whenever wanted. Some of the post go out to shoot them, or Indians bring them. Wild fowl is abundant. There were hanging up in the larder of the kitchen, geese, ducks, the common wild duck & the canvas backed, teal & wild muscovy. A fine wild goose can be had for half a dollar if you buy [one], later they will be much cheaper.

We had luncheon, after which I rode out with Lieutenant Sparshott to a lofty spot wherein could be seen the whole lower part of the island spread out, as well as the various islands of the lovely archipelago. In the distance, to the East & South were the magnificent elevations of Mount Baker & Ranier. The former some fifty miles, the latter 100 miles distant, being respectively 11,000 & 13,000 feet high. The light played upon the snowy heights & formed all sorts of colours. Upon the elevated ground which runs through the island I had a view of the lower portion which is more open. There were large flocks of sheep & settlers houses. The American camp lay also at a distance before me of some twelve miles.

At the 'Hermitage,' a settler's house about half way towards the American camp, situated on a lake, was a French Canadian half breed, named Louis, another named Antoine. The former has been out thirteen, the latter twenty-four years. They live by hunting the deer & beaver. They take the venison to Victoria & get four pence half-penny a pound. There were 422 sheep belonging to the Hudson's Bay Company.

In coming back I passed a wolf trap, formed by a horse shoe of stakes firmly driven into the ground, the front open. On the top of a huge block, below, the bait of a piece of sheep. The wolf comes in, begins to eat, moves a prop & brings down the stone which crushes him.

By the kindness of Captain Bazalgette arrangements were made for divine service. The store was cleared, benched & lighted & filled by seven [o'clock]. Mr. Dundas read prayers, I the lesson & preached. We sang the canticles & the hymns right lustily. The men were attentive. Several of the crew of the *Forward* were outside the door & could not get in. I took for my text the words of Jesus, 'I am the Door.'

Next morning some of the Indians asked if they could be visited sometimes. It was hard to be cut off from the means of grace. Some of them when in Victoria not only attended the morning, but the evening service, & enjoyed it. I promised to see what I could do.

October 11, Thursday.

After breakfast, I walked out to a lake about two and a half miles from the encampment.

THE BEAVER

The object of our walk was to see a beaver dam. These animals build their houses in the water. To keep up a sufficient depth they create, most ingeniously, a dam across the water. In this case they have raised a bank some ten feet high & 150 feet in length across the end of the lake where the water was inclined to be shallow & pass away. The beavers had cut down trees & brought them to the spot. They had cut lengths of three & four feet to lay on the top & across the larger pieces. Then they had filled [it] in with caulk & mud. The result is a perfect bridge of about from three to four feet wide. I walked over it. I saw the trees which had been cut, one ten inches in diameter. I brought away with me a piece about six or eight inches in circumference which had been cut by the teeth of these animals. At first sight the cutting has the appearance of an axe, but close inspection shows the marks of the teeth working like a gouge or hollow chisel. It is said they can fall the tree in any direction they please.

Another wonderful [piece] of instinct was a channel which they made to carry off the water when inclined to overflow the dam which would be in danger of being borne away.

Yesterday I saw the skin of a beaver, shot by Louis the hunter. Also a tail which is a flat stiff leather '∩' [drawing of a beaver tail] thing used by the animal for carrying the mud & otherwise as a trowel.

After visiting the men & partaking of an excellent luncheon in the mess room, I embarked again on board the *Forward* & reached Victoria at shortly after six, having started at three.

October 12, Friday.

INDIAN SCHOOL

Visited today & taught in the Indian school. There were present about fifty. A considerable improvement was manifest in the faces of the girls! They had allowed soap & water to do their work. I heard many say their letters & small words. They are very apt at writing. Some already write good copies. One fine young man was there, the son of Edensor [Edenshaw], a Chief of the Haidas. He seems most anxious to learn. He told others what to say & kept them quiet.

NEWSPAPER ATTACK

The attack upon me in the *Colonist* appears to have excited a great interest so that today & yesterday have appeared portions of the *Occasional Paper*, in extenso. I cannot but feel thankful that a paper hostile to religion should admit for the perusal of its readers so much matter on religious subjects & be instrumental in circulating my own feelings & wishes & plans for the spiritual good of the colony. After the very blackening process with which it commenced, the present publication cannot fail of producing an impression less unfavourable. Possibly, even some hitherto hostile may be changed. Friends will I trust be interested & strengthened.

May God grant that this may be realized. I trust I may be ever ready to endure & to suffer for the cause of Christ. I may have to suffer too for my own shortcomings, but if [given] to the work of God, if the knowledge of the Saviour's name be thereby advanced I shall rejoice, yea & do rejoice, however much my own motives may be infringed, my own conduct criticised & reproached.

CHRISTIAN TEACHING AND THE JEWS

At the Collegiate School are some twelve boys, sons of Jews. The Scriptures are read every morning & each boy is required to bring a Bible. One boy did not do so. Mr. Woods several times desired it & then said non compliance would be noted by a bad mark. This brought up the father. He declared, sooner than his son should read the Scripture, he would take him away & not only him, but all the other Jews would act in the same way. Mr. Woods told him nothing would move us from the principle of religion as the foundation of education. He then said he would consider.

October 13, Saturday.

Today two young men coming to begin business as druggists, from Norwich, called on me, Mr. Searby & Mr. Livock. A letter of introduction from Rev. Mr. Biscoe of Edlington, Lincolnshire, stated Mr. Searby's family to be upright & constant adherents of the church.

I was served today with a writ in conjunction with Mr. Cridge & Messrs. Churchwardens, Pemberton & Wood by Bishop Demers for damages 500£, for blocking up his way to [the] cemetery. This will I presume try the question of the Church Reserve.

October 14, Sunday.

I preached at Christ Church morning and evening.

October 15, Monday.

I sent today a letter to Bishop Demers respecting the extract from a private letter of mine, quoted in the *Occasional Paper* reflecting upon him. It was expressive of regret. However it is received, I feel I am only doing right in this course. Mr. Cridge & Messrs. Wood & Pemberton were with me some time respecting the writ above named. We agreed to try conciliatory measures first.

I saw Mr. Crease, the Barrister afterwards.

In the evening I gave an address at the Devotional Meeting upon 'The Temptations of Christians'!

October 16, Tuesday.

Last night a violent storm of thunder & lightening lasted for several hours. Such occurrences are very rare here. Thunder & lightning being scarcely known for years.

A letter in the local paper today from Bishop Demers attacking me for a statement in the remarks of my Commissary in the *Occasional Paper*. The Bishop shows an exasperated tone. I am glad I wrote to him before this came out. He does not appear to be a wise man for he has selected for animadversion two points, which really are spoken in compliment of the zeal of the Romist Church.

October 17, Wednesday.

Rain all day. Preached at Christ Church. The Governor had kindly asked me to dinner but, having engaged to preach, I thought it best to decline, in accordance with the rule I have always adopted of letting duty have precedence over pleasure.

THE JEWS AND THE COLLEGIATE SCHOOL

Some twelve fine children, sons of Jews, have been sent to us. Our rule is to have Scripture read & explained as a first work in the daily routine.

Some parents of the Jewish persuasion have objected & today Mr. Woods called to tell me the parents threaten to remove all the Jewish boys unless we concede the point. I am thankful to say Mr. Woods has been firm & decline[d] to concede the Christian character of the school. I fancy the threat of removal & obtaining a teacher from Francisco is an American mode of pressure which, however well it may have told elsewhere, will fail in this instance & I expect the greater part of the Jewish boys will continue. They told Mr. Woods they had tried to get Bishop Demers to give way but he declined to agree.

October 18, Thursday.

REV. MR. MACFIE AND THE COLOUR QUESTION

I had a visit today from an Independent Minister, Mr. Macfie. He is the individual who formed a separate congregation from that of Mr. Clarke on the question of colour, he taking the side of the American prejudice. It seems that a certificate given by me to Mr. Clarke & remarks of mine in a published letter have reflected severely upon Mr. Macfie in the English Papers. I fancy also the [Congregational British Colonial] Society which supported him against Mr. Clarke is pressed by rebuke for the part taken by the Committee. Mr. Macfie came to ask me to hear his view & to modify my opinion. He said it was very hard that he, who had kept silent when Mr. Clarke went to print, should suffer reproach. Mr. Clarke had disgusted his people by his political agitation. He had openly proclaimed his protest against the colour prejudice, & in consequence of these & various other matters affecting his reputation his congregation in two months [time] had well nigh left him when Mr. Macfie arrived. Mr. Macfie said he had never in his heart sanctioned the prejudice & had never in his chapel had a negro pew. Coloured people had sometimes been seen there & on one occasion a coloured man was told he might sit where he liked. He thought the best way of meeting a prejudice was not by preaching about it but by holding forth the Gospel as the best corrective. Our Saviour & his disciples did not proclaim against slavery, although in the midst of it. He asked whether aristocrats in England would sit in the same pew with their servants.

I told Mr. Macfie he had only himself to blame for the unhappy notoriety attached to his name. Why had he been silent when he was publicly charged with countenancing the prejudice? He was silent because he would otherwise have offended the prejudice[d] & lost some of his congregation. He chose that line, the line of human expediency & now suffered the consequence. It was a new light to say he never sanctioned the prejudice, it was also new that Mr. Clarke left for other reasons. These were not [the] grounds set forth to the Society, but the one question of colour. Did he not represent these things to the Society? If so, why were they not published. I had seen the correspondence. I knew what the feeling here of the coloured people was, & what was the general feeling in the town. It all told me that Mr. Macfie was the champion of the 'separation party' & that the second chapel was erected upon that ground. It was wrong to calumniate Mr. Clarke. If a prejudice was wrong it was the duty of a minister to witness against it. St. Paul broke down the partition wall, & proclaimed 'all were one in Christ Jesus' & 'everyone members one of another.' This was the gospel principle. In England it was now very common to see rich people sitting side by side with working people. There were now many churches where seats were not appropriated & all went equally about.

Mr. Macfie said he had not heard of such churches, but there was such a thing as people doing a sort of penance, as a work of merit, in such humility. I said that could not be in the Church of England because the principles of the church were against justification of that sort. Nothing but the merits of Christ were looked to for justification.

He said the coloured people expected too much. One of the most respectable of them had told him he should expect, if he were a rich & educated man & had a worldly position, to be received on an equality with persons of the same position!

I said he was quite right, if a man of character, no one should hesitate to receive him on an equality. Of course this did not mean he should thrust himself with society, any more than a white man could thrust himself where he pleased. He must take the usual course, people choose their friends, but I should have no hesitation in asking such a man to my house on a perfect equality. I had had coloured gentlemen at my table. He was rather surprised.

I gather,

- that Mr. Macfie had become somewhat tainted with the prejudice, though he denies entertaining it.
- that having taken what he thought the politic line he has lost his character in England, though he has kept a congregation here.
- that he is anxious to get me to say something to counteract the impression caused by my strictures.
- that he still will allow the negro corner men to look upon him as their champion.

VISIT TO BARCLAY [BARKLEY] SOUND

I came on board the *Grappler* Gun Boat at about six o'clock, having through the kindness of Captain Speran, who commands on the Station, obtained passage. The Lieutenant [Commander], Helby, had made preparation to receive me. Captain Stamp, the founder of the Barkley Sound settlement also came on board.

CHAPTER 10

*This will one day be the
great fishing station of the colony*
19 October – 31 October

October 19, Friday.

At daylight this morning we left Esquimalt Harbour. The weather was
beautiful & so continued the whole day. The coast of Vancouver Island
was one mass of timber & a rolling mountain region inland covered also
with timber. Here & there were openings, as though of streams, probably leading from lakes. As we advanced towards Port San Juan a fringe
of lower land lay along the shore, which, when cleared, offered an
opportunity of cultivation more promising than some we had seen
previously. Yet probably very fair land may be more widely spread, as the
outside appearance of Sooke & Metchosin have much the same appearance from the sea.

We anchored about half past six a little short of Bonilla Point in
sixteen fathoms of water for the night.

SERVICE AT SEA ON BOARD THE GRAPPLER

At half past seven, a comfortable awning being placed over the deck, we
had service. I read the litany & preached. We sang three hymns heartily.
I took for my subject 'Encouragement to the Penitent,' illustrating it by
the parables of the fifteenth [chapter] of St. Luke.

October 20, Saturday.

BARKLEY SOUND

At six we left our anchorage & proceeded northwards towards Barkley
Sound. The land of Vancouver Island on our right was undulating
mountain ranges covered to the summits with interminable pine. Here
& there were openings where probably tracts of land may eventually be
cultivated. We observed several rivers pouring their waters into the sea.
We entered the bay about half past ten. It is some miles in width & twelve
[miles] in depth. One entrance is about two miles wide, a chain of
islands runs up the middle & another entrance still wider is to the north.

After twelve miles, we entered the Alberni Canal which is eighteen miles long, by about a mile to two miles wide. The sides are formed by high land, covered with Douglas Pine. Here & there, valleys where land might be cultivated are seen, but all covered with timber. The scenery was essentially Scotch. Rather upon a larger scale but similar to the loch & inland seas of the West Highlands.

At the head of the lake there is a bay & a circular shore & a river & a striking mountain range which is part of the backbone of the island. There is evidently considerable tracts of land which might be cultivated. We anchored about five o'clock. A schooner was lying at anchor & a large store and several other buildings had been erected. Men were at work laying the foundation of a saw mill to be worked by steam. I went on shore with Captain Stamp & Mr. Sproat, the proprietors, & with Captain Helby. We visited the works & walked over the excellent site for a town. Altogether the commencement is good & the undertaking seems likely to prosper. They have only begun about six weeks [ago].

The new town is to be called *Somass*, the Indian name.

LAY HELP

Mr. Sproat has been used to have a service every Sunday and all the men have attended, some forty. Mr. Sproat had spoken to them about preserving their settlement from the evils that had characterized some others. The men expressed great interest & suggested various ways in which they might accomplish this.

NEW WESTMINSTER

Captain Stamp, whose authority is good, says vessels, of as large burden as go to London, can go to New Westminster. At high water there is twenty-three feet upon the bar of the Fraser.

October 21, Sunday.

SERVICES AT SOMASS — BARKLEY SOUND

Rain all day. At half past ten we had service in a large upper room of the mill store lately erected. All the settlers were present, some forty, and with the ship's crew made about seventy-five, a goodly congregation in the midst of this wild country, in the very heart of Vancouver Island. I read the morning prayer & litany. We sang three hymns & the three canticles, & there seemed a hearty appreciation of the service. My text was from Romans 10:13-15.

BIBLE CLASS ON BOARD SHIP

At half past two, the Captain's Cabin was filled with men for a Bible class. There were two officers besides the Captain present. We read round. The portion taken was the seventh [chapter] of St. Luke & I trust a blessed & profitable time was spent in drawing forth the lessons of that beautiful chapter. It was pleasing to see the old quartermaster with big Bible & spectacles on, and the young man, taking their turn in reading the Word of God with evident delight. One young man, Agar [Aguilar], I remarked as particularly clever & good in his answers. I learned that he had been a drunkard, but had lately reformed & this was one fruit of his improvement. He had been carefully trained in a clergyman's family in Ireland.

EVENING SERVICE ON SHORE

At half past six we had service again in the 'large upper room.' It was lighted up & adorned with flags of all nations from the ship, as though [an illustration] of the Saviour's kingdom gathering up all people & the preaching of the gospel for a witness in all the world. We had evening prayer. Three heartily sung hymns & the canticles showed how much all entered into the service. I preached upon prayer, & illustrated & explained the Lord's Prayer from St. Matthew 6.

During the day Indians were about. I saw one or two present in the morning & several boats full were under the store listening & wondering at our psalmody & perhaps asking for what intent.

ROMIST USE OF INDIAN FEAR

The Indians are easily worked upon by superstitious fears. Lately there has been a sort of panic amongst them. There came down, from a northern tribe, a box, & in it a priest's hat, a surplice & some other articles. These had been passed on from one tribe to another all round the coast. It was said to have been started at Nanaimo by the priests. The mysterious character of the box produced a profound consternation. Each tribe made haste to pass it on to the next. About here the consternation was such that the men all cut their hair in token of anxiety. The object of the priests was, I imagine, to create an anticipatory dread of them that they might be objects of veneration & fear. This was in fact using the superstition of these poor creatures to introduce another. How inconsistent with the truthful & simple message of the Gospel of peace & love. The above fact was communicated to me by Mr. Banfield the Indian Agent who has lived here some years amongst the Indians.

October 22, Monday.

CANOE EXCURSION ON THE CLEESTACHNIT RIVER

Visit to the Sheshat [Seshart] Indians

Mr. Sproat, Lieutenant Helby & myself with three Indians started about half past twelve for the River Cleestachnit, which runs into the head of the bay. Near the entrance we landed on the left bank upon a rich prairie & walked some way till the wood began. The river for some miles was about 200 & 300 feet across. On the same side, the left bank (coming down) we penetrated up two small streams the Mallsette and the Kentsuksose, the former about twenty or thirty feet across, the latter fifty. We got out on the right bank some way up the latter & walked across one of the most beautiful prairie meadows I ever saw. It contained about 500 acres of the choicest land, covered with grass & ready at once to be occupied with herds of cattle. Towards the end of it, nearer the main river, were occasional clumps of trees, as though planted & having the aspect of a cultivated park. Our canoe had gone back & round & we again proceeded. On the opposite side was clear land of the same sort. Further on, the varied trees bowered down upon the water. Noble Douglas pines, 150 & 200 feet high, cedars, maples with the brightest yellow tints of autumn, the alder and a tree with bright red leaves clothed the banks. Occasionally the land was entirely clear & open. At other times the trees stood not thickly, but inviting the wood-man & husbandman. The banks were generally flat, but not so as to be ever overflowed.

Wild fowl flew around in abundance, geese, & ducks, innumerable. The river seemed to swarm with salmon which continually jumped out of the water in sizes which must have been from ten to twenty pounds weight. The gentle winding of the stream, its placid flow, the noble trees reminded us of the Thames between Richmond & Windsor.

This is by far the most beautiful, the most promising country I have yet seen for agriculture. We must have seen at least 1500 acres of entirely clear, rich prairie land with an extent of lightly timbered land of many thousand acres.

Seshart Indians

About five miles up the extent of our excursion today was the Seshart Village, a large place, some 400 yards long situated near a rapid on a picturesque bend of the river. We visited the lodges.

They are a fine race, but miserably clad, men & women being nearly naked. The poor creatures were somewhat alarmed, but on the whole were pleased to see us. Great quantities of salmon were in all stages of preparation for winter consumption. Some were opened out & undergoing the operation of smoking, over their heads. Heaps of fresh fish just caught were in the lodges. The women were making oil & cooking & mat making. They have no metal pots, so instead of boiling the pot over the fire they have wooden boxes, the sides of which are sewn together in lieu of nails. In these is placed the articles to be cooked, [&] upon these, red hot stones & then water is thrown in. They catch salmon by weirs which are ingeniously contrived. They also spear them. The small delicious *oulachan [oolachin]* is found in great abundance & is caught by passing through the water a blade on the edge of which are teeth of some fish [used] as spikes, these stick the fish & bring them up, [Drawing in manuscript omitted] this is their fishing fork.

Mr. Sproat told me they have brought down 300 salmon in one morning as the produce of the night's fishing. They get beads & trinkets in return & some blankets. There were some very fine children.

October 23, Tuesday.

VISIT TO THE CENTRAL LAKE

At nine o'clock we were in readiness for a start. A good canoe with three Indians was alongside containing old Jacob, a Seshart, Togreat one of the tribe of that name & Hallorvish, the Chief of the Opachesettes [Hopachisat]. My three European companions, Lieutenant Helby, Mr. Sproat, [&] Mr. Banfield (Indian agent) felt it right to arm themselves with revolvers, & armed also for the inner man with a supply of eatables we pushed off & made for the River Cleestachnitt. The day gradually improved till it broke out a lovely clear October morn & continued bright & cheerful for the remainder. To the Seshart village we had the same route as yesterday. We visited some of the people there but we found them somewhat disturbed & one man came past us with his face blackened, a sign of anger & war. We heard there was a great excitement. The cause we learned to be, in part, the coming of the gun boat & the notice which had been given them of an investigation respecting the ill conduct of two of their body. We saw the Chief Wiccanamish, however, & we heard afterwards from old Jacob, whom we left till our return, that the conference ended in good intentions & a desire to pacify the angry gun boat.

We got into our canoe again above the rapids & resorted to poling for the rest of the way, on account of the rapidity of the current. The river about eighty yards wide meandered through a rich country. We got out & walked over an extensive prairie meadow of about 150 acres. Here & there were beautiful groves of maples bright with yellow autumnal foliage. Stately dark leaved Douglas pines formed the background. The timber was not thick & might easily be cleared the whole extent along. At about eight miles we came to the forks of the river, one branch tending to the east, the other to the west. The former leading from an expansive lake twelve or fifteen miles away & extending many miles till it could not be far distant from the Gulf of Georgia. Communication certainly is easy in that direction for the Komuck [Comox] Indians were in the habit of making invasion upon those of this locality. A mountain range running parallel with the lay of the island was on our right, or east, beyond which was the Gulf of Georgia. This range is called by the Indians *Chetannos*. We went up the west branch. At this point of the forks is the village of the Hopachisat. The wife of Hallorvish, their chief, brought him a box of food, consisting of fish. A smaller canoe was sent on to get up some difficult rapids & be ready for us on the lake which we reached at two o'clock. We left our large canoe lower down & walked up by a trail about a mile & [a] half.

We passed several weirs for catching salmon. Canoes too, with Indians spearing the fish, which were in great abundance, leaping out of the water continually. We saw very many of large size, some weighing not less than twenty pounds. We saw many in canoes & in the Indian houses. An idea of the abundance of this kind of food may be known from the fact that in one morning 300 have been brought over to the mill, the produce of one night's labour.

We lunched on a bank of the lake, from which was a delightful view. Islands & bays & distant mountains with several sorts of trees & placid water & a bright day & blue sky form the items of this pleasurable scene.

We went across the lake, some six or seven miles & inspected two arms running north & south, the latter joining a valley lying at the back of the Seshart village to which there is a trail & communicating with the prairie near to the Mill Bay. We saw the opening to the northern part of the lake extending probably some twenty-five miles in that direction & receiving a river. We calculated the lake to be six to seven miles in its widest breadth & some thirty miles long. Taking the whole valley of both lakes & branches of the river, with the river lands, we considered the valley to be from ten to twenty miles in width & from thirty-five to forty in length, the whole of which appeared to be suitable for settlement. The banks of the lake on the west side were not so suitable. The Indians call the lake Cleecoot, the further extremity is not far from a lake coming out of Clay-o-cot [Clayoquot] Sound.

Fish abound in the lake. Lieutenant Helby killed a martin with [a] revolver. We paddled on the lake till sunset & then by the light of the moon made our way back. With some few tumbles, [and] led by Indians, we found the path through the dark forest [for] the two miles & then got into our canoe & reached the ship at nine o'clock, having spent really a pleasant day & gratified to find Vancouver Island possessing so attractive & so extensive a tract of country.

October 24, Wednesday.

TRIAL OF AN INDIAN — ADDRESS TO THE SESHARTS

A short time since an Indian was removed from the store where trade was wont to be carried on. He struck the Indian agent, Mr. Banfield. Afterwards the necks of two tame geese were found wrung, which belonged to him. Today the greater part of the tribe came by appointment to have the matter investigated. They brought the culprit. There were present three chiefs. The matter was laid before Lieutenant Helby on board the *Grappler*. He heard the evidence & appointed the prisoner to be tied up. There was much excitement during the process. The Indians thought he was going to be killed. Some were for jumping into the water & swimming away. It was observed some had knives. One approached where the prisoner was tied, whispered something, he had a knife. At length the chiefs brought forward three skins & desired to make reparation for the geese. It was very interesting to see them come forward in a solemn manner. Then Mr. Banfield, advanced, & begged the sentence might be remitted. Lieutenant Helby, assented, & ordered the prisoner to be untied. The interpreter explained all this. The man was free. I then addressed the people. They were attentive. I spoke of God, who was good & hated evil, of Jesus Christ, who had died & exhorted them to do well, & that one day there would be blessing & reward for the righteous & condemnation for the wicked. I showed them the Bible, told them it was the word of God & that my desire was [that] they should know it.

All, at length, went away with good feeling, but not before Wiccanamish had address[ed] those present, saying there were some of other tribes there. Let them not go away & suppose that the Seshart were alone to be blamed. Amongst them were many quite as bad as the man brought up that day who deserved to be punished. It was interesting to see his anxiety that the honour of his tribe should not suffer in the estimation of his neighbours.

WALK IN THE WOODS — A BEAR

Mr. Sproat & I took a walk into the forest at the back of the mill. We found extensive openings where but little was needed in preparation for the plough. We walked for several hours & in returning found ourselves entangled in the dense forest. Luckily I had a compass. After many tumbles over huge trees, we came upon the trail. It was nearly dark. Presently we heard a noise, a cracking of the wood. It was a bear.

He ran across our path at a short distance, an easy shot, & passed round at the side of us. At length the beach was reached & we were safe.

SPIRITUAL MEANS FOR THE SETTLEMENT

I had much talk, about the provision to be made for this place, with Mr. Sproat. He is anxious about it. He has given a Service on Sunday evenings. I asked what would be done when he went. He said that was his trouble. It was refreshing to see such interest taken. He said, before coming out, he & his partners had had a conversation about the moral & religious welfare of the people & they had resolved to wait & ask what I proposed. He requested me to put on paper what I wished & address the letter to him & he would lay it before his partners, with his recommendation. I proposed there should be a church, a school, a mission house for Indians, a glebe, a piece of land for the parsonage & gardens, several acres. The people must support the minister in part. Collections to be made every Sunday, pew rents & [...], a sum to be added to make up [the] deficiency.

AMERICAN WANT OF RELIGIOUS MEANS

One of the most important settlements in the lumber business is at Port Gamble. The proprietors have kept out the use of spirits. None of their workmen can get it. They have, however, no church or minister. Mr. Banfield told me much regret was expressed by some living there at their want of spiritual means. I earnestly trust in this settlement we may do better. Mr. Banfield expressed his pleasure at hearing there was the chance of a clergyman here. 'It will be a good thing Sir, not only for the [savages?] but for others. I am a bad man myself. It will be a blessing for me I know.' This he said under strong feelings evidently. I was able to encourage him.

October 25, Thursday.

WORD TAKING

I had two hours today with Mr. Banfield & a couple of Indians getting words. I have got about a hundred. I was pleased to find Mr. Banfield anxious about the spiritual welfare of the Indians. Before concluding he asked me to have prayer. 'I should like,' he said, 'these Indians to hear prayer & then it will [also] do me so much good.' I read a portion of Scripture, John 3:13-21 & explained it & then offered up prayer for God's blessing upon the settlement & for the poor Indians that they may be converted to Christ. Two workmen came in & joined us. I had [some] earnest conversation with Mr. Banfield about his spiritual state.

I went round amongst the workmen. Some were felling trees, others rolling logs, others preparing machinery for erection. I called upon Mrs. Fuller and Mrs. Young. They are young people, both from Norfolk, well brought up, confirmed, & the latter a communicant. They are attached to the Church of England. The husband of Mrs. Fuller is also a churchman. They say, they think, they are the only church people, but that there is a good disposition towards the church in the rest & they have been pleased with the Services already held. They are very anxious for a clergyman.

EVENING SERVICE

Notwithstanding the rain we had a goodly attendance of some forty persons in the 'Upper Room' of the store this evening. I gave the evening service. We sang three hymns and the canticles. The singing was hearty & the service devotional. I preached from St. Matthew 22:42, 'What think ye of Christ?' There was much attention, all were men but one. May the gracious Spirit bless his own word of faith to some present tonight!

ROMIST PRIESTS AND MORALITY

The Indian Agent informed me there was no doubt of the fact of immoralities having been committed by the Romist missionaries. He mentioned the Cowichans as one tribe amongst whom this had been the case.

PROVISIONS AT SOMASS MILL

The people said provisions were reasonable. A goose, 1 shilling; a duck, six pence; flour, 2 shillings a stone & better than in England. Fresh meat at present, they only get occasionally.

[Mr.] Fuller, a carpenter, got 6£ a month in London. Now he gets 10£ a month & his board & house. The chief engineer gets 16£ a month & board & house.

October 26, Friday.

CANOE EXCURSION UP THE KENTSUKSOSE

I went with Lieutenant Helby up the Kentsuksose. We had three Indians, Manekies & Tetechett & a boy. We entered first the Clee-stack-nitt & then up the branch on the right. The Kentsuksose meandered first through prairie meadows covered at this time with lofty ferns. It was low water & many Indians at different points were spearing salmon. The salmon, of the largest size, swarmed in the stream. They ran against the canoe, they scrambled out of the way, they rushed up to shoal water where they floundered about & swam together in shoals.

The Indian stands in a canoe or on the shore, or in the water with a long rod [Drawing in manuscript omitted] at the end of which are two strong bone spear heads with [barbs] from which a string is attached & held in the hand. A fish passes, he hurls the spear as a man would a javelin, strikes the fish in the side, the barbed spear head is fixed & the line drags the fish in. I saw several fish caught of perhaps from ten to twenty pounds weight.

At one place a weir of upright rods was placed across the stream, no fish could get through except in one place & that enclosed them in a cul-de-sac. They were here taken out of the water by hand. Some, however, continually forced their way out & an Indian stationed at the point kept spearing them. It appeared to me any possible number could be got & if nets were used, millions of the finest salmon would be easily secured.

At the river we got out of our canoe & walked across the prairie to follow the river, we struck into a trail, it was the road to Nanaimo. We crossed the river on a tree & after walking some short distance came to some beautiful falls over which is a bridge. Up these falls the salmon of all sizes were leaping. It was exciting to see every second a fish leap, sometimes failing & falling back. Occasionally they jumped on to a ledge part of the way up & then made another spring. Their leaps were about five feet & some times more. One of our Indians caught three with his hands. Over this bridge we went & ascended a picturesque bank, at the top of which was open land of large extent, probably from 500 to 1000 acres, for it seemed to reach to the mountain several miles off. It was not prairie, but burnt woodland. There was a large growth of grass & fern & the trees were dead. This fine tract might be speedily brought into cultivation, watered for some distance by the Kentsuksose, which from the quantity of water at these falls, must have its source several miles away.

Last night & this morning was much rain. Rain is falling heavy tonight.

October 27, Saturday.

Continued rain, with thunder & lightning. Went up the stream close by the settlement. The land on each side is good & thinly timbered, maple being in abundance. Visited the people of the settlement.

INDIAN FRIENDSHIP

After the Indians returned on shore from the ship, the offender having been released, & kind words having been spoken, the tribe had a great *wahwah* amongst themselves. When they [returned they] resolved to give up lands to [the] King George men [and] they gave up considerable tracts to various persons who had taken part in the proceedings. Of course we did not accept the farms which had been allotted but were pleased to find these poor creatures ready to appreciate what was in fact meant in kindness to them. They are reputed generally to be without gratitude.

October 28, Sunday. 21st after Trinity.

Fine clear day.

SERVICES AT SOMASS. BARKLEY SOUND

The upper room of the mill store was again in requisition & two hearty services were held. In the morning I gave the morning prayer & litany & preached from St. Mark 2:27 [on] 'The Sabbath.' In the evening was the evening prayer & sermon on the 'Risen life in Christ,' Colossians 3:1-4. From forty to fifty persons were present at each service & some Indians.

PREACHING TO THE SESHART INDIANS

In the afternoon, at two o'clock, the Indians of this tribe were collected in the upper room of the mill store. There were present the two principal chiefs. Hy-you Panuel and Wiccanamish. I spoke to them in their own language, upon a few simple subjects of religion, such as God made all things, made man good, sin came & death. God displeased, Jesus came, his work, God reconciled, heaven, hell.

The Indian agent, Mr. Banfield, said they understood what I told them. I trust some glimmer of truth may have reached them & that Christian Services in the midst of them may have excited enquiry.

The last named chief brought me presents, and I gave both him & the others a blanket each.

In the evening Hy-you Panuel was at the service & I spoke to the people, the settlers present, about the Indians calling on them for sympathy & pointing out the Indians in the very midst of them, ready to be instructed.

I feel greatly interested by these poor people & sometimes I am impelled with a desire to come & live amongst them & devote myself much to their evangelization. I trust my God may give me an increasing interest in their spiritual welfare.

October 29, Monday.

Morning fine, rain in afternoon.

Left the Somass moorings at half past six. Found the schooner which had left on Friday, not above seven miles on her way. Towed her to the Sound. She went out to sea. We went into an arm of the Sound to visit the chief of Ohyats [Ohiats], Cleeshin.

THE OHIATS — BARKLEY SOUND

Mr. Banfield, [the] Indian agent, Mr. Aguilar & myself went in the ship's boat to visit the Ohiats. We pulled about a mile & [a] half along the windings of a romantic inlet. On either side were fine trees, principally cedar. We passed, at one point, a house built by Mr. Banfield, where he resided & had a garden, & was clearing the ground at the back when the new settlement at Somass called him away. We gathered some of his cabbages & turnips.

The principal village of the Ohiats is higher up the Sound. We saw it in passing. Here, however, lived the Chief Cleeshin & a few families, a part of the year.

We landed & found the old chief in bed. He seemed frightened, but was soon assured of our good intentions. The interior of his lodge was the same as the universal type. Salmon hanging up to dry. Fires burning in the midst. Women engaged in diligent mat making. Men lying sleepily on their couches, wrapped in blankets. Filth of all sorts lying about & perfumes unbearable arising from oil and decayed fish.

Mr. Banfield invited the chief & others to come off to the ship, which they did. We had with us Hy-you Panuel, the Chief of the Sesharts. He is connected with the Ohiats by marriage. His presence with us, proud of the distinction, took away fear from them. Before starting Cleeshin dressed himself in a suit of sailor's clothes given him by Governor Douglas. He had not been happy & had not only blackened, but scraped his face with some instrument till the skin was bruised. Some trouble had afflicted him. He told Mr. Banfield his heart had been sad. Poor creatures, self mutilation seemed a refuge. He brought in the canoe two interesting little girls, his daughters. When Lieutenant Helby had impressed them with reference to good behaviour & by a sight of the big gun, biscuits were given to the little girls, with which all were pleased.

I spoke to Cleeshin & the other men upon a few points of religious truth & I believe they understood me tolerably well. When we parted, Mr. Banfield went with them & was to stop in their village tonight. It seemed a strange thing for a single white man to go away with several canoes of uncivilized Indians & to trust himself amongst them. Yet so good is the prestige of the English name that he is safe. Yet near here was the scene of the capture of the *Swiss Boy*, an American ship, last year & it is said, the well nigh massacre of the crew.

INDIANS IN BARKLEY SOUND

On our way down we passed a canoe of Indians. These were the You-cluch-liets [Ucluelets], who inhabit a valley in the Alberni Canal on the left going up & whose river Nahwuit flows from a lake some fifteen miles away situated not far from & westward of Cleecot Lake.

A canoe of three Indians we also passed, who live in the canal, these were the How-cheak-lesets [Chicklisets?]. They are fair haired. One fine youth was like an English lad & had colour in his cheeks. They are the only fair haired Indians hereabouts. They overtook us in their canoe, though we were steaming seven knots.

FISH IN BARKLEY SOUND

The fish are very numerous. Two whales kept company with us for some distance. They are very abundant. Salmon are plentiful. Herrings in the season are in extraordinary abundance. The receding tide leaves the shores white with millions of this fish. The natives take them by a spiked blade [small drawing in manuscript omitted] which they slice through the water & each time stick a number, with nets, any quantity might be got.

Halibut are also numerous & grow to great size, weighing two or three [pounds] each. There is also good cod & oysters, also the oo-lachin, a delicious fish like sardines. I have little doubt that this will one day be the great fishing station of the colony.

BARKLEY SOUND

Barkley Sound is about twelve miles broad by sixty-two deep. It is studded with islands & indented with winding arms. Some twenty or thirty rivers flow into it and much land might be used for cultivation. One breadth of land I saw [was] nine miles across to the sea by twenty [miles] from the mountain range to the entrance. This, Mr. Banfield assures me, is excellent land. It is covered with timber but not rocky or swampy. It lies immediately on the south side of the entrance to the Sound.

We anchored for the night in an arm of the Sound.

October 30, Tuesday.

A dismal day, rain, wind & fog. Our vessel rolled about & made even several of the crew sick. We reached Port San Juan & took shelter for the night.

Captain Stamp informed me that thirty-two Chinamen returned recently to China, having been but few months in British Columbia, & took with them 23,000 dollars as the amount of their earnings, being 4600£ or about 143£ each, a fortune to a poor man in China. He can get a passage to China for thirty dollars, [or] 6£.

October 31, Wednesday.

Arrived at Sooke [at] half past ten.

VISIT TO SOOKE

The *Grappler* reached Sooke at half past ten. Lieutenant Helby & I went up to the farm. We found Mr. & Mrs. Muir, two old worthy Scotch people. There was a complete old country farmyard. We dined with them, venison, fresh butter, milk & cheese, all off the farm, were placed before us. There are some thirty [people] in all, their sons & dependents working the farm & the saw mill. Mrs. Muir tends twenty-five cows. After the meal I read a portion of Scripture & explained & then offered prayer. The old man saw us down to the boat. The Sooke river he said was 100 yards wide & comes from a lake some miles away. It abounds in fine trout & salmon. They get about three deer a week.

We left Sooke at two and reached Victoria in the evening.

CHAPTER 11

A bishop is more agitated by cares & storms than the sea is by winds & tempests

1 November – 31 December

November 1, Thursday.

Fine day. Had [a] visit from Mr. Crease about the law suit now going on as to the Church Reserve. Rode with Mr. Dundas who dined with me.

LARGE TURNIP

A turnip taken up in my garden (white) weighs twenty-six pounds & is forty-two and a half inches in circumference.

THE OCCASIONAL PAPER

I have been attacked for writing to a friend & stating the fact of widespread infidelity in America, Oregon in particular, and the fact of the Wesleyan Chapel being built by a large proportion of subscriptions from people of the Church of England.

In the Oregon paper published at Portland (*Christian Advocate*), the same number which finds fault at my statement respecting infidelity has a notice of an address in another column, 'To the Infidels of Oregon!!'

Mr. Garrett told me that a member of the Wesleyan congregation, Dr. Dickson, informed him that the chief part of the money came from [Upper] Canada, & that not above 1000 dollars were collected here, & that about 400 dollars only came from people of the Church of England. By their own showing, therefore, nearly half of the Victoria subscriptions came from Church [of England] people.

November 2, Friday.

Visited the Governor. Gave account of excursion to Barkley Sound. Discussed Bishop Demers, the *Occasional Paper*, etc. He said he had read the latter & could see nothing to object to. He had read Bishop Demers letter in the *Colonist* & could not understand what he meant.

THE JEWISH BOYS AT THE COLLEGIATE SCHOOL

Mr. E. Mallandaine called to state he had heard the Jews were going to remove their boys & this he thought unfortunate. 'Better to have them for a part of the time than not at all. Could not a concession be made?' I replied the school was a Christian school in connection with the mission here of the Church of England. Religion was made the basis, & the tone & the motives of the teaching was to spring day by day from religion, & that [was] the only standard of truth, viz. the Christian.

If the Jewish boys [were] allowed to omit the religious half hour, on what principle of justice could we refuse the Deist, the Roman Catholic, the Socinian, the Mormon. A door would thus be opened which would destroy the very character of the school.

If the Jewish boys [were] allowed to omit the religious teaching, they would come in with a contemptuous reference to the previous instruction. The inference might be drawn that religion was not absolutely necessary, if it could be dispensed with. Some, would envy those [who are] exempt & look upon the first half hour as hardship. The religion of Christ would be viewed as a matter of choice & opinion. Hence the great principle of the school & the law & discipline founded upon it would be weakened.

As it is, a liberal character is given to the school, as a Church of England school, by not insisting upon all attending the special church instruction. If the concession asked for [was] granted, we should lose the sympathy & support of many in England.

November 3, Saturday.

Rainy day.

November 4, Sunday.

Much rain last night. Preached morning & afternoon at Christ Church. St. John's in the evening. A dull day. Rain. Small congregation. Measles are prevalent.

November 5, Monday.

Rain in the morning. Fine afternoon. At the devotional meeting gave address on the subject 'The Throne of Grace.'

November 6, Tuesday.

Reverend Mr. Dundas, Messrs. Green & Hornfray, Churchwardens of St. John's, & Mr. Burnaby dined with me & we discussed the affairs of St. John's which are satisfactory. They agree to give their Rector 400£ a year.

A Swede, named Lind, who has a farm at Saanich met me today and offered me an acre of land to build a church upon in the neighbourhood of his residence, a spot he says suitably situated for the other settlers.

November 7, Wednesday.

Walked to Esquimalt. Called upon the officers of the *Topaze*, pleasing & intelligent men. Also upon those of the *Alert* who have just returned from Sitka.

SITKA

The officers of the *Alert* which has just returned from the Russian settlements at Sitka were much pleased with their visit. There are about a thousand inhabitants. The Governor has a large & comfortable house. He & several of the leading officials are Lutherans. The wives of himself & the next in command are English ladies (on one side). There is a Lutheran minister, but he is prohibited from any outward display of zeal, & is not allowed to instruct the Indians. There is a Bishop of the Greek Church & priests. They baptize the Indians but no means of instructing them seems to be resorted to. They say the Indians are in the same state as formerly except they have learned freely the vices of the white man.

I saw sketches of Sitka & another place near, also dresses from birds skins, & fish bladders & bow & fishing implements. One of the latter was a spear for whales. A loose barbed head attached to a string at the end of which was a bladder. These bladders, filled with air, gradually exhaust the fish by weighing him up to the surface where he receives more & more harpoons.

The officers were received with great kindness & refined cordiality. English was well spoken. Sitka is the seat of the Russian Fur Company. The sea otter skin is the most choice of the acquisition of the settlement.

I preached at Christ Church this evening. The day was dull. At night there was a storm of rain & wind.

November 8, [Thursday].

The mail [ship] *Brother Jonathan* came in. Mrs. Woods arrived. I dined with the Governor. Much wind & rain.

November 9, [Friday].

Stormy day.

November 10, Saturday.

Storm & rain.

November 11, Sunday.

Preached at St. John's in the morning, Christ Church in the evening. Rain in the afternoon.

ENQUIRERS

I received a visit from Lieutenant Stubbs of the *Alert*. He is in an anxious state as to his spiritual welfare. I had some interesting conversation with him. I had spoken to him on board the *Alert* & found him then eager to speak upon religious subjects.

Lieutenant Helby of the *Grappler* was also most anxious about himself & desired aid. I gave both to him & Lieutenant Stubbs, [the book] 'The Pathway of Safety.' It is pleasing to see such instances.

November 12, Monday.

A fine day.

November 13, Tuesday.

INDIAN SCHOOL

I spent several hours in the Indian school. There were assembled the members of three different tribes, the Haida, the Tsimshian, & Songhees. The latter are the natives of this locality, the two former are from the north. The writing of some is really good. Many know their letters & some small words. There were young persons of all ages, from the child of five years old to the grown man & woman. One boy, I was much struck with, named [Rou?], the son of a Chief of the Haida called Edenshaw. A young woman of the Tsimshian can read small words. I questioned her as to elementary points of religion. She knew of God, of heaven & hell. She asked me to teach her the Lord's Prayer. Her name is Shee-il. She said she tried always to do right.

They sang several hymns, 'There is a happy land,' 'Rock of Ages,' etc. The school owes credit to Mr. Garrett, seeing it has been in operation only so short a time.

Rain most of the day.

FEMALE COLLEGIATE SCHOOL

Had [a] conversation with Mrs. Woods, the Superintendent of the Female School. She appears an intelligent person & has her definite ideas of instruction. We spoke about several departments. I especially pressed the anxiety I felt that all should go forth with clear views on religion & well taught as members of the Church of England. She said the school she had been brought up in, at Dublin, had made a great impression on her from much attention having been paid to this branch. The Reverend Mr. Maturin regularly attended, to give religious instruction. He was a high churchman but was greatly valued by all & made a deep impression. She should like a similar plan to be pursued here.

November 14, Wednesday.

Had conference with Mr. Cridge in drawing up burial ground regulations, also with Mr. Garrett about the Indian work.
    Day fine.

November 15, Thursday.

Visited the Indian school. Went with Mr. Garrett & Mr. Glover to look at some land on the Esquimalt Road. The Governor's son sent today to the Collegiate School. Paid Mr. Cochrane for assessed taxes [on] six [New] Westminster lots, $152.50.
    Slight frost last night.

November 16, Friday.

A fine day. Two of my horses ill.

November 17, Saturday.

A mail [ship] in. Letters from Mr. [John] Garrett. A lovely day. Rime frost last night.

November 18, Sunday.

Beautiful weather, clear & slight frost. Preached & administered Holy Communion at St. John's. Preached at Christ Church in the evening.

November 19, Monday.

Frost last night, fine day. Gave exposition from Ephesians 4:1, on 'Unity of the Spirit.'

November 20, Tuesday.

Fine day. Frost at night. Drank tea with Mr. & Mrs. Cridge. The *Oregon* mail steamer left.

Having last night been asked for advice upon this subject, I, today, consulted authorities (Bingham) & wrote out directions in four rules for the guidance of the missions. May God give me wisdom in these difficult points.

November 21, Wednesday.

Fine bright day. Frost at night. Attended a meeting of the Indian Improvement Committee. I preached at Christ Church in the evening.

JOHN WESLEY AND THE 'EPISCOPAL METHODISTS'

I read today the letter of Wesley to Dr. Coke & Asbury when he appointed 'Superintendents' of the Wesleyan body in America with 'power to ordain.' He says, he was some years before convinced, by Lord King's book on the Primitive [Methodists], that bishops & presbyters were the same office & therefore the latter could transmit the succession, & [he] ground[ed] his act upon there being no bishops & no jurisdiction of English ecclesiastical, or any other authority there, to clash with. We see how injurious was the neglect of [England's] Church in refusing bishops to her daughters in America. Had there been such, Wesleyanism would never have usurped the practice of Episcopacy, perhaps America would never have fallen away in hatred & bitterness from the motherland.

This letter of Wesley directs the itinerant minister,

1. To use a Liturgy on Sundays.
2. To administer the Holy Communion every Sunday.
3. To say Litany Wednesday & Friday.
4. To have extempore prayer at other times.

Allusion to this act of Wesley is made in Wilberforce's *American Church*. The above letter is quoted in *Church Journal* September 26, 1860, p.286.

A BISHOP'S CARES

Chrysostom says, 'a bishop is more agitated by cares & storms than the sea is by the winds & tempests.' It is some consolation to know that one is not singular in the burdens that weigh heavily upon the mind. It is our lot. We trust He who hath called us will also give us strength. Yet we must ever feel with the apostle, 'who is sufficient for these things?'

November 22, Thursday.

Another lovely day. Frost at night, bright clear vigorous sunshine in the day. The mountains of Olympia highly picturesque & beautiful. I was engaged all today laying out my garden.

November 23, Friday.

Beautiful bright bracing day.

INDIAN DECAY

I visited today the various Indian camps with Mr. Garrett. There is much sickness amongst them at all times & particularly at present from bronchitis. I saw today several poor creatures whose condition was most distressing to witness. There was one little girl of about ten evidently not long for this life, the hectic flush on her cheek betokened her malady. She had attended the school. Another was a woman, sitting, very miserable & evidently in pain, much wasted. A third was a man lying on a mat. A fourth was a horrible object. A man some weeks ago had been shot in the leg & knee. The leg was shrivelled, & the foot dead. The knee was [swollen] & livid & [had] shot openings [from which] matter came. There the poor fellow sat & groaned & no proper treatment had he, or perhaps, would he receive it. Their superstitious fear of European treatment is great. If a patient dies they attribute death to intention & seek the life of a medical man or some white person in revenge. Mr. Garrett, however, has acquired influence & their confidence & administers medicine.

The want of proper remedies, & neglect is one clear cause of decay to these people. Their dwellings are on the ground, the wet comes freely in, their clothing is scanty, their dwellings are crowded, they frequently want food, & hence are victims to preventable diseases.

CUSTOMS WITH THE DEAD

When any one dies, it is a custom with the Haida Indians to take out the intestines & burn them, sear the inside of the dead & then pack up, in the closest manner, the body & deposit it in a box which they keep by them. I saw today a small recess, built out from the wooden wall of the hut, with opening inside like a small cupboard, in this was a body. Sometimes they place the box under a tent outside their house. I saw several of these today. They pass them softly & speak in a hushed manner. Sometimes they keep a body for several days dressed up & painted & sitting in a chair. They take their meals with the deceased who has a portion set before him. They do this with children, several lately were to be seen.

LIFE'S UNCERTAINTY

I went today to visit a mourner. It was the same house where nine months ago I married a youthful couple, the daughter of Captain

Langford with Mr. Bull, an officer of the Navy. A few days ago, with hardly an hour's illness, he, in the full flush of health, was struck down & was no more. Here was the young widow. In the same room where took place the wedding breakfast was now the sight of tears & sorrow. Where had been offered the felicitations of the company, & hopes of long life & happiness [at the wedding], now were the consolements of friends & the *habillement* of mourning. I ministered to the mourner & the family, showing to her how God was pointing out her path. Nine months ago he seemed to strew it with flowers, now he appoints a cup of sorrow. See in all [this] his hand & his love, ordering for the best. Have patience in 'running the race,' not of our choosing, but of his setting & look to Jesus 'the author & finisher of our faith.'

THE MINER'S END

In [the diary entry for] June (29th), on my journey to Lytton, between the Halfway House & that place I met a miner, a fine young man of twenty-six years of age & six feet, six inches high. He sat down & we had [a] talk by the way. I spoke of his home & touched his feelings. He did not like the miner's life. He said nothing improper. There was a store near. He was in there, shortly afterwards, & found out who I was. He affected to be greatly concerned, for he had been talking to the Bishop & the Bishop had touched his feelings & made him swear. He professed to be shocked at swearing before a Bishop! The fact was he supposed he had sworn for it was habitual with him to do so.

The paper of this week gives an account of the upset of a boat in the river & amongst others who were drowned this young man's name & description (Farringdon) is given. Poor fellow, he longed to be out of that life & be again at his peaceful home in Maine, where his father is a farmer. One is thankful to have had an opportunity of meeting him by the way & casting forth the seed of the word of life, whether any fell into good ground, then which took root & planted, persisted or not, we cannot tell, the day will reveal. Perhaps his parents will never know his end, the end of many miners, some violence or terrible danger frequently hurries them away. No class of men need more to be followed & spoken to of God, their Saviour, their souls & eternity.

ARE INDIANS IN A STATE OF NATURE?

You enter an Indian abode. You are struck with the fine manly form, the bright & intelligent countenance, the majestic gait, the eloquent attitudes of the Indian. In the women too, there is a grace, a softness of voice, a truly feminine submission, and sometimes even beauty. But all else is utterly out of place. These noble forms are crouched upon the damp & filthy ground. Fish & decayed flesh render unbearable the atmosphere, they are eaten up by vermin & dirt. They paint their faces, sometimes all of the brightest red, or striped, or black. They scrape their faces at times till the skin is torn, they make cuts in the lip to make it protrude in the most forbidding manner, of clothing they have little or none. Yet the cold winds & frosts & rain mercilessly enter & spread death around. Infants are subjected to the torture of flattening the skull, till the head is squeezed into all sorts of shapes.

All these customs, & many horrifying habits & their squalid condition, are evidently not the true native character which belongs to those beautiful specimens of the Creator's work. No they are fallen from nature. Their habits are unnatural & it is Christian civilization which alone can bring them back to true nature & to teach them to live for the true object of human existence & to show forth the true graces of restored & redeemed manhood.

November 24, Saturday.

A fine day.

November 25, Sunday.

Day fine. Preached at Christ Church in the morning. St. John's in the evening.

November 26, Monday.

Meeting of Chapter. Agreed to have a College Institute, with course of lectures to begin. Day fine. A shower in the night.

November 27, Tuesday.

Captain Richards called to ask me to write a certificate of the necessity of the Admiralty granting a pension to poor Mrs. Bull, the young widow of Mr. Bull. In two months more she could have claimed it, but [she] was married only ten months.

Rain began about four o'clock & continued the night.

November 28, Wednesday.

A good deal of rain. Thunder was heard. Signs of snow in the clouds.

November 29, Thursday.

Rain. At twelve this night went on board the *Otter* to sail for New Westminster with Reverends Cridge, Dundas [&] Garrett.

November 30, Friday.

Expected to be near New Westminster, instead found we had been almost stationary outside Victoria harbour, owing to fog. Arrived at [New] Westminster in pouring rain at about three. The people had given up the idea of the Consecration [of Holy Trinity Church] for today. [I] was kindly received by Colonel Moody & Mrs. Moody.

December 1, Saturday.

With [the] exception of slight & partial fog, a fine day & not cold.

December 2, Advent Sunday.

CONSECRATION OF HOLY TRINITY, [NEW] WESTMINSTER

Fine weather was our privilege today for the interesting event of the first Consecration in British Columbia. At eleven o'clock the Church was full. The Royal Engineers, [a] fine corps, had arrived. The Bishop was met at the porch by a body of the inhabitants who presented the Petition. This was read by the Acting Registrar, Hopson P. Walker Esq., Barrister-at-law. The procession then advanced, the bishop leading, five clergy in surplices following. They repeated the twenty-fourth Psalm. The consecration service then proceeded with the morning prayer & communion. The proper Psalms were chanted. Richardson's anthem 'O How Amiable Are Thy Dwellings' [based on the] eighty-fourth Psalm was sung admirably. Mr. Sheepshanks, the Rector, read Prayers, Messrs. Pringle & Garrett the Lessons, Mr. Cridge & Mr. Dundas the epistle & gospel. The sermon was preached by the Reverend A. C. Garrett from the text John 3, 'God so loved the world, etc..' It was an effective & eloquent address. The collection was $124, about 25£. Communicants, including clergy, eighteen.

At three, [we had a service of] the litany & a Baptism. Reverend Mr. Pringle preached. Congregation about fifty. Coll[ection]: $12.

In the evening, at half past six, a goodly congregation again met. The anthem, [based on] Isaiah 49:13, 'Sing Oh Heavens' [by] Kent, as well as the Psalms & hymns were most effectively sung. The choir are mostly soldiers. Sermon, by the Rector, an excellent address from the Prayer of Solomon in I Kings 8. All these sermons were unwritten.

A deep impression was made & altogether seldom has passed a day more effective in the solemnity, the simplicity, the order, [and] at the same time practical application of the service of Consecration. Under the Blessing of God I trust confidently some heart will be truly awakened, & upon many, an improving influence be brought to rest, which may lead to ultimate good.

December 3, Monday.

A characteristic of Governor Douglas is a minute inspection of the details of every department, so much so as to give himself immense trouble. He, however, preserves what is also a congenial element in his character, a despotic [absolute] authority.

This, however, is not to be taken in a bad sense. He has been trained to rule arbitrarily & has not experienced till recently the contact of educated gentlemen, officers of the [. . .] & others from England, accustomed to attend to the details of their own department.

The [Royal] Engineers are served by contract. They brought out flour from England which is not good. The men are particular. They are promised rations of certain goodness. They insist upon the fulfilment of the promise. Colonel Moody spoke to the Governor about this flour & suggested that it should be sold. It had been got cheap in England & would probably fetch a price not much below the cost.

Some little time after, it came out that the Governor had, through another party, unknown to Colonel Moody, sent for some of the flour. He gave it to a baker in Victoria to make a loaf. The baker returned a loaf of excellent bread. The Colonial Secretary & the Governor eat [ate] of the loaf & were well satisfied of the fastidious daintiness of the Royal Engineers. The Colonel says the baker, wishing the Governor to be pleased with his skill in baking, took of his own best flour & produced a very different sample of bread.

The above incident, related to me by Colonel Moody, is an index to a good deal in the character of Governor Douglas.

I visited various people in New Westminster. The impression made by the Consecration appears to have been good.

THE CONSECRATION — EVENING LESSONS

The lessons at the evening service on Sunday were very appropriate, although not selected. In the second [chapter] of Isaiah the allusions to the mountains & hills, the land being full of silver & gold, full of idolatry, the cedars, were singularly descriptive of our mining land, the timber & the heathen, while the prophecy 'They shall beat their swords into plowshares & their spears into pruning hooks' in the fourth verse had its fulfilment in the presence of the military who have been employed in the peaceful occupation of making roads, building bridges & laying out towns & some of whom formed the choir in this church.

The second lesson, Hebrews 8, compares the spiritual temple of the church with the Jewish Tabernacle & refers to the new covenant of the gospel.

I visited Captain & Mrs. Pritchard. The former is Governor of the jail. With the latter I had interesting conversation as to her desire to change from the church of Rome to that of England. She is a Spaniard, born at Cadiz. She has for some time ceased to attend the Roman worship. I had observed her yesterday at the service, & her husband attentively guiding her in the use of the Prayer Book. They had a Spanish version of the New Testament & wanted other books. There is no doubt of her intellectual deliverance from the errors of Rome, I trust also the [. . .] will be found satisfactory in a deeper sense.

December 4, Tuesday.

CONFERENCE OF CLERGY AND LAITY

A number of laity met today at Colonel Moody's to confer upon sundry matters connected with the church. We were six Clergy (Messrs. Cridge, Sheepshanks, Dundas, Garrett, Pringle & myself), Colonel Moody, Captains Gossett, Luard, Parsons, Grant, Dr. Seddall, Captain Spalding, Messrs. Sproat, O'Reilly, Bushby, Hamley.

The laity had had a meeting previously & resolved upon certain points on which they desired information. Colonel Moody stated these:

1. their desire for me to reside more in [the Colony of] British Columbia
2. to have a collegiate school
3. as to a cemetery
4. marriages, [and the] mode of procuring licences

I answered their questions as to their particulars, and also explained certain other matters & requested their opinions—viz.

1. Parochial organization
2. Diocesan or Synods, Church Society
3. Maintenance of Church & Clergy
4. Duties of Churchwardens
5. Sources of income for religious objects

Colonel Moody also introduced the subject of Indian Missions.

I dined this evening at the Mess of the [Royal] Engineers [Camp] where I met a large party.

Mr. Sheepshanks, Mr. Garrett & I walked out on the North Trail to see a newly arrived family, from [Upper] Canada, six fine girls well brought up, as Church people.

December 5, Wednesday.

Visited with Dr. Seddall & several families of the Engineers.

Dined at the Colonial Restaurant with Captain Gossett. Attended the evening service at [Holy] Trinity [Church]. There was a good congregation. Mr. Dundas preached.

CONFERENCE MEETING OF LAITY AT NEW WESTMINSTER

A conference was held at the Court House, of friends of the Church of England, to meet the Bishop on subjects connected with the church. There were present amongst others Colonel Moody, Chief Commissioner & Lieutenant Governor, Chief Justice Begbie, Captain Gossett, Treasurer of the Colony, Reverends Sheepshanks, Pringle, Cridge, Dundas, Garrett, Captain Spalding, Messrs. Holbrook, Armstrong, Brown, Manson, Homer (Members of City Council), Messrs. Hamley, Hopson Walker, O'Reilly, Sproat, Dewdney, Holmes, Armstrong senior, Powell, Captain Cooper, Bacon, Bushby, Dr. Seddall, McCrae, & others.

Colonel Moody was in the Chair. I gave particulars very similar to my address, yesterday, at Colonel Moody's house. Colonel Moody summed up very well my plan of organization. Three Canadians spoke in favour from their experience in [Upper] Canada. Mr. Holbrook pressed upon me the feeling of the Colony [of British Columbia] as to my non residence, [and] also expressed anxiety for a school. There were several other speakers. The whole passed off harmoniously. It was resolved on Tuesday evening to have a meeting of the pewholders to select a Church Committee & Churchwardens.

I felt very thankful at this opportunity of meeting so many laymen, of explaining the principles of the church, of interesting them in its affairs, of showing how much we looked to them, and I was thankful for the apparent hearty response which was made to the suggestions placed before them.

BRITISH RIGHTS

One of the speakers at the meeting at the Court House, in pressing a more constant residence on my part in New Westminster with some vehemence, delivered himself of the following sentiment. 'We claim the rights of British subjects & one of these rights is to have a Bishop resident amongst us.'

THE COMMUNION TABLE AT HOLY TRINITY

On Saturday December 1, in visiting the church before [the] consecration, I observed the communion table to be made closed in front with panels, all in fashion. I remarked to Mr. Sheepshanks, in the presence of Mr. Dundas, that if any person objected on the ground of conscientious feeling, to that form, I should be compelled to decide against the

Rector & for the objector, in as much as that was not in strict accordance with the idea of a [communion] table, as contemplated by the Church of England.

December 6, Thursday.

VISIT TO INDIANS

Mr. Garrett, Mr. Sheepshanks & myself visited in a canoe, two lodges of Indians, on the opposite side of Quortlan [Kwantlen] & Musqueam. We spoke to them upon religion & morals.

December 7, Friday.

Colonel Moody left home to go to Victoria. This evening I attended [the] service at the new church, [Holy Trinity]. Mr. Garrett preached. Fine clear frosty day.

December 8, Saturday.

Another clear frost. I dined at the [Royal] Engineers mess.

December 9, Sunday.

Beautiful day, clear frost. I preached at the new church [in New] Westminster in the morning. There was a good congregation, my text [was] Ephesians 2:19-22. A collection was made for the church.

I preached at the [Royal Engineers] Camp in the afternoon, Matthew 22:42. Mr. Garrett preached in the evening at [Holy Trinity, New] Westminster.

December 10, Monday.

Fine frosty day, clear sunshine.

December 11, Tuesday.

Fine frost & sunshine. Visited people in [New] Westminster & at the [Royal Engineers] Camp.

MEETING OF PEWHOLDERS TRINITY CHURCH,
[NEW] WESTMINSTER

This evening at seven a meeting was held in the church for electing Churchwardens & Committee. The Rector, Rev. J. Sheepshanks in the Chair. Messrs. Bushby & Manson were elected [Church]wardens & Messrs. Colonel Moody, Captain Gossett, Brown, Armstrong, Holmes, Captain Cooper [formed] the [Church] Committee. I attended & gave points as to proceedings.

At the services, the clergy have been in greater force than ever seen here before, of course. We hear the opinion expressed has been favourable. Mr. Maclure, the town President, told Mr. Sheepshanks everybody was surprised at the sight of so many superior educated men who had come out from England for the simple desire to do good. In all other bodies, such men, he said, stay in the populous & rich places. Mr. Hooper said he had heard Spurgeon. 'But Sir, Spurgeon is not fit to hold up a candle to Mr. Garrett.' Mr. Powell said 'go through Canada & you would not find two clergy of the Church of England equal to any of those who preached.'

This favourable impression, I am thankful to hear. It is one of the important things at the commencement of our work.

December 12, Wednesday.

Day frosty & clear, called upon persons in New Westminster.

December 13, Thursday.

Day dull & cold. Received letters from England.

December 14, Friday.

Left New Westminster by the *Otter*. Rain most of the day. Voyage eight hours & three quarters, reached Victoria at a quarter to five.

NEW ROUTE FROM COAST TO ALEXANDRIA

Conversed with Captain Travallier who recently travelled from Alexandria to the coast in six days, he says. He first went to Lake Chilcotin. He took an animal to pack his things & saw no mountains, but a fine open country the whole way, considers the distance about 120 miles. He struck the coast somewhere below Salmon River.

Mr. Way, contractor for the road to Spuzzum & the ferryman, told me that the gallant captain is telling the tale to himself & another [man]. A short time before, [he] said he had done the journey in four days [and] a half & [Mr. Way] suggested there might be other variations. It is very difficult to get truth, people here are so sadly unscrupulous & stick at nothing when they have an object in view.

INGOTS OF GOLD

I saw today a fine ingot of 111 ounces of gold which had been assayed at the Government place, [New] Westminster & stamped, another also, smaller, but [it] seems valuable in quality.

I had [a] conversation with several miners who have been working at the Cariboo mines. All agree as to the rich mineral character of the country & are returning early in the year.

A SWEDE INTERESTED FOR THE CHURCH — SUNDAY OBSERVANCE

Mr. Peterson, of Cayoosh, was on board [the *Otter*]. He is one of the Church Committee at that place & is doing his best to get up a church. He considers the English Church just like his own. He said they had determined at Cayoosh to close the stores part of Sunday. I said I trusted they would one day close all Sunday. He said that would be very difficult. It was the custom for the miners to do their business that day & they came in from a distance.

In Germany, he said business went on part of the day, though in his own country there was entire cessation. Of course, his reasoning was unsound, as I told him, but when so large a proportion of the people are French, German, Italian, etc. & so few of English training, the difficulty of a strict observance of the Sunday is very great. It is difficult even in England in some places. I fear we can only hope to accomplish the entire [day of] rest by degrees.

December 15, Saturday.

Day fine, though dull, had a walk with Mr. Dallas & talked about Mr. Cridge's matter of difference as to stipend. He [Mr. Dallas] has been offered the Headship of the [Hudson's Bay Company] territory, in succession to Sir G. Simpson, lately deceased.

December 16, Sunday.

Preached at Christ Church morning & evening. In the afternoon attended the Indian School & was greatly delighted to see a full attendance & to observe the great improvement. There were men & women & children of all ages.

December 17, Monday.

Rain first part of day, fine from twelve [o'clock]. Had meeting of [the] Chapter.

December 18, Tuesday.

Day fine, rain the evening.

December 19, Wednesday.

Rain most of the day.

December 20, Thursday.

Day fine throughout.

December 21, Friday.

Day fine.

EXAMINATION OF THE BOYS COLLEGIATE SCHOOL

This day, the half yearly examination of the Collegiate School took place. There have been forty-six boys, forty-one in actual attendance. The Governor was present & distributed some of the prizes. I presided. There was a good number of parents & friends. Several addresses were made. I stated, in giving the Scripture prizes, that the instruction of the school was based upon the word of God.

Today the *Oregon* steamer arrived, bringing the Reverend Christopher Knipe, a welcome addition to our body.

December 22, Saturday.

Day cold.

EXAMINATION OF THE INDIAN SCHOOL

A gathering of the Indians took place today. The building was well occupied. The Governor was present. Three tribes were examined. The Haidas, the Tsimshians & the Songhees. They spelled & pronounced small words. They were examined in Scripture. Their copy books were shown. They sang 'Rock of Ages,' 'There Is a Happy Land,' & 'Here We Dwell in Grief & Pain.' The order was remarkable. At a word from Mr. Garrett the whole school, old men, young men, women & children stood or sat, or ceased conversing. Afterwards the prizes for good attendance were given, principally clothing worked by the Dorcas Society or sent from England. The Governor address[ed] the Indians in Chinook & [also] the company present. 'There is hope for the Indian' was the happy substance of his address. Truly the whole scene was touching & [a] cause of thankfulness.

December 23, Sunday.

A beautiful day. Preached at Christ Church in the morning. Rev. C. Knipe preached in the evening.

December 24, Monday.

Chapter meeting: considered education, & agreed upon the course to take.

Fine day.

December 25, Christmas Day.

Fine clear frosty day.

Service was held in Christ Church & St. John's, morning and afternoon. I preached in the morning at Christ Church. There was a fair congregation. The Holy Communion was administered in both churches.

Mr. Garrett, Mr. Pemberton, Mr. Dundas, Mr. Knipe, & [two] Miss Penrices dined with me.

December 26, Wednesday.

Rode with Mr. Garrett & Mr. Knipe to Cedar Plains. Arranged about a service there on Sunday. We have, hitherto, had service once a fortnight, & now propose once a week.

OPPORTUNE VISIT

In going round to give notice of the service, Mr. Garrett knocked at a door. 'Come in' said several voices. There were assembled persons in close conversation. 'Sir, we are having a religious discussion. Here are Baptists, Presbyterians & Episcopalians & we have different opinions.' 'Oh have you, let me hear them,' [said Mr. Garrett]. They were speaking of immersion in baptism & original sin. The latter was denied by one, the former advocated by another.

Mr. Garrett explained. One said, 'Sir, do you remember what Agrippa said to Paul, well that is what you have done to me 'I am almost persuaded.' Another said, 'I will come six miles to Church if you will speak to us in this way.'

One said he had been brought up a Baptist, but he had seen Presbyterians & Episcopalians having [such] different opinion[s], that he did not know which was right & so had given up religion altogether.

How important & opportune is the visit of a faithful & sound pastor under such circumstances. We trust such may be the case in this [. . .].

On our way home the Governor joined us & we rode in with him.

Day delightful.

December 27, Thursday.

Day fine, clear & frosty. There dined with me Mr. & Mrs. Cridge, Mr. & Mrs. Woods, Messrs. Reverends Glover, Dundas, Knipe. Lieutenant [. . .], Dr. Wallace, Alston.

About half past ten, a magnificent halo appeared round the moon in which were the prismatic colours.

December 28, Friday.

A beautiful day after hard frost & bright moonlight night.

December 29, Saturday.

Fine clear day. Lieutenant Helby & Mr. Bushby dined with me. Mr. Knipe not well.

December 30, Sunday.

Rain all day. Preached at St. John's morning, & Christ Church evening. Ministered at the hospital in the afternoon.

INDIAN SERVICE

I visited the Indian Mission this afternoon. On entering I was much struck. The building was full. Service was proceeding. Mr. Garrett was preaching in the Chinook. There was a quiet & even solemn attention as he unfolded to them the truth of God & of Christ. I was struck by the manifest influence he has attained & the interest with which they appeared to understand & to drink in his words. I afterwards instructed a class, illustrating my remarks by reference to the [Society for the Promotion of Christian Knowledge] S.P.C.K. scripture prints. Amongst others present, was a respectable man who took much interest. He said he lived near & had seen with great delight the improvement that was taking place. The Indians now would frequently pass his home singing Christian hymns which they had learned at school.

INDIAN MISERY

On passing away towards my duties at the hospital, I went through the Indian Camp. Sad & dreadful was the scene. Noises & screams of fighting & revel resounded on all sides. The crowded lodges were full of confusion. It seemed exactly as if the place was Bedlam & a multitude of dangerous lunatics were incoherently & loudly talking & at the same time wounding & injuring each other. Occasionally there were men & women outside raving in an excited manner. The cause of all this misery is drink. Terrible are the consequences. The poor Indian is literally insane under the influence of drink. Undisciplined naturally, he is utterly unrestrained when in liquor & most distressing is the sight. This it is which is the cause of Indian misery & numbers are hurrying prematurely to their graves, literally poisoned by the vile [concoction] which is prepared for the purpose.

December 31, Monday.

Rain most of the day. Held [a] Chapter [meeting] which lasted above two hours. We discussed the education question, & were unanimous, for which I feel thankful in view of a future struggle.

A[t] seven we held a devotional meeting at which Mr. Cridge, Mr. Garrett, Mr. Dundas & Mr. Woods took part, as well as myself. The proceedings lasted two hours. I think as a closing of the year it was useful. Certainly, there seemed a good impression, for which I am thankful.

The Hills Enigma

ONE hundred and thirty-five years have elapsed since Bishop George Hills arrived to take up his duties. During the first four years, between 1860 and 1863, he travelled to most of the settled places in colonial British Columbia. Although Hills recorded a great variety of observations of colonial life in private notebooks, most of what he wrote has gone unnoticed.

The diaries written between 1860 and 1863 show Hills at the peak of his career. They convey his eagerness to discharge his duties, but also his interest in such activities as the routine of miners, how to set up a camp in the bush, native customs and handmade items and the abundance of fish. For this period, there is more material concerned with settlers, natives, miners, merchants, military men and government leaders than with the church.

Contemporary descriptions of Hills imply that he was dynamic and energetic. He was described as "a man of splendid physique, very tall, at least six feet, four inches tall and broad and strong in proportion."[1] His "voice and enunciation" were "admirably clear [and] . . . powerful."[2] A clergymen who worked under Hills in Victoria for twelve years said that with regard to "travelling in Indian canoes, on horseback, and often walking while fulfilling the duties of his office, there were few who could beat him."[3] Another clergyman described him as "a kind friend and a thorough gentleman, with sympathetic feelings in his heart, but arbitrary to a degree if opposed in any matter on which he had set his mind."[4]

Others among Hills' contemporaries were less positive;[5] they were not enthusiastic about the arrival of a colonial bishop. But a sufficient number of the contemporary comments are positive enough and seem so far removed from the image of Hills presented in most articles and books available today that they raise questions about why there is a marked difference of opinion. Why is the image of Hills conveyed by his contemporaries, and the earliest diaries, so different from more recent views of Hills? This is due in part to the general trends of historiography that have marginalized the churches, and partly to a narrow focus on several incidents in Hills' life that epitomize him as eccentric and aloof.

Very little has been written about Bishop Hills. What does exist concerns a few events and these tend to be repeated. For example, one of the following four items can be found in nearly every book that discusses Bishop Hills: (1) the account of the Rev. John Sheepshanks' whistling, (2) the idea that a state church was planned in British Columbia, (3) Hills' high church outlook, and (4) the Hills-Cridge conflict that occurred in the 1870s. These have functioned as a filter through which Hills has been seen.

There are two important consequences of this focus. First, Hills tends to be treated as a colonial bishop who was out of step with the society around him, or at worst, as an unwanted but necessary relic of colonial domination. Second, this focus tends to create an impression that there is very little of significance to explore about Hills' years in British Columbia and that the importance of the role Hills played in colonial society has been overlooked. Although some of the people Hills encountered were relatively unknown, others were important figures of colonial society, and they are still recognized as such. Hills met with men like Governor James Douglas, Chief Justice for British Columbia Matthew Begbie, Colonel Richard C. Moody, Chief of the Royal Engineers, the Reverend Edward Cridge who was Bishop Hills' Dean, and William Duncan, missionary to the Tsimshians at Metlakatla on a regular basis, and these men have been seen as the pioneers and influential men of the time. But Bishop Hills, whose role was of equal importance, has not been treated in the same manner. Although Hills was a prominent person, he is one of the least-known individuals of the colonial period.

Some colonial figures have retained a prominence because their names have become place names. Books such as Walbran's *British Columbia Coast Names* and the Akriggs' *B.C. Place Names* are filled with examples of places that have taken the names of people who lived in the Province. Some of these individuals were resident for a very brief period, in comparison to the thirty-three years Bishop Hills lived in colonial British Columbia. However, there is no well-known place in British Columbia that has been given Bishop Hills' name.[6]

Other colonials are remembered because their biographies or memoirs have been published.[7] In the nineteenth century it was common practice to write a biography of a bishop soon after his death. Usually it was written by relatives or close associates of the deceased. In the case of Bishop Hills, a biography was not planned until fourteen years after his death.

A draft manuscript for a biography of Hills was prepared in England, but it was never published, primarily because of a decision made in Victoria. The British Columbia Church Aid Society, an English association founded to assist the development of the Anglican church and to raise funds, commissioned a journalist to write a biography of Hills for the fiftieth anniversary of his installation. When the book, by W. H. Skipton, was ready for publication the Society wrote to ask the Bishop of British Columbia (John C. Roper) if he would write a preface. Bishop Roper refused, partly because Edward Cridge, then Bishop of the Reformed Episcopal Church in Victoria, was still alive. The effects of the dispute between Bishop Hills and Dean Edward Cridge that had occurred in the 1870s still swayed public opinion towards Cridge. The Society then decided to purchase and store the book. They intended to publish it five years later, but nothing further was done with the manuscript.

The treatment of Hills in periodicals and books has also tended to reinforce the idea that he as a leader of a colonial church was not significant in the general development of British Columbia. Historical studies of Canada and British Columbia have, until recently, had little need to consider the role of the churches in the colonial period. While some change of emphasis is evident among historians of Canada, there is still a need for a clearer understanding of the role of the churches in British Columbia.[8]

Few writers have taken an interest in the activities of clergymen in the Church of England during the colonial period. In the words of a prominent Canadian church historian, it "has been possible to tell the Canadian story without much reference to the presence of the churches," mainly because "most of our ancestors were attracted here by such tangible assets as fish, furs, gold or wheat, or came here in desperation to escape famine or unemployment."[9]

Studies concerning gold mining societies in colonial British Columbia suggest that there was very little positive interaction between miners and the churches. For this period, the Church of England has been seen by some writers as more concerned to gain political privilege than to provide "spiritual leadership."[10] Others have argued that miners, who formed the largest portion of the first large wave of immigration in British Columbia, were different from pioneers in other parts of North America.[11] Very few held the "belief that the encounter with the wilderness marked a fresh start, the beginning of a new and better society," a view "that was tied one way or another to Christianity."[12]

When these views of gold mining societies are compared with Hills' descriptions of the response he encountered in 1860, a different picture emerges. He was welcomed by many settlers, miners and natives that he met in the Colony of British Columbia.[13] Hills' accounts of the discussions he had with miners is generally positive.

Opposition to Hills was located chiefly in Victoria where the Hudson's Bay Company had a strong influence, and his diaries clearly reflect the different responses. Even when consideration is given to the human tendency to leave out negative situations and record the more positive ones, this pattern holds.

Trends in writing about the history of British Columbia[14] have also contributed to the lack of attention given to Hills. Studies about the churches in British Columbia have been left outside the mainstream of scholarly work. This has marginalized the historical interest in Hills and leaders of other denominations in British Columbia.

In addition to the general absence of studies about the colonial period and the churches, the image of Hills presented in the few studies that mention his name have tended to portray a view of Hills that discourages further studies. The earliest material about Hills came from letters and extracts of his diaries that were published in England through the Columbia Mission. Because the extracts were the first[15] and most available sources, they have often been consulted.

One Anglican scholar noted that those extracts "which have appeared as Occasional Papers or Annual Reports of the Columbia Mission have been edited by missionary society secretaries with such loyalty and tact that the human courageous figure of the original tends in the published version, to emerge as a sanctimonious prig."[16] This original editorial work has not improved the view of Hills held by later writers, but repeated use of the published diary extracts as the major research source tends to reinforce a negative view as the only possible one.

The most often repeated anecdote about Hills shows him as one who was pompous and full of complaints. The earliest known version of the story regarding the "tall, grave, dignified Bishop" who censured the Rev. John Sheepshanks for being "so undignified, so unclerical" because he was "whistling as they rode along the trail" appeared in a book honouring Sheepshanks, the Bishop of Norwich.[17] This anecdote, based on Sheepshanks' diaries, has been repeated in publications for more than eighty years.[18]

A variation of the idea that there was an Anglican attempt to introduce a state church is outlined in a recent article. It claims that Hills was "naive" and thought he was the head of "Vancouver Island's and British Columbia's supposed 'established' church"; according to this view, Hills "did not realize that the Pacific Northwest was not the United Kingdom."[19] The idea expressed in the article, that there was an attempt to introduce an Anglican state church in the colonial period, is not new. This recent version attributes the intention primarily to Bishop Hills while an earlier version argued that British Columbia was "threatened with the possibility of having a State Church" just prior to Bishop Hills' arrival, that is between 1854 and 1859, when Edward Cridge was Chaplain for the Hudson's Bay Company.[20]

There is ample evidence that Hills had no intention of introducing a state church in British Columbia. The discussions held at the Mansion

House meeting in London, prior to Hills' departure in 1859 clearly demonstrate this, as well as the fact that Bishop Hills raised a large fund during 1859 from private donors for the Columbia Mission. These supporters were well aware that Hills intended to introduce a permanent self-supporting church; the funds they contributed were given to help achieve that end. Hills was very opposed to church establishment in colonial British Columbia and he was clear about his reasons. In 1861, he insisted parishioners in the towns of Douglas and Lillooet return the land Governor Douglas gave them and took pains to see the letter which contained his request was published.[21]

Another often repeated comment about Hills is that he was high church.[22] This term, and Hills' association with the Tractarian movement, has little meaning outside theologically informed circles and it adds to the notion that Hills' central concerns were far removed from the needs of ordinary people. Hills is often described only as high church, without other comments. Some writers add that he was influenced by the Tractarian movement. Hills has been labelled "moderate tractarian,"[23] "high church";[24] a "high churchman" who "emphasized ritual";[25] and one with "Anglo-Catholic tendencies."[26]

The Tractarian movement began in 1836 as a result of the British government's suppression of the rights of several Anglican bishops in Ireland. The group of men who wrote a series of public papers, or tracts, in response to the government's action hoped to "restore to the public mind the sense that the Christian ministry possessed a divine authority independent of the state."[27] It emphasized apostolic succession as the basis of a bishop's authority, and this was, of course, beyond the state's authority.

The strongest years of the Tractarian movement, which began at Oxford, coincided with Hills' years of study at Durham University.[28] Around 1843, when Hills was a curate under Dean Hook, the movement became more preoccupied with the medieval church and shifted its emphasis away from the primitive, or first century, biblical church. Hook was quite outspoken about his disagreement with the changes in Tractarian ideas and the movement's interest in the medieval Roman Catholic church.[29] This influence would have been felt by Hills because he was then a curate under Hook. By the 1850s when Hills was attracting attention for his work with working class people at Yarmouth, the movement had become a major force for change in the Church of England: it was considered "a spirit or power which permeated the whole country . . . [it] raised up a whole body of men, not only clergy . . . but the laity also, full of devotion to the church."[30] Every clergyman would have been influenced to some degree by the Tractarian movement.

Bishop Hills' understanding of his ecclesiastical authority can be seen in his accounts of meetings with the Rev. Edward Cridge in 1860. Within the first week of his arrival Hills made changes to the worship service that brought it in line with what was happening in the colonial church in Canada.[31] He also explained to Cridge that he wanted "the regulations of the church fully carried out" and that his decisions would be made "in accordance with the Prayer Book."[32] A few weeks later Hills informed a Quaker gentleman: "my principles are those of the Church of England which I sincerely believe are those of the pure gospel and my desire is distinctly & honestly to preach Christ and lead ever according to his will."[33] This remark is one of the clearest expressions of what he termed "pure Christianity."[34] Hills' explanation that the Thirty-Nine Articles formed the basis for his decisions in matters of church policy indicates his understanding of the duties of a bishop, as well as his loyalty to the teachings of the Church of England.[35]

A Tractarian influence can be seen in Hills' writing in 1860. He identified with the role of the early church bishops as founders of the church. On the evening before his arrival in Esquimalt he wrote, "May I be faithful . . . laying in all their just proportions the foundations of his church. May I myself more & more build upon the one foundation rock, rooted and grounded in him."[36] From Hills' point of view his ministry was similar to that of Abraham, the founder of the Hebrew nation: "the morning was very hot . . . I sat in the tent door in the heat of the day. So did Abraham in a strange land far from the house of his birth."[37] On the first anniversary of his consecration the diary entry describes his thoughts about the event: with the "vast multitude in Westminster Abbey . . . I see the venerable, the Archbishop & bishops of the Anglican church solemnly entrusting, to one most unworthy, the sacred office of a bishop & laying it on him with their hands, all its weighty responsibilities and cares."[38] The importance of apostolic succession as the basis for Hills' authority is evident.

Edward Cridge thought of Hills as a Tractarian, and remarked to one man who questioned this view, "Ah, you cannot see it—the tractarianism is hidden. I can see it."[39] Cridge saw Tractarianism and ritualism as essentially the same. However, Hills did not support the "extreme ritualism" that he encountered in England in 1871.[40]

Although many writers have regarded Hills as high church, there was some difference of opinion among his contemporaries. One knowledgable woman did not describe Hills as a high churchman. When Sophia Cracroft visited Victoria in 1861 with her aunt, Lady Franklin, the wife of the lost explorer Sir John Franklin, Sophia commented on the Bishop in one of her letters to relatives in England.

He is a strict Churchman, tho' by no means High Church. But his firmness is guided by so much tact that he has gained great respect fm [from] all; and in some instances has literally won his way. He is not anxious to have his clergy all of one way of thinking—thinks it good for all that they should differ.[41]

Her view stands in contrast to some of his contemporaries' and most later opinions.

In 1874, an American clergyman who hoped to find work under Hills spoke to the bishop about views of the church. When the clergyman informed Hills that he had heard the Bishop was "broad church," Hills informed the clergyman that he was mistaken. Hills said he had "distinct views . . . and disliked what we called broad church views" but he was "obliged as bishop to allow the latitude of difference of opinion which the church allows."[42]

The Hills-Cridge court trial and the rupture that followed has been seen as a high church and low church conflict. Major differences between Cridge and Hills became apparent in 1872. On the day that Christ Church Cathedral was consecrated, at the evening service Archdeacon Reece gave a sermon commending the revival of ritualism as a safeguard against extremes within the church. Dean Cridge objected to the comments on ritualism.

> At the close of the sermon, instead of giving out the hymn, the Dean, from the reading desk, in an impassioned manner, said he desired to protect against the teaching of Archdeacon Reece. That was the first time ritualism had been preached in that church & it should be the last. He declared ritualism was contrary to the law of scripture, the law of the church & the law of the land.[43]

Relations between Hills and Cridge were severed, a lengthy exchange of letters between the two followed and eventually a highly publicized schism. An ecclesiastical trial and a Supreme Court trial were held in 1874. Bishop Hills' authority was upheld by both courts.[44]

The Dean rejected the authority of bishops. He argued the church had no need of a bishop; a congregation and a clergyman were all that was necessary. When Cridge left the Church of England many of the parishioners went with him. A year later the former Dean became the Bishop of the Reformed Episcopal Church in Victoria.

At the time of the trial, and for the remainder of his life, Cridge was well liked in Victoria. Cridge received popular approval. This has been attributed to his early arrival in the colony and his position as Chaplain for the Hudson's Bay Company, while the response to Hills reflects his independence from the company.

> He [Cridge] was a Hudson's Bay Company Chaplain before he was a church rector. He had 'the company' solidly behind him. If he left the church many of the old stalwarts would leave with him. . . . Even in 1874 the company's power was still felt. Cridge belonged to them; they would take care of him. Bishop Hills had no association with the company; he was regarded as an outsider.[45]

Although Hills was proved legally correct in the actions he had taken, he appears to have lost much of the good opinion he had built in the eyes of the public during his earlier years. Hills could not be faulted because he carried out his duty and was proved correct and yet the loss of popular support seems to imply he must have been at fault in some undefinable or unknown way.

The 1874 trial has had a major impact on views of Hills and the church. One of the main consequences is that Bishop Hills has been cast as the high church antagonist, against the low church, Dean Edward Cridge. The schism that resulted created such a disturbance that one church historian wrote of Hills, "his faults may be omitted"[46] while another commented that the diaries had not been published, "partly because they have been so faithfully guarded."[47] Hills tends to be interpreted by the effects of the Hills-Cridge dispute. This event is often repeated; at times it is only referred to briefly, in articles and books. The negative view of Hills that this event has produced is so entrenched that it seems nearly a consensus.

The 1870s began a period of decline for the church and for Hills. In addition to the troubles at Christ Church Cathedral with Dean Cridge, the wooden cathedral burned in 1869 and the stone cathedral that was proposed did not materialize because of a lack of funds.[48] Other changes occurred as a result of the change in the size of Hills' diocese and the introduction of two new bishops to oversee the new dioceses created in 1879.[49] After this time Hills' area of responsibility consisted of Vancouver Island and some of the surrounding small islands. Hills also lost one of his most faithful supporters and lifelong friends during this decade.

Henry Press Wright (1816-1892) was a close friend of Hills for fifty years. Between 1861 and 1864 he was the Archdeacon of British Columbia. His work was interrupted by a recall to England for assignment as a military chaplain,[50] and later he returned to British Columbia to serve as Archdeacon again, between 1877 and 1880. However, after his return to British Columbia, Archdeacon Wright discovered that many things had changed.

Earlier, in 1861 Wright wrote that "the general quality and zeal" of the Anglican missionaries was commendable and "the bishop, in addition to visiting remote areas himself, had shown foresight in placing clergy at key points so that all significant centres were served by the church."[51] Two days before Wright returned to British Columbia, he spoke of Hills as "the good Bishop of Columbia, the friend of my boyhood, of my manhood, and of my old age."[52]

Wright thought that "the diocese had changed too much" from the years when he had first served as Archdeacon; there were "setbacks and problems that had not existed before."[53] He cited several reasons for the problems the church faced in the 1870s.

In Victoria, the dispute between Hills and Cridge had caused a "severe split among church people."[54] The Bishop's support of one local clergyman, the Rev. F. B. Gribbell, who had "roused considerable hostility among leading laymen," ran counter to the advice of most other clergymen.[55] Also, Wright observed, the church had become "too respectable," There were a number of important upper class people who attended the church, such as the "Governor, the Chief Justice . . . [and] leading professional men" but, he wrote, "further we cannot go, for the artisans and hand-workers [labourers]" were not "with us."[56] In Wright's eyes this was a major change from former days and a great loss.

With regard to the Church of England on the mainland, Wright thought the work was also in decline. The clergymen were "less effective than their predecessors," large areas were without a clergyman, church buildings were deteriorating: "the feeling towards the church which years ago was so warm is now fast growing cold, I may add even careless. . . . The past liberal assistance of the Bishop and his frequent visits years ago seem to be utterly forgotten."[57]

In 1878 Wright wrote, in a letter to the Secretary of the Society for the Propagation of the Gospel in Foreign Parts, "the sad part of the story is that the Bishop is a truly good man but as ignorant of his fellow man as he is obstinate in having his own way. Of this I am quite certain that G. Columbia can never more do any real good on this coast."[58] According to Archdeacon Wright, Hills had become virtually a different man by the 1870s. Wright resigned as Archdeacon and returned to England in 1880.[59]

There is a noticeable shift in the content and the length of the diary entries throughout the 1870s. There are fewer entries and they are often brief. Hills made journeys less often and these are shorter. The diary entries reveal very little about the places he visited. Only occasionally does Hills include his conversations with settlers in the diary entries. Instead Hills records mainly visits to clergy, inspection and consecration of churches, examinations and confirmations of natives. The novelty and freshness of the encounter with a new world that is so striking in the 1860-1863 diaries is absent.

After 1865, Hills had a wife to consider, and this undoubtedly had some influence on the shorter number and length of trips he made to the Colony of British Columbia. It has been suggested that the change in the quality and length of Hills' diary entries was probably due to Hills' sharing his thoughts with his wife, instead of writing them on paper.[60] Some of the clergymen who worked closely with Hills thought his wife had too strong an influence on his activities.[61] However, there were other factors that influenced the way Hills conducted his journeys to distant places.

The means of transportation changed. What had previously required months of difficult travel could be accomplished in a few days or weeks, especially in colonial British Columbia. For example, the 1866 journey to Yale was just over three weeks long, in comparison to the 1860 journey which was three months in duration; another trip between Victoria and Lytton in 1874 was completed in twelve days time.[62] The improvement in transportation meant greater ease of access, but it also allowed for shorter stays and, therefore, less opportunity for the bishop to become involved with local people. In contrast to the 1860 journey to the golds fields when Hills said "I was everywhere kindly received & in some cases I believe kindly welcomed for religion's sake,"[63] much of his time on the brief later trips involved administration of the diocese.

The change in Hills' outlook can also be seen by comparing his early and later diary entries. The enthusiasm and openness Hills expressed in 1860, especially after his trip to the gold mining region, is very different from his evaluation of his ministry in later years.[64]

In 1876 Hills evaluated his episcopate as "one very barren of results to the eye if judged by many other episcopates." However, he also saw that the general economic state of British Columbia had influenced the growth of the Church of England: "the colony has been unparalleled in its disappointments & slowness of growth—indeed it has been in a state of chronic stagnation & of course this has affected the Church of England as it has affected every interest."[65]

In 1880, while Hills was on an extended trip to England, he reflected on the twenty-one years of his episcopate. He acknowledged, "alas, I know of many shortcomings, much sloth, neglect & cowardice in the work of my ministry. How far short have I come of the most moderate standard of a Bishop's office & work."[66]

By 1880 Hills had lost much of his earlier enthusiasm and energy for the work in British Columbia and he was increasingly aware of his failings. Hills was approaching the end of his career. Eight years later he submitted his resignation and then withdrew it, after the death of his wife in the same year. Finally in 1892, he resigned and left for retirement in England.

The full text of the early diaries, between 1860 and 1863, has the potential to alter current views of Hills' life and work. In their unabridged state, the diaries provide a balance to the entrenched views of Hills as eccentric and aloof. They show he had an interest in life and people that more than surpassed the obligations he had as the colonial bishop. The record of Hills' private thoughts about the world he inhabited indicates there is much interesting material still to be uncovered, more than has been supposed.

NOTES

[1] Notes of Bishop Schofield's conversation with the Rev. W. P. Arden, 15 September 1909. Text 57, Archives of the Diocese of British Columbia.

[2] Dorothy Blakey Smith, ed. *Lady Franklin Visits the Pacific Northwest: Being Extracts from the Letters of Sophia Cracroft, Sir John Franklin's Niece, February to April 1861* and April to July *1870*, (Victoria: Provincial Archives of British Columbia, 1974), 32.

[3] Letter of the Rev. W. C. Ellison to request recollections of Bishop George Hills, advertised in the *Guardian*, 8 February 1909. Bishop Hills Collection, Archives of the Ecclesiastical Province of British Columbia and Yukon.

[4] *Ibid.*

[5] Among these were Matthew Macfie, author of *Vancouver Island and British Columbia: Their History, Resources and Prospects*, 1865 rpt. (Toronto: Coles Publishing Co., 1972), 82-83. See also references in *Diary*, 18, 23 March and 18 October 1860.

[6] John T. Walbran, *British Columbia Coast Names 1592-1906: Their Origins and History*, Ottawa, rpt. 1909 (Vancouver: J. J. Douglas, 1977). Also see Bishop Hills Diary, April 11, 12, 1863. Hills mentions that Bishop's Cove was named by Captain Pike of the *Devastation*. Saint Mary the Virgin Church in Vancouver is dedicated to the memory of Bishop Hills, but this is not apparent from its name alone. Bishop Hills' name is inscribed on the grave monument of his wife Maria Philadelphia Louisa Hills (1823-1888) in Ross Bay Cemetery, Victoria.

[7] See Helmcken, John Sebastian, *The Reminiscences of Doctor John Sebastian Helmcken*, ed. Dorothy Blakey Smith (Vancouver: University of British Columbia Press, 1975); Susan Allison, *A Pioneer Gentlewoman in British Columbia: the Recollections of Susan Allison*, ed. Margaret A. Ormsby (Vancouver: University of British Columbia Press, 1991).

[8] Chad Gaffield, ed., *The Invention of Canada: Readings in Pre-Confederation History* (Toronto: Copp Clark Longman, Ltd.,1994), xvii. This book contains articles on churches and societies in Ontario, Quebec, Nova Scotia and Newfoundland. The one article on the Pacific Northwest concerns the fur trade between 1821 and 1849.

[9] John Webster Grant, "Introduction," in *The Cross in Canada*, ed. John S. Moir, (Toronto: Ryerson Press, 1966), vii.

[10] S. D. Clark, "Mining Society in British Columbia and the Yukon," ed. W. Peter Ward and Robert A. J. Macdonald (Vancouver: Douglas & McIntyre Ltd., 1981), 224.

[11] Harris, R. Cole and John Warkentin, *Canada Before Confederation: A Study in Historical Geography* (New York: Oxford University Press, 1974), 300.

[12] *Ibid.*

[13] *Diary*, 30 June 1860.

[14] Allan Smith, "The Writing of British Columbia History," in *British Columbia: Historical Readings*, ed. W. Peter Ward and Robert A. J. McDonald (Vancouver: Douglas & McIntyre Ltd., 1981), 5, 15-16.

[15] The Hills diaries were returned to British Columbia in 1959 when the British Columbia and Yukon Church Aid Society in England ceased to exist.

[16] Simon H. D. Carey, "The Church of England and the Colour Question in Victoria, 1860," *Journal of the Canadian Church Historical Society*, XXIV, No. 2 (1982), 63.

[17] D. Wallace Duthie, *A Bishop in the Rough* (London: Smith, Elder & Co., 1909), 45-46.

[18] See G. H. Cockburn, "The Founder of the Church in British Columbia," *Across the Rockies*, xxix, No. 4 (1937), 7; Walter N. Sage, "The Early Days of the Church of England on the Pacific Slope, 1579-1879," *Journal of the Canadian Church Historical*

Society, II, No. 1 (1953), 13; Frank A. Peake, *The Anglican Church in British Columbia* (Vancouver: Mitchell Press, 1959), 34; G. P. V. Akrigg and Helen B. Akrigg, *British Columbia Chronicle, 1847-1871, Gold & Colonists* (Vancouver: Discovery Press, 1977), 185; Lyndon Groves, *Pacific Pilgrims* (Vancouver: Fforbez Publishing Co., 1979), 22-23. Godfrey P. Gower, "The Anglican Church in British Columbia," in *Circle of Voices: A History of the Religious Communities of British Columbia*, ed., Charles P. Anderson, Tirthankar Bose, Joseph I. Richardson (Lantzville: Oolichan Books, 1983), 42. Joan Weir, *Catalysts and Watchdogs: B.C.'s Men of God 1836-1871* (Victoria: Sono Nis Press, 1995), 18.

19 Vincent J. McNally, "Church-State Relations and American Influence in British Columbia Before Confederation," *Journal of Church and State*, 34, No. 1 (1992), 98-99.

20 F. W. Howay, *British Columbia From Earliest Times to the Present, Vol. 1* (Vancouver: S. J. Clarke Publishing Co., 1914), 616-17.

21 *Diary*, 12 June, and 1, 15 August 1861. See also *Columbia Mission Report*, 1861, 34-35.

22 The terms high church and low church are expressions used by Anglicans to indicate adherence to different emphases of Anglican worship. High church is used to describe Anglicans who have a high regard for sacraments, ritual, and the authority of bishops and priests. The term low church describes Anglicans who attribute less significance to high church principles and place greater importance on evangelism. There is a wide range of views within these two groups.

23 Jean Usher, *William Duncan of Metlakatla: A Victorian Missionary in British Columbia* (Ottawa: National Museums of Canada, 1974), 98. See also, Jean Friesen, "George Hills," *Dictionary of Canadian Biography*, vol. 12, 1891-1900 (Toronto: University of Toronto Press, 1990), 440, 442.

24 Philip Carrington, *The Anglican Church in Canada* (Toronto: Collins, 1963), 125; L. G. Thomas, "The Church of England and the Canadian West," in *The Anglican Church and the World of Western Canada*, ed. L. G. Thomas (Regina: Canadian Plains Research Center, 1991), 18-19.

25 Henry Roper, "The Anglican Episcopate in Canada: An Historical Perspective," *Anglican and Episcopal History*, 57, No. 3 (1988), 269.

26 "The Early Days of the Church of England on the Pacific Slope, 1579-1879," 9.

27 Owen Chadwick, *The Victorian Church: Part I, 1829-1859* (London: SCM Press Ltd., 1987), 71. All the material in this paragraph is based on Chadwick's book. See also *William Duncan of Metlakatla: A Victorian Missionary in British Columbia*, 98.

28 The comments on Hills' education and work are based on an undated letter from W. H. P. Arden, to "My Dearest Carry." "Correspondence—Bishop Hills Collection," Archives of the Ecclesiastical Province of British Columbia and Yukon.

29 W.R.W. Stephens, *The Life and Letters of Walter Farquhar Hook* (London: Richard Bentley & Son, 1885), 341-42.

30 *The Life and Letters of Walter Farquhar Hook*, 439.

31 *Diary*, 8 January 1860.

32 *Diary*, 7, 8, 11 January and 13 February 1860.

33 *Diary*, 21 January 1860.

34 *Diary*, 17 July 1860.

35 The Thirty-Nine Articles are printed in the back of *The Book of Common Prayer*.

36 *Diary*, 5 January 1860.

37 *Diary*, 21 July 1860.

38 *Diary*, 24 February 1860. The Hills-Cridge Supreme Court trial is also an indication of Hills' view of the responsibilities that were tied to apostolic succession.

39 *Diary*, 20 March 1874.

40 *Diary*, 19 February 1871.

[41] *Lady Franklin Visits the Pacific Northwest*, 22.

[42] *Diary*, 8 June 1874.

[43] *Diary*, 5 December 1872.

[44] *Diary*, 17 September, 23 October 1874.

[45] Patricia M. Johnson, "McCreight and the Church," *British Columbia Historical Quarterly*, xii, No. 4 (1948), 299.

[46] G. H. Cockburn, 7.

[47] "The Church of England and the Colour Question in Victoria, 1860," 63.

[48] *Columbia Mission Report*, 1870 shows the proposed stone cathedral; see p. 14. Also see *Columbia Mission Report*, 1871, 72.

[49] Bishop Hills initially tried to divide the diocese in 1864; he was successful in 1879. From the one diocese of British Columbia consisting of all the British colonial territory, two additional dioceses were founded: the Diocese of New Westminster and the Diocese of Caledonia.

[50] Donald H. Simpson, "Henry Press Wright: First Archdeacon of Columbia," *British Columbia Historical Quarterly*, xix, Nos. 3 & 4 (1955), 156. All the information about Archdeacon Wright is from this source.

[51] "Henry Press Wright," 151.

[52] "Henry Press Wright," 164.

[53] "Henry Press Wright," 167.

[54] "Henry Press Wright," 168.

[55] "Henry Press Wright," 169.

[56] "Henry Press Wright," 170.

[57] *Ibid.*

[58] Letter of H. P. Wright to the Society for the Propagation of the Gospel in Foreign Parts, 8 May 1878, in "Henry Press Wright: First Archdeacon of Columbia," 171.

[59] "Henry Press Wright," 175.

[60] This is the observation of Jean Barman.

[61] "Henry Press Wright," 171.

[62] See *Diary*, 25 September to 10 October 1866 and 28 April to 9 May 1874.

[63] *Diary*, 8 August 1860.

[64] *Diary*, 30 July 1860.

[65] *Diary*, 24 February 1876.

[66] *Diary*, 24 February 1880.

Bibliography

ARCHIVAL MATERIAL

ARCHIVES OF THE ANGLICAN PROVINCIAL SYNOD OF BRITISH COLUMBIA AND YUKON

British Columbia Church Aid Society Yearbook, 1912

Diaries of Bishop George Hills, 1858-1864

Notebooks of Bishop George Hills:
'A Run into Scotland—1858'
'British Columbia Including Vancouver's Island, 1858-1860'
'Visit to British Columbia, 1860'
'Synodal Notes and Memorandum Book,' 1860
'Notes & Heads & Thoughts on Matters Affecting Christ Church—Begun January 12, 1860'
'Notes on Ministry and Ordination,' 6 March 1861–17 August 1892

Hills' Correspondence and Papers:
Letter from Maria T. King to Reverend G. Hills 18 November, 1858.
Letter from Bishop G. Hills to Caroline, 3 December, 1859.
Letter from Bishop G. Hills to Caroline, 18 November, 1860.
Letter from Bishop G. Hills to the Reverend J. Xavier Willemar, 14 May, 1867.
Letter from E. Bulwer Lytton to Governor Douglas, 31 January, 1859.
Letter from E. Bulwer Lytton to Governor Douglas, 24 March, 1859.
Letter from Rev. W. C. Ellison to the *Guardian*, 8 February, 1909.

A Manual of Ethnological Inquiry Being a Series of Questions Concerning the Human Race, Prepared by a Sub-Committee of the British Association for the Advancement of Science, appointed in 1851, and Adapted for the Use of Travellers and Others, in Studying the Varieties of Man. London: Taylor and Frances, 1852

Skipton, H. P. K. 'A Life of George Hills, First Bishop of British Columbia,' unpublished manuscript, 1912

Trial of the Very Reverend Edward Cridge, Rector and Dean of Christ Church Cathedral, Victoria. Victoria: The Victoria Standard Office, 1875

Columbia Mission Reports:

Report of Proceedings at a Public Meeting Held in the Egyptian Hall, Mansion House, on Wednesday, November 16, 1859. London: Rivingtons, 1860

Speeches at the City Meeting, 30th November, 1860. London: Rivingtons, 1861.

'Extracts of Speeches Delivered in England by the Bishop of Columbia, 1863-4.' *Fifth Annual Report of the Columbia Mission for the Year 1863.* London: Rivingtons, 1864.

Ninth Annual Report of the Columbia Mission for the Year 1867. London: Rivingtons, 1868.

Occasional Paper. London: Rivingtons, 1860.

ARCHIVES OF THE DIOCESE OF BRITISH COLUMBIA

"Royal Letters Patent Founding and Constituting the Bishopric of British Columbia and Naming and Appointing the Rev'd. George Hills D.D. the First Bishop Thereof." Date Jan'y 12th, 1859 (copy) 86-13.

Bishop of Columbia Correspondence 1859-1876.

Bishop of Columbia Correspondence Out 1860-1891.

Bishop C. Schofield Notes of Conversation with Rev. W. P. Arden, 15 September, 1909.

Bishop Hills Papers:

Grant for the Site & Endowment of Christ Church &c. Victoria, Vancouver Island, 6 May 1864.

Letter from Bishop G. Hills to Mr. McSwiney, 27 October, 1860.

Letter from Bishop G. Hills to Reverend E. Hawkins, 1 June, 1861.

Letter from Bishop G. Hills to His Excellency Governor Douglas, Victoria, 1 Jan. 1862.

Letter to "My Dearest Uncle" from Arthur R. Lempriere, 12 June, 1859.

BRITISH COLUMBIA ARCHIVES AND RECORDS SERVICES

British Columbia Blue Book, 1860-1871.

Letter from the Rectory, Eythorn, Devon. England to "Dear Sir," 6 November 1934.

Mallandaine, Edward *The First Victoria Directory.* Victoria: Edward Mallandaine & Co., 1860.

Occasional Paper, One Letter from the Honourable Lady Lavinia Skewton, London to The Lord Bishop of Colombia [sic]. Victoria: British Colonist, 1860.

Brown, Rev. R. C. Lundin. *British Columbia: An Essay.* New Westminster: Royal Engineers, 1863.

OBLATE PROVINCIAL HOUSE ARCHIVES

'Catholic Ladder' Files.

BOOKS AND ARTICLES

Adams, John. *Historic Guide to Ross Bay Cemetery.* Victoria: Morriss Printing Co. Ltd., 1983.

Akrigg, G. P. V. & Helen B. Akrigg. *British Columbia Chronicle, 1847-1871: Gold & Colonists.* Vancouver: Discovery Press, 1977.

Bagshaw, Roberta L. "Church of England Land Policy in Colonial British Columbia." *British Columbia: Geographical Essays in Honour of A. Macpherson.* Ed. Paul M. Koroscil. Burnaby: SFU, 1991.

Berger, Carl. *Science, God and Nature in Victorian Canada.* Toronto: U of Toronto P, 1983.

Belyea, Barbara. *Columbia Journals: David Thompson.* Montreal: McGill-Queen's UP, 1994.

Bridge, Kathryn, "Two Colonial Artists," *British Columbia Historical News,* 16, No. 4 (1983), 6-13.

Carey, Simon, H. D. "The Church of England and the Colour Question in Victoria, 1860." *Journal of the Canadian Church Historical Society,* XXIV, No. 2 (1982), 63-74.

Carrington, Philip. *The Anglican Church in Canada.* Toronto: Collins, 1963.

Chadwick, Owen. *The Victorian Church, Part 2, 1860-1901.* London: SCM Press Ltd., 1987.

Clark, S. D. "Mining Society in British Columbia and the Yukon." *British Columbia: Historical Readings.* Ed. W. Peter Ward and Robert A. J. McDonald. Vancouver: Douglas & McIntyre, Ltd., 1981. 215-31.

Cnattingius, Hans. *Bishops and Societies, A Study of Anglican Colonial and Missionary Expansion, 1689-1850.* London: S.P.C.K., 1952.

Cockburn, G. H. "The Founder of the Church in British Columbia." *Across the Rockies,* XXIX, No. 4 (1937), 3-7, 10.

Dictionary of the Chinook Jargon or Indian Trade Language of the North Pacific Coast. Victoria: T. N. Hibben & Co., 1899; rpt. 1972.

Downs, Barry. *Sacred Places: British Columbia's Early Churches.* Vancouver: Douglas & McIntyre, 1980.

Duff, Wilson. *The Indian History of British Columbia: Vol. 1, The Impact of the White Man.* Victoria: Provincial Museum of Natural History and Anthropology, 1964.

———. 'The Fort Victoria Treaties.' *BC Studies,* 3 (1969), 3-57.

Duthie, Rev. D. Wallace. *A Bishop in the Rough.* London: Smith Elder & Co., 1909.

Farley, A. L. *Atlas of British Columbia: People, Environment and Resource Use.* UBC Press, 1979.

Fingaard, Judith. *The Anglican Design in Loyalist Nova Scotia: 1783-1816.* London: S.P.C.K., 1972.

The First Century of the Colonial Episcopate, 1787-1887. Westminster: S.P.G., n.d.

Fisher, Robin. *Contact and Conflict: Indian—European Relations in British Columbia, 1774-1890.* Vancouver: UBC Press, 1977.

Friesen, Jean. "George Hills," Editor, Francess G. Halpenny. *Dictionary of Canadian Biography, XII, 1891 to 1900.* Toronto: U of Toronto P, 1990.

Gazetteer of Canada: British Columbia. Ottawa: Department of Energy Mines and Resources, 1985.

Gough, Barry. "Sir James Douglas as Seen by His Contemporaries." *BC Studies.* No. 44 (1979-80), 32-40.

Gower, Godfrey P. "The Anglican Church in British Columbia." *Circle of Voices: A History of the Religious Communities of British Columbia.* Eds. Charles P. Anderson, Tirthankar Bose, Joseph I. Richardson. Lantzville: Oolichan Books, 1983. 34-52.

Grant, John Webster. "Introduction." *The Cross in Canada.* Ed. John S. Moir. Toronto: Ryerson Press, 1966. vii.

———. *Moon of Wintertime: Missionaries and the Indians of Canada in Encounter Since 1534.* Toronto: U of Toronto P, 1984.

Groves, Lyndon. *Pacific Pilgrims.* Vancouver: Fforbez Publishing Co., 1979.

Gray, Rev. Charles. *Life of Robert Gray: Bishop of Capetown and Metropolitan of Africa, Volume 1.* London: Rivingtons, 1876.

Hacking, Norman R. "Steamboating on the Fraser in the Sixties." *British Columbia Historical Quarterly,* 10 (1946), 1- 41.

Harris, Barbara P. & Andrea R. Giles. *An Annotated List of the Acquisitions and Holdings of the Chinook Jargon Project at the University of Victoria.* Victoria: UVic, 1990.

Harris R. Cole & John Warkentin. *Canada Before Confederation: A Study in Historical Geography.* New York: Oxford UP, 1974.

Hawkins, Ernest. *Historical Notices of the Missions of the Church of England in the North American Colonies, Previous to the Independence of the United States: Chiefly from the MS. Documents of the Society for the Propagation of the Gospel in Foreign Parts.* London: B. Fellowes, 1845.

Hazlitt, W. C. *The Great Gold Fields of British Columbia.* 1862; rpt. Victoria: Klanak Press, 1974.

Healey, Edna. *Lady Unknown, The Life of Angela Burdett-Coutts.* London: Sidgwick & Jackson, 1984.

Henderson, J. L. H. "The Abominable Incubus." *Canadian Church Historical Society*, 11, No. 3 (1969), 1-13.

House of Assembly Correspondence Book: August 12, 1856-July 6, 1859. Victoria: Archives of British Columbia, 1918.

Howay, F. W. *British Columbia From Earliest Times to the Present: Vol. 1.* Vancouver: S. J. Clarke Pub. Co., 1914.

———. "The Negro Immigration into Vancouver Island in 1858." *British Columbia Historical Quarterly*, 15 (1951), 101-13.

The Invention of Canada: Readings in Pre-Confederation History. Ed. Chad Gaffield. Toronto: Copp Clark Longman, Ltd., 1994.

Jessett, Rev. Canon Thomas E. "A Concise History of the Church in the Pacific Northwest." *Historical Magazine of the Protestant Episcopal Church*, 36, No. 2 (1967), 111-26.

Johnson, Patricia M. "McCreight and the Church." *British Columbia Historical Quarterly*, 12, No. 4 (1948), 297-309.

Kilian, Crawford. *Go Do Some Great Thing: The Black Pioneers of British Columbia.* Vancouver: Douglas & McIntyre, 1978.

Koroscil, Paul M. "Boosterism and the Settlement Process in the Okanagan Valley, British Columbia, 1890-1914." *Canadian Papers in Rural History* Ed. Donald H. Akenson. Gananoque: Langdale Press, 1986. 5, 73-103.

Lai, David Chen-Yan. "Chinese Communities." *British Columbia: Its Resources and People.* Ed. Charles N. Forward. Victoria: UVic, 1987. 335-57.

Lamb, W. Kaye. "The Census of Vancouver Island." *British Columbia Historical Quarterly*, 4, No.1 (1939-40), 51-58.

Macfie, Matthew. *Vancouver Island and British Columbia: Their History, Resources, and Prospects.* 1865 rpt. Toronto: Coles Publishing Co., 1972.

McNally, Vincent J. "Church-State Relations and American Influence in British Columbia Before Confederation." *Journal of Church and State*, 34, No. 1 (1992), 93-110.

Mayne, Richard Charles. *Four Years in British Columbia and Vancouver Island.* 1862; rpt. Toronto: S. R. Publishers Ltd., 1969.

Merrens, H. Roy. "The Physical Environment of Early America: Images and Image Makers in Colonial South Carolina." *Geographical Review*, 59 (1969), 530-56.

Millman, T. R. & J. L. H. Henderson. "Ernest Hawkins." *Dictionary of Canadian Biography, IX, 1861-1870.* Ed. Francess A. Halpenny. Toronto: U of Toronto P, 1976. 378-79.

Murray, Peter. *The Devil and Mr. Duncan: A History of the Two Metlakatlas*, Victoria: Sono Nis Press, 1985.

Ormsby, Margaret A. "Some Irish Figures in Colonial Days." *British Columbia Historical Quarterly*, 14, nos. 1 & 2 (1950), 61-82.

———. *British Columbia: A History.* Vancouver: The Macmillan Company of Canada, Ltd., 1958.

———. ed. *A Pioneer Gentlewoman in British Columbia: Recollections of Susan Allison.* Vancouver: UBC Press, 1976.

Pascoe, C. F. *Two Hundred Years of the S.P.G.: An Historical Account of the Society for the Propagation of the Gospel in Foreign Parts, 1701-1900, Volume 2.* London: S.P.G., 1901.

Peake, Frank A. *The Anglican Church in British Columbia.* Vancouver: Mitchell Press, 1959.

Pemberton, J. Despard. *Facts and Figures Relating to Vancouver Island and British Columbia, Showing What to Expect and How to Get There.* London: Longman, Green, Longman & Roberts, 1860.

Reid, Robie L. "The Chinook Jargon and British Columbia." *British Columbia Historical Quarterly*, 6, no.1 (1942), 1-12.

Roper, Henry. "The Anglican Episcopate in Canada: An Historical Perspective." *Anglican and Episcopal History*, 57, No.3 (1988), 255-71.

Rothengerger, Mel. *The Wild McLeans*. Victoria: Orca Book Publishers, 1993.

Rowley, Owsley Robert. *The Anglican Episcopate of Canada and Newfoundland*. Milwaukee: Morehouse Publishing Co., 1928.

Sage, Walter N. "The Early Days of the Church of England on the Pacific Slope, 1579-1879." *Journal of the Canadian Church Historical Society*, II, No. 1 (1953) 1-17.

Simpson, Donald H. "Henry Press Wright: First Archdeacon of British Columbia." *British Columbia Historical Quarterly*, XIX, Nos. 3 & 4 (1955), 122-85.

Slater, G. Hollis. "New Light on Herbert Beaver." *British Columbia Historical Quarterly*, 6, No.1 (1942), 13-29.

Smith, Alan. "The Writing of British Columbia History." *British Columbia: Historical Readings*. Eds. W. Peter Ward and Robert A. J. McDonald. Vancouver: Douglas & McIntyre Ltd., 1981. 5-34.

Smith, Dorothy Blakey, "The Journal of Arthur Thomas Bushby, 1858-1859." *British Columbia Historical Quarterly*, 21 (1958), 83-198.

———. ed. *Lady Franklin Visits the Pacific Northwest: Being Extracts from the Letters of Miss Sophia Cracroft, Sir John Franklin's Niece, February to April 1861 and April to July 1870*. Victoria: Provincial Archives of British Columbia, 1974.

———. ed. *The Reminiscences of Doctor John Sebastian Helmcken*. Vancouver: UBC Press, 1975.

Stephens, W. R. W. *The Life and Letters of Walter Farquhar Hook*. London: Richard Bentley & Son, 1885.

Thomas, L. G. "The Church of England and the Canadian West." *The Anglican Church and the World of Western Canada*. Ed. L. G. Thomas. Regina: Canadian Plains Research Center, 1991. 16-28.

Underhill, Stuart. *The Iron Church: 1860-1985*. Victoria: Braemar Books, 1984.

Usher, Jean. *William Duncan of Metlakatla: A Victorian Missionary in British Columbia*. Ottawa: National Museums of Canada, 1974.

Walbran, John T. *British Columbia Coast Names: 1592-1906*. 1909; rpt. Vancouver: Douglas & McIntyre, Ltd., 1971.

Weir, Joan. *Catalysts and Watchdogs: B.C.'s Men of God 1836-1871*. Victoria: Sono Nis Press, 1995.

Wilson, Alan. *The Clergy Reserves of Upper Canada*. Ottawa: The Canadian Historical Association, 1969.

Woodward, Frances M. "The Influence of the Royal Engineers on the Development of British Columbia." *BC Studies*, 24, Winter (1974-5), 3-51.

THESES AND UNPUBLISHED MATERIAL

Bagshaw, Roberta L. "Settlement and the Church of England in the Bishopric of British Columbia, 1859—1863." M.A. Thesis, SFU, 1987.

"Handbook of Indians of British Columbia, Vol I, A-K." Draft Copy, B.C. Native Studies Bibliographic Centre, 1978.

"Handbook of Indians of British Columbia, Vol. II, L-Z." Draft Copy, B.C. Native Studies Bibliographic Centre, 1978.

Harley, Philip. "The Catholic Ladder & Missionary Activity in the Pacific Northwest." M.A. Thesis, U of Ottawa, 1965.

Wrinch, Leonard. "Land Policy of the Colony of Vancouver Island, 1849-1866." M.A. Thesis, UBC, 1932.

Index

Pringle, Rev. David (1828-1908), 24, 57, 64, 66, 78, 95, 104, 120, 121, 122, 123, 124, 126, 153, 154, 155, 201, 202, 203, 210, 272, 274, 275; family, 219
Puget Sound Agricultural Company, 57
Puseyite, 58

Quakers, 48, 57, 61, 62, 288
Quayome Indians, 162-63, 164, 166, 182, 196
Queen Charlotte Islands, 56, 215
Queen's birthday, 112
Quesnel, 149-50, 157, 177, 178

Reformed Episcopal Church, 24, 285, 289
Richards, Captain George Henry (1820-1896), 56, 67, 271
Ridley, Bishop William, 24
Rivieccio, Rev. Louis, 102, 103, 104, 105, 109, 203
Roads (and trails), 76, 78, 82, 116, 118, 120, 121-22, 125, 142, 143-44, 149, 153, 154, 168, 175, 199, 200, 201, 207, 274
Robson, Captain [Lieutenant] Charles Rufus (?-1861), 223, 227, 232, 235, 242
Robson, Rev. Ebenezer, 122, 228
Roche, Lieutenant Richard, 66
Rock Creek. *See* Gold
Roman Catholics, 33, 54, 81, 83, 84, 85-87, 93, 100-01, 102, 103, 105, 109, 110, 123, 125, 143, 145, 151, 170, 180, 183, 185, 188, 192, 193, 198, 205, 227, 229, 230, 231, 232, 236, 242, 246, 251, 257, 264
Romist Church. *See* Roman Catholics
Roper, Bishop John C., 285
Royal Engineers, 17, 27, 65, 112, 118, 143, 273
Royal Engineers Camp, 72, 73, 74, 76, 77, 111, 114, 115, 116, 274, 276; school, 117
Royal Letters Patent, 18, 22

Saanich, 27, 100, 110, 265
Saanich Indians, 57, 100
St. Ann, Sisters of, [85], 222
Saloon, 30, 36, 113, 181, 186
Salt Spring Island, 13, 26, 222, 223, 224, 225, 226, 227; Ganges Harbour, 27
San Juan Island, 13, 20, 26, 60, 65, 66, 72, 82, 104, 220, 242-44

Sappers, 114, 143, 144, 145, 169
Schools, Anglican, 20, 63, 100, 101, 123; for boys, 25, 27, 53, 110, 220, 236, 245, 246-47, 267, 279; female collegiate, 25, 27, 99, 221, 222, 239, 241, 266; for Indians, 27, 31, 236, 245, 266, 267, 278
Scott, Bishop Thomas, 47, 83, 232, 234
Seddall, Dr. John V., 75, 274, 275
Seemium, Chief, 115
Semiahmoo Bay, 66, 82
Seshart Indians, 38, 252, 253, 254, 255, 259, 260
Settlers, 72, 73, 100, 255, 227, 241, 243, 257, 291
Sheepshanks, Rev. John (1834-1912), 24, 53, 73, 75, 77, 95, 107, 108, 109, 110, 111, 112, 114, 118, 154, 179, 180, 181, 182, 183, 187, 188, 194, 195, 200, 201, 233, 272, 274, 275, 276, 284, 286
Ships,
  Alert, 265, 266
  Athelstan, 69, 80, 87
  Brother Jonathan, 93, 242, 265
  Columbia, 68
  Cortez, 219
  Douglas, 154
  E. Anderson, 239
  Forward, H.M.G.B., 222, 223, 242, 244
  Ganges, H.M.S., 49, 50, 52, 56, 67, 106, 218, 219, 221
  Glimpse, 84
  Grappler, H.M.S., 13, 32, 38, 219, 248, 249, 255, 262, 266
  Heather Bell, 37, 85, 97, 98, 99
  La Planta, 119
  Maria, 112
  Moody, 117, 119, 205
  Northerner, 54, 59
  Oregon, 9, 212, 279
  Otter, 71, 78, 79, 227, 271, 277, 278
  Pacific, 13, 49, 57, 59, 67, 79, 82, 102, 108
  Panama, 61, 79, 82, 102, 107
  Perkins, 111
  Plumper, H.M.S., 49, 67, 240
  Princess Royal, 69
  S. L. Stephen, 97
  Satellite, H.M.S., 49, 51, 66, 104, 106, 107, 108, 225
  Silent, 119
  Swiss Boy, 262
  Termagant, 219